Mrs Dizzy

the Life of Mary Anne Disraeli
Viscountess Beaconsfield

MOLLIE HARDWICK

ST. MARTIN'S PRESS
NEW YORK

This book is dedicated, with love,
to my husband,
'my severest critic . . . whose taste and judgment
have ever guided its pages'
and whose photographic skill has enriched it

ST. MARTIN'S PRESS   NEW YORK

© Copyright 1972 by Mollie Hardwick
All rights reserved.
Library of Congress No. 72-89422

Manufactured in the United States of America.
No part of this book may be reproduced without
permission in writing from the publisher.

St. Martin's Press
175 Fifth Avenue
New York, N.Y. 10010

Affiliated Publishers:
Macmillan & Company, Limited, London
—also at Bombay, Calcutta, Madras and Melbourne—
the Macmillan Company of Canada, Limited, Toronto

CONTENTS

ILLUSTRATIONS

† Source unknown.
* In the possession of the author.

FOREWORD

If happiness can linger in bricks and mortar, in furniture and ornament, as tragedy is said to do, the mutual love of Mary Anne and Benjamin Disraeli will pervade Hughenden Manor, in Buckinghamshire, so long as it stands. Without wishing to sound too fanciful, I felt it there on my first visit a few years ago, and came away intrigued and determined to find out more about the lady whose charming, enigmatic face, between its vine-clusters of ringlets, had looked down upon me from portraits in her riotously cheerful drawing-room.

Printed sources told me hardly anything beyond that she had a talent for wifehood and a degree of eccentricity in her old age, was apparently courted by Disraeli for her wealth, and was some years older than he was. As a complete personality she failed to come to life.

But investigation of the immense store of Disraeli Papers in the National Trust's archives at Hughenden revealed the woman behind the legend: a woman who was a striking original all her life, who could inspire passion and give it, from girlhood to old age; and, I found, had done so with more men than her two husbands. The other men in her life, hitherto unknown and unchronicled, reveal in their correspondence with her a side of her character quite unsuspected, and fascinating in its unlikeness to her popular image.

In writing this book I have had the inestimable benefit of access to the Hughenden Papers. They include more than ten thousand letters, documents, commonplace books and miscellaneous items of Mary Anne's alone, not to mention an enormous amount of Disraeli material. Relatively few of those belonging to Mary Anne have been, it seems, consulted or used by previous authors, and I am most grateful to the National Trust for permission to bring their contents to light here, and to photograph various items on exhibition at Hughenden. The house's custodian, Mr T. A. Jefferson, and his wife have given me their kindest and most patient co-operation.

In retrospect, I feel considerable gratitude to Disraeli's nephew, the late Major Coningsby Disraeli, and to his successors at Hughenden who have kept it, and its charm, for the delight of visitors and scholars.

Highgate   MOLLIE HARDWICK
1972

'Henceforth confide in me,' she smiling said.
'My sunlit destiny shall glance on thee,
    In spite of all thy gloom.'
                        And those sweet words
Brought faith and solace to the mournful life
Fortune had ever crossed.

Disraeli to Mary Anne
on her birthday, 11 November 1846

'Little Whizzy'

It was only right and proper that Mary Anne, who was to be so lively and so lovely, should have been born in one of the liveliest of English cities, in the heart of one of its loveliest counties, Devon. Exeter, in 1792, was still largely a medieval city, a place of leaning old houses, Tudor gables, a handsome cathedral with graceful precinct-dwellings, a famous coffee-house and numerous winding alleys and steep flights of steps. It was even appropriate in its strongly Royalist politics for the future wife of the greatest of Tory leaders. Always strong for King and Church, it had fought Cromwell with underground plots, and Exeter's own General Monk had been largely responsible for bringing back the exiled Charles II to be welcomed and fêted in an Exeter bright with garlands and banners and merry with wine-flowing fountains. Mary Anne would have enjoyed the scene hugely, as no doubt her ancestors did.

In the year of her birth England was on the verge of war with France. The French Revolution was at its height: France's King and Queen, Louis XVI and Marie Antoinette, were awaiting the guillotine. England was full of unrest and fear. The Devon folk, who had been supplying men to the Royal Navy for so many centuries, knew that sons, fathers and brothers would soon be at sea.

But on 11 November 1792, Exeter was quiet enough; and on that day Mary Anne made her first appearance. She was christened three days later in St Sidwell's Church as 'Marianne, Dar. of John and Eleanor Evans'. Her birth may have taken place in the St Sidwell's district beyond the East Gate, devastated by bombs in 1942 and now completely rebuilt, or she may have been born in a farmhouse at Brampford Speke, a village a few miles north of Exeter. Her father was a native of Brampford Speke, where his family had farmed for generations, but he had chosen the Royal Navy as his life. Born in 1760, he had joined H.M.S. *Alarm* as captain's servant in 1771, the year in which the twelve-year-old Nelson shipped on the *Raisonnable* as a midshipman. Had he lived his career might well have paralleled Nelson's in more than youthful enlistment, for he rose to the rank of lieutenant when he was only twenty-one (Nelson had been nineteen).

In 1788 he felt secure enough to marry, and chose Eleanor Viney, a well-connected young lady descended from Wiltshire landowners. Her father had been the Rev. James Viney, vicar of Bishopstrow, Wiltshire, and she brought her husband a considerable fortune for those days; no less than £5,300, with a promise contained in the Deed of Settlement that 'she hath great expectations of being possessed of considerable fortune from her aunt, Mary Anne Viney, of the city of Gloucester, and otherwise'.

No portraits of Mary Anne's parents are known to survive. A young man in naval uniform, a young woman becomingly capped, they may hang unrecognized in some Exeter house or antique shop. It was Mary Anne's habit to keep everything remotely connected with herself, her family, and her friends, which makes their lack remarkable. But among her papers are letters which provide a glimpse of her parents' courtship, and suggest that she may have inherited her vivacity from her exuberant, voluble father. In 1786 he writes from Gosport to Miss Viney, at Charlewood House, near Plympton, facetiously ordering her to have her portrait painted.

> You profess much vanity, no doubt—but pray give me leave to figure to myself the pleasing sense of admiring you under all forms, and at every point of view. I am the best judge of your Deformity, and will keep you totally in my own Opinion. Therefore, as your picture will gratify me when the original is beyond my view, it is my particular command that it shall be done. Does this look like beginning to show my lordly authority? O yes, I find I shall improve rapidly under my teacher P–n in the act of 'Wife obey your Husband'—otherwise called good husbandry.
>
> So you presume to think that you will keep the Hut vastly neat; be careful, Madam, lest rash promises bring on severe correction. This style of speaking seems to sit very easy on me, do you suppose you are strong enough to bear it? Oh! No!

—fear not, I have other Language for Nora, she whose tender Bosom fondly moves to make me happy—shall I not, O Heaven-born sympathy, devote my hours, my life, my soul to cherish, serve that dr. Girl where all my future joys are centred. Nora, you found me truly in the rough, and it is your business to bend, burnish and shape me to whatever form will make you most happy, and if you are not completely 'twill be your own fault.

Adieu—eternally and affectionately I am Eleanor Viney's John Evans.

In another letter he looks forward to the happy moment 'when I hold my adorable Wife in these fond arms . . . my good little housewife will have ready all the receipts for her husband to mix. . . .'

His pre-marital dictates have a flavour of Mirabel's to Millamant.[1]

You are, Nora, perfect clockwork—do you think, you little Hussey, I will allow you to be so regular when I am your acknow-ledged Master? Do you imagine I will go to bed at 10 and rise by 7? Don't mistake me, I am grown quite a drone, beside it is in bed the moments fly and I almost wish to pass my time totally in bed till we meet—but peradventure the temper of my body as well as my mind will alter after a little matrimonial balsam . . . a quick mastery would greatly add to my happiness, and you are very sensible that was it in my power to fold you in these longing arms before the time appointed, I wou'd—but that cannot be—we must patiently wait till our money matters are in better order.

A lottery ticket was evidently intended to be the foundation of John's fortunes, but on 20 March 1787 he writes:

At length, Nora, all my dreams and expectations are vanished. My ticket is drawn—a blank! Therefore no more faith in dreams, they are not from Heaven, they are only founded upon the sleeping fancy by some subtle tantalizing Demon. . . . O that you cou'd hear me gently murmuring on your Bosom—but we shall soon I hope clasp each other never to part again.

To this courtship period, perhaps, belongs a very long song 'with music by Miss B[ridget] Viney', with an equally long chorus.

[1] In William Congreve, *The Way of the World.*

Blush not, turn not in confusion,
Kindly to my vows attend,
Let Love plead for this intrusion—
Who can love and yet offend?
Love more sweetly yields confession,
Glows the cheek, illumes the eye,
Glances own the fond impression,
Blushes paint the kind reply.

In later years Mary Anne told people that her parents made a runaway match. It may have been so, for neither Evanses nor Vineys appear in the list of witnesses to the ceremony in St Charles's Church, Plymouth. But at the same time and before the same altar, Eleanor's twin sister Bridget was joined in matrimony to John Evans's friend, Thomas Munn, a lieutenant in the East India Service. It seems highly improbable that both couples should have eloped, and even more so that a runaway bride should have brought with her such a handsome Deed of Settlement, drawn up beforehand. Mary Anne was somewhat given to romancing about her origins and youth, possibly prompted by her highly individual sense of fun. Indeed, it may well have been Mary Anne herself who started a rumour that she began life as a factory girl.

The newly-weds made their home in St Sidwell's. It was convenient for John's journeys to London or Plymouth, and for visits to his parents at Brampford Speke. Their first child was born on 10 February 1790, a boy who was christened James at the village church. On 21 March John and Eleanor carried him there again, for his burial.

Here another mystery arises, for Mary Anne grew up with a living brother, John Viney Evans, whose name appears in the Army Lists as both John and James. The discrepancy is probably explained by the fact that a child would often be given the name of one previously dead; John, born on 12 April 1791, was perhaps given the unofficial name of James as well, though John alone appears on his certificate of baptism, and John was the name by which his sister called him.

In the year after John's birth Eleanor bore a daughter, who was probably called after her great-aunt Mary Anne Viney, as James had been called after his uncle Captain James Viney. Soon after her appearance, John Evans was promoted to first

4

lieutenant, and in January 1793 he was commissioned to H.M.S. *Ceres*, a fifth-rate of 32 guns. What appeared to be a fortunate promotion turned out to be the reverse. *Ceres* sailed for the West Indies to join John Jervis (later Earl St Vincent) in his expedition against the French West Indies. During the voyage there was such a severe outbreak of malignant fever that the ship was ordered to Bermuda in an attempt to save her men. John, who died on 17 April 1794, was probably a victim of the fever, for there is no evidence that he was killed on active service.

The young widow, left alone with her two-year-old son and baby daughter, appears to have moved to the home of her husband's parents at Brampford Speke. Old Mr Evans owned or rented the farms of Sowdons and Moors, in one of which he, his wife, and widowed daughter lived. Among the Disraeli papers is a print of a thatched house, probably Sowdons (now rebuilt) with a long garden ending in a ha-ha. The inscription on the print reads 'where Mary Anne was born', and is accompanied by a wisp of soft brown hair from her head, 'cut when a child, 1793'.

Apart from the new face of Sowdons, Mary Anne would find little change in her birthplace today. After the noise of modern Exeter, largely rebuilt since the destruction that came upon it from the air in 1942, it is strange to come to a little village almost untouched by the passing of two centuries. The surrounding countryside is green, lush and hilly, with the soft, sensuous look of rural Devon. The sturdy church, the cottages and farmlands, are much as Mary Anne knew them. Even the village inn has escaped modernization, remaining a little alehouse of the kind George Morland painted for the price of a pint. The churchyard in which little James Evans lies is peaceful and pretty.

No trace of Mary Anne remains at Brampford Speke, just as no record of her childhood appears among her papers, other than a letter written to her mother, perhaps when Mrs Evans was visiting relations.

My Dear Mama,
   Our school is broke up and I am very comfortable with three pleasant companions with whom and my brother I shall spend the holidays very agreeably. He unites with me in duty to you

5

and all kind friends and in wishing they may enjoy the pleasures
of the season I am my dear Mama your Dutiful daughter
Mary Anne Evans.

In spite of her fatherless state, Mary Anne's childhood was
certainly 'very agreeable'. As a woman she wore that sunny
confidence which is the heritage of the child who has never had
reason to mistrust its elders, even admitting, with cheerful
complacency, that nobody in her life had ever crossed her. There
was great family affection between the three Evanses. In their
letters Eleanor is always 'My darling Mamma' or 'My dearest
Mamma', and Mary Anne's pet name is 'Little Whizzy' or
'Tiddy': a bestowal which evokes more vividly than description
the merry little girl whose high spirits sometimes subjected her
to the disapproval of her rather pious young brother. A gay
little spinning-top, she flashed and whirled with an affectation
of feather-headedness which concealed a shrewd brain and a
warm heart.

Perhaps she picked up the local Devon burr, and it clung to
her sweet voice for life, her accent later causing as many
raised eyebrows in London society as her provocatively frank
speech. Queen Victoria, entertaining her to dinner for the first
time, was to remark that '*she* is very vulgar, not so much in her
appearance, as in her way of speaking', a way which we may be
sure Mary Anne exaggerated in the cause of amusing people or
shocking them. But her beauty, which caused her lovers to
compare her to a fairy, can never have been of the red-cheeked
rustic kind, nourished though it was by the fresh Devon air.

At Brampford Speke she played, galloped through the
meadows, learned to read and write as fluently as she talked,
and in as dashing a style. Her spelling was perfect, but her
handwriting must have been the despair of her teachers. Every
attempt of theirs to force her into the fashionable copper-plate
script was useless; to the end of her life she wrote an execrable
scribble of heavily slanting black down-strokes and faint up-
strokes, more like hieroglyphics than handwriting. Her contemporaries, used to their own and other people's small clear
letters, must have found it baffling, though most of her corre-
spondents were too polite to say so. Only her cousin Walsh
Porter was frank· enough to tell her, 'I could not read some of

6

the hieroglyphics in your letter; if there is any merit in writing illegibly, you shine.' And, later, 'I should not care what colored paper you wrote on, so that I could read the contents, but I cannot.'

There must have been many visits to Exeter for Mary Anne: shopping expeditions with her mother, riding to market with her grandfather, playing with John in the old pleasure-ground of Northernhay, watching the hands of the clock at St Mary Steps Church creeping up to the hour, when the three mechanical figures called by Exeter folk 'the Miller and his Sons' would come out and strike. The sailor's children would stop to gaze at the Ship Inn, where Drake used to drink, and wander on the Quay, watching the boats come up the Exe to unload at the fine Customs House. Under firm escort by servants, they might go to a fair in the Crolditch, or to the great Lammas Fair which was Exeter's annual revel, to ride on hobby-horses and watch the Punch and Judy and the travelling actors ranting out melo-drama, acrobats dancing on tightropes, and pathetic moulting bears lurching clumsily to the scraping of a fiddle; then, happily tired, back to Brampford Speke laden with fairings, a doll and ribbons and trinkets for Mary Anne, a tin soldier and a lambkin made of plaster and wool, exactly like Grandpapa's lambs, for John. There was always plenty of money to spend and plenty of fun to be had. The widowed lady who had been Lieutenant Evans's dear Nora was deeply religious, but far from narrow-minded; and the years were the pleasant ones before Georgian freedom gave way to Victorian sobriety. Mary Anne's early years were blessedly uneventful. A happy childhood, like a happy marriage, does not make history; but the latter truism Mary Anne was by her life triumphantly to refute, not once, but twice over.

2

'You captivate me beyond description'

In 1807, when Mary Anne was fifteen, her grandparents died. At once the fortunes of the Evans family changed. There was now no point in continuing to live at Brampford Speke, and Mrs Evans took the natural step of transporting herself and the children to her nearest relative, her brother Captain James Viney. His home was Cathedral House, adjoining Gloucester Cathedral Close, a pleasant old place which had been in the Viney family for the best part of a century. The original Viney of Gloucester had been a barrister-at-law of the Middle Temple, but the present one had chosen the Army, and distinguished himself on active service. He fought under Wellington in the Peninsular War and was awarded the medal and clasp for the battles of Rolera, Vimiera, and Corunna, at which he commanded the Royal Artillery. A grateful country then awarded him the Companionship of the Bath and a knighthood; by 1830 he was a Major-General.

James Viney is one of the shadowy figures in Mary Anne's story. He was obviously on good enough terms with his sister to share his home with her, at such times when he was in England, and it may have been the example of his gallantry which fired his nephew John to enlist in the Army. In September 1808, at the age of seventeen, he received a commission as ensign in the 29th Regiment of Foot. From this time onward John seems to have lived away from home, and to have become an increasing source of anxiety to his mother and sister. There are indications that money was no longer very plentiful in the Evans and Viney families, and that John was better at spending than at saving. His portrait at Hughenden Manor shows a delicate, sensitive face with a look of pathos in the blue eyes, and hair that appears prematurely grey.[1] His mother worried, Mary Anne worried,

[1] But may have been powdered, for the lock framed with his miniature is brown.

and his long, neurotic letters, sparing them nothing of his troubles, did little to reassure them.

For only three years they lived in Gloucester, where Mary Anne, a very well-educated young lady by now, is said to have taught in a Sunday school established to improve the minds and morals of Gloucester pin-factory girls. Then came another drastic change, for Eleanor Evans married for the second time.

Of Thomas Yate, her new husband, little is known. In the copy of his will for Probate he is called a surgeon, but no record exists of any Bristol medical man of that name. Perhaps he was an Army surgeon, for one version of his career makes him a lieutenant of Militia; if so, Mrs Evans may have met him through her brother. Another tradition makes him Master of Ceremonies at Clifton Assembly Rooms. He is hardly mentioned in the family letters, and seems to have brought no money with him, for his wife's anxiety about her son's debts and the money due to her from Gloucester properties increased with the years. They now lived at 50 Park Street, Bristol, in a plain, tall, terraced house (now, like its neighbours, a shop) in the steep street rising from the quayside to the Cathedral. To Mary Anne, with the sea in her Devonshire blood, it must have been an exciting place to live, after the ecclesiastical solemnities of Gloucester. It was five years since Trafalgar. Sailors who had served with Nelson still swarmed in the streets, fought and whored in the Backs along the river, and drank in the Llandoger Trow, the inn which Robert Louis Stevenson was to people with Ben Gunn and Long John Silver and Jim Hawkins. Mary Anne certainly never went into it, or any other Bristol tavern, for no lady could be seen in places where songs resembling 'Yo ho ho, and a bottle of rum', only a great deal less inhibited, were roared out, and where knives were still drawn at the slightest provocation.

Bristol had become rich by the slave trade, as well as by tea and tobacco. The splendid houses of Berkeley Square and Great George Street had been built from the profits of the sale of black flesh. Merchantmen lying in the dock brought goods and money to Bristol; the merchants themselves were the only class to have been enriched by the Napoleonic Wars. Fashionable life abounded, particularly in Clifton, whose beautiful

9

rows and crescents were set in green downs, so high and airy that even hopeless consumptives like Sarah Siddons's dying daughter came there in the hope of cure. The Spa at Hotwells, Clifton, was patronized by a livelier set than the lower-lying and more torpid Bath. Beaux and belles rode in neat turn-outs to routs at the Assembly Rooms, the streets were gay with spangled muslins and feathered bonnets, swallow-tail coats and dazzling white tight pantaloons. Mary Anne, for the moment, could only look on.

Various people who knew Mary Anne, or knew those who knew her, received the impression that at some time in her youth she had been either a milliner or a milliner's apprentice. Sir Stafford Northcote said that while staying at his home, Pynes, near Exeter, she asked to be taken for a drive through the town, and pointed out to him 'the shop where I was a milliner'. Either his memory or hers must have been vastly at fault: she left Exeter at fifteen, and before that had no financial need to be apprenticed to any trade. Another rumour ran that an old lady, who had once been Mary Anne's companion, said that before her first marriage she kept a milliner's shop in Bath or Exeter. Yet another story links her with a shop at Chepstow. All these may be entirely apocryphal, perhaps stemming from some facetious statement made by Mary Anne in one of her Cinderella moods. But they are so persistent that they may have some foundation. Miss Doris Leslie's[1] researches in Bristol archives revealed that one Mary Evans, mantua-maker, had a shop in Culver Street, Clifton, which ran parallel to Park Street. But neither Mary nor Evans was an uncommon name.

If she was for a time a milliner, she chose a most apt trade for a pretty, frivolous, money-wise young woman. Money-wise she certainly learnt to be at this time, and the knowledge served her well when the administration of a great town house and a fine country house came into her hands. She was learning to be a good housekeeper. She kept an Occasional Book, copying into it useful hints such as her mother's 'Strengthening Receipt'.

Take a bottle of port wine, and an ounce of isinglass, a small piece of cinnamon and sugar to your taste, put all the ingredients together on the fire, and when half is gone, it will be sufficiently

[1] See Bibliography: *The Perfect Wife.*

done. Take every morning at eleven o'clock, the quantity about the size of a nutmeg.

A recipe for Devonshire junket jostles directions for reading a set of *trompe-l'œil* cards.

Raise the edge of the card to the level of the eyes, about a foot from you, glance along the surface, and the words will be legible.
1. Happy may we part,
    And happy meet again.
2. May I kiss you my dear,
    Yes, if you please.
3. You are politely requested
    to mind your own business.
4. Slap Bang, Here we are again,
    What jolly dogs are we.

That, of course, was for recreative moments, like the riddles she noted down.

Why is a poker and shovel like a consort?—Because it is an appendage to the Grate.

Why is the Prince of Wales like a cloudy day?—Because he is likely to reign.

(As indeed he was: King George III had relapsed into the terrible illness which has now been diagnosed as hereditary porphyria rather than madness[1] after the death of his beloved daughter Amelia in the year Mary Anne came to Bristol.) More soberly, she records a maxim to be borne in mind by the sick:

Doctor Air and Doctor Diet,
Doctors Merriment and Quiet.

At their first meeting Disraeli was to call her 'a flirt and a rattle'. She was obviously both, even at this early age, for among her notes are verses copied out by her, with wicked glee, from disappointed admirers (though at least one, as we shall see later, had a certain success). A poem from one of the unfortunates, sarcastically entitled 'A Pleasing Memento of yr. friendship', informs her that

[1] See Bibliography: C. C. Trench, *The Royal Malady.*

My waking daydreams thought they found thee
With truth's bright halo wreathed around thee,
But foul deceit, I saw the token,
The vision's fled, the dream is broken.
Faithless, from my heart I sling thee,
Worthless, to the winds I fling thee!

It may have been the same disillusioned swain who sent her
the lines 'On Friendship; to Miss Evans',

You call yourself my friend, and say
You glory in the name;
But tell me, will you, on the day
When Poverty, in drear array,
With sorrow drives each smile away
Preserve the sacred flame?

Poverty, in drear array or otherwise, was soon to be no longer
any concern of Miss Evans. She made her way into good Clifton
society, probably through her mother's aristocratic connections.
She danced and laughed and flirted with the best of them, as
merry as the richest nymph in Clifton; or possibly merrier. She
must have charmed many hearts. Of one, she made a complete
and dazzling conquest.

It was 1815. The occasion was a ball in celebration of the
victory of Waterloo, given in Clifton by the Vernon-Grahams,
visitors to the Spa. General Vernon, who had hyphenated his
name the year before, was half Welsh, and had invited as one of
his guests a fellow-Welshman. Wyndham Lewis was thirty-
seven, son of a country squarson of Newhouse, Llanishen,
Glamorganshire. The land itself was not particularly profitable,
being suitable neither for grazing nor building, and somewhat
remote in its situation; but Wyndham's father also had sub-
stantial holdings in the Dowlais iron works, the profits of which
brought Wyndham something like £11,000 a year, in those days
a very handsome income.

Wyndham had read Law and was to be called to the Bar in
1819, but would never practise, preferring to take a vigorous
part in local affairs as a magistrate and deputy lieutenant of
Glamorgan. He was also squire of Greenmeadow, the house near
Cardiff which he leased from a brother, modernized and renamed Pantgwynlais (the Welsh translation of Greenmeadow).

12

His inclinations were political, but at this time he seems to have had no serious thought of indulging them at a national level. He had few recreations other than hunting and scribbling verse. The only scandal that could remotely be attached to his name was connected with an illegitimate daughter being brought up in Ireland. He had never married, perhaps because of a certain shy and withdrawn quality in his character, though there must have been hot competition for him among the young ladies of Llanishen and Cardiff. His closer friends called him Tony, an improbably frivolous name for this man of grave, melancholy aspect. Not even a well-cut coat, waistcoat of shot silk, and draped black cravat could make him look handsome or romantic. Deep-set, weak eyes, unfashionably cropped hair, a long wandering nose and an elderly mouth, combined with prominent ears, gave him the aspect of a failed Lake Poet. But his face, like his nature, was kindly, and under the shot-silk waistcoat beat a tender, susceptible heart.

From the moment he bowed over Mary Anne Evans's tiny hand and led her into the dance he was her slave. She was twenty-three and at the height of her beauty. Short in stature and of slight build, though with an excellent figure, she was endowed with every grace favoured by taste and fashion. Her face was a perfect oval, her complexion radiantly clear. Enormous dark blue eyes, under curving brows, a straight nose, a small, sweet mouth with the very slightest look of sensuality about it, were crowned by brown hair, parted smoothly above her high brow and gathered into great clusters of shining ringlets, falling to hide a swan-like neck and white, sloping shoulders. Her bodice, in the fashion of the time, was very low-cut, giving the world the full benefit of her shoulders and not a little of a charming bosom. She affected long earrings, peeping tantalizingly between the ringlets, and was much given to lace frills and pink and blue satin bows. Just as her manner could change in an instant from encouraging sweetness to cold rejection, her face had the enchanting quality of repose and stillness, almost gravity, when it was not breaking into smiles. This 'face without a frown' may well have helped to preserve her beauty so long from the wrinkles of middle-age. And, more potent than loveliness, she radiated sex and incited men by her very presence.

If she had intended to deal out to Wyndham Lewis the hot-and-cold treatment with which her other suitors had been tormented, she soon discovered her mistake. Here was a man who, despite his mild looks, would not take 'No' for an answer: besides, his intentions were strictly honourable. The violence of his passion for her was literally irresistible, it would seem, and he must have had some attraction for her, for no force on earth could impel Mary Anne along a road she did not want to take. Perhaps she found an older man more interesting than the youths who had pursued her, and his quiet manner a perfect foil for her own exuberance. There may even have been a kindred quality that drew them together. Disraeli was to comment that Wyndham Lewis 'is one of the oddest men I ever met, but I like him', and Mary Anne certainly had some quirks of character which would one day earn her a reputation for eccentricity.

There was also, of course, his money. Behind Mary Anne's fair white brow lay a keen, practical brain. Wyndham Lewis was the richest suitor she was ever likely to find. Her youth was no longer in its early morning by contemporary standards, and life at 50 Park Street might well be improved upon. One of the riddles copied out in Mary Anne's Occasional Book had been: 'How is the best way to keep a man's love?—Not to return it.' Now, she decided, was the moment to disprove this. Very soon after their first meeting, it seems, Miss Evans consented to become Mrs Wyndham Lewis.

The transported lover lost no time in establishing himself in his lady's life. He stayed in Clifton, leaving affairs at Pant-gwynlais to take care of themselves. He made himself agreeable to Mary Anne's relations, bestowing on her mother hare and woodcock, hunted by his brother. He visited her uncle, Colonel Viney, in Plymouth, writing from the Colonel's home on 22 October that although he was receiving the greatest attention from his host, he could not help regretting his absence from the object of his 'fondest and tenderest affections'. A fortnight later, from Cheltenham, he is wistfully chiding 'my dearest most charming darling' for a lapse into coquetry.

How much happier I am in musing over your virtues, how delighted I am with recalling to my memory those pathetic

14

tones which on our way from Mead Park on Sunday made so
indelible an impression on my heart; but what would induce the
angelic eyes of my charmer to triumph in her conquest? by their
frown on the same evening, surely she was not *aware* of her
conquest, and I shd. have been convinced she was not, but that
dear Token which she drew from her Bosom, with so much
modesty, renewed every kinder emotion of my soul.

O do not, my own angelic Mary Anne, harbour a thought which
can excite such another look! if you could see into my heart
you would be assured that you have no cause to entertain the
slightest doubt of the unalterable Love of your most afftionate
W.L.

On 14 November he writes that at their last meeting 'you
look'd at me with such scornful anger . . . but I thought you
lov'd me precisely the same as *the one at Redcliff* led me to
doubt. . . .' On 30 November, more cheerful, he tells her, 'On
Monday my dearest Mary Anne I hope to be delighted with
another kiss from the object of my most affectionate love.'

Day after day the post brought Mary Anne long poetic
effusions which made up in rapture what they lacked in scansion, and blended the Bible with Roman mythology and a touch
of the romantic balladry from the popular *Waverley* novels.

> Propitious God of Love, my breast inspire
> With all thy charms, with all thy pleasing fire;
> Propitious God of Love, thy succour bring,
> While I my darling, my Mary Ann sing.
> Mary Ann lovely, modest, easy, kind,
> Softens the high, and rears the abject mind . . .
> Wherever she arrives, soft peace she brings,
> From her the Heav'n of softest passion springs.
> With virtue strong as hers had Eve been arm'd,
> In vain the Fruit had blush'd, the Serpent charm'd.
> Nor had our Bliss by Penitence been bought,
> Nor had frail Adam fall'n, nor Milton wrote . . .
> From distant shores repair the noble youth,
> And find report for once had likened truth.
> By wonder first, and then by passion mov'd,
> They came, they saw, they marvell'd and they lov'd.
> By public praises, and by secret sighs,
> Each own'd the general power of Mary Ann's eyes.
> With knowing skill, they each with ardour strove
> By glorious deeds to purchase Mary Ann's love . . .
> In vain they combated, in vain they writ,

Useless their skill, and impotent their wit.
Great Venus only must direct the dart,
Which else will never reach the fair one's heart.
Spite of the attempts of force, and soft effects of art,
Great Venus must prefer the happy one,
In Wyndham's cause her favor must be shewn,
And Mary Ann, of mankind, must love but him alone.

This heroic version of courtship in Clifton may well have caused Mary Anne's elegant eyebrows to arch even higher; but it was gratifying to have on record that however warmly she bestowed 'the Heav'n of softest passion' upon Wyndham, she knew where to stop. He gave her a locket, accompanied by some rhetorical questions.

To whom should I the Locket take
But her who 'joys the gift I make
And boasts she wears it for my sake?
What Nymph can I admire or trust
But Mary Anne, beauteous, true, and just?
What Nymph should I desire to see
But her who leaves the plain for me?
For whom should I compose the lay
But her who listens when I play?
To whom in song repeat my cares
But her who in my sorrow shares?
In love am I not fully blest?
Mary Ann, prythee tell the rest.

Irrepressibly he poured out his love in touchingly awful stanzas.

On flow'ry banks, by ev'ry murmuring stream,
Mary Ann is my Muse's softest theme . . .
When she is near, all anxious trouble flies,
And joy's renewed by her consoling eyes . . .
But on the plain when she no more appears,
The plain a dark and gloomy prospect wears . . .
Dear lovely girl, I cry to all around,
Dear lovely girl, the flattering vales resound.

Mary Anne obviously enjoyed Wyndham's courtship, even to the extent of banishing her mother from the room when he called, drawing from him a mild reproof. 'I can assure you from my heart,' he wrote, 'that it will afford me most unfeigned pleasure to enjoy your charming society, but I must beg that of your mother is at hand—she will not be driven from her fireside.' That her kisses and caresses were freely given is clear from a paean by Wyndham which also records her reputation.

Of her, they cry, I'm often told,
'See there the maid with bosom cold!
Indifference o'er her heart presides,
And love and lovers she derides . . .'
Ah, ever be they thus deceived,
Shall be her bosom cold believed!
And never may enquiring eyes
Pierce through her faithful Love's disguise.
Yet could they all her bosom share
And see each grateful tumult there,
Ah! never should I then be told
That she is the maid with bosom cold.

Still she could not quite break herself of teasing and tormenting. 'You captivate me *beyond description*,' wrote poor Wyndham, 'and no shadow of doubt ever clouds my thoughts— indeed I often accuse myself of cruelty in reverting to what occurs in your *other moods*. . . .'

Her brother, now Major Viney Evans, approved of the match. 'My dearest sister,' he wrote:

I must congratulate you on your approaching nuptials to a gentleman you seem to have a particular regard for, as he is the finest out of so many admirers you have at last fixed on as your husband, and I am sure Mr. Lewis must be very superior, having engaged a heart as *particular* as yours, and I assure you it gives me no small satisfaction to hear you express yourself in such warm and affectionate terms of him, as it convinces me that your whole heart is wrapt up in and concentrated on him, and to tell you the truth I used to think you very cold, but at the same time was always sure that if any gentleman *could* insure your affections, no young Lady would really be more warm.

Your very timely description of Mr. Lewis has pleased me beyond measure, because I know your discrimination is so great that you do not speak like a blind lover, but as a sincere Friend, which, my dearest Mary Ann, is a very scarce article, in this weathercock age. . . . As of course my Uncle will be acquainted with this business, I hold it advisable for him to give you away, particularly as he has always shown so marked a partiality to yourself. . . . You are now, my dear sister, about to enter an entirely new state in this life, where you will be obliged in many things to be responsible. The charge of a house and perhaps a family conducted in a proper manner require the utmost exertions; neither should a wife ever find her time unemployed, being always studious in the education of her children or doing good to her neighbours.

I need not tell you to be always uncommonly regular in your devotions to God, as from Him all blessings flow; but it is your duty also to impress on the minds of your servants and all that are about you the high consideration and regular attendance at church or Chapel. . . . I am sure in this last respect the example you have had from our excellent Mother is engrafted on your mind, that yourself and Mr. Lewis will make one of the happiest couples in Wales. . . . I hope one of these days, when resting from the fatigues of my Campaigning (or our holiday as we soldiers call it) I shall have the honor of being introduced to Mr. Lewis. . . .

We shall next Friday have a grand Review of the whole British Army by the Duke of Wellington in the Champ de Mars.

Poor, pompous, pious John, so unlike his volatile sister; he was never to have practical experience of the married state about which he so gravely lectured his 'Whizzy dear'.

In the winter of 1815 Mary Anne was married. 'Friday, at Clifton,' reported the *Bristol Mirror*, 'Wyndham Lewis, Esq., of Green Meadow, near Cardiff, to Mary Anne, only daughter of the late John Evans, Esq., of Brampford Speke, Devon.' The witnesses were James Viney and A. Yates, whoever he or she may have been. It has been suggested that Thomas Yate may have celebrated his step-daughter's happiness rather too freely the night before, and consequently been unable to remember his own name at the ceremony; but Thomas's sister, Ann, may have been present and signed the register, in the excitement of the moment adding an extra 's' to her name. Mary Anne's Uncle James gave the bride away, Mrs Yate no doubt wept, though not bitterly, and the happy couple left for a honeymoon, probably spent at Greenmeadow.

3

'The lady will try her utmost to please'

Life at Greenmeadow suited Mary Anne. For the first time she had the opportunity of using her practical mind to administer a fine large house, and the money to carry out her schemes. It had been built on the site of a Cistercian monastery, in a position carefully chosen for its advantages. Wide, lovely panoramic landscapes surrounded it, the river Taff flowed through a green valley, and busy Cardiff was only four or five miles away. In a different direction, at about the same distance, was New House, the Wyndham Lewis family home. Here Wyndham's father had lived and died, as had Wyndham's elder brother Thomas, who had died seven years before, leaving a baby heir, John.

John's guardian was not Wyndham, perhaps because he had been a bachelor at the time of his brother's death, but the Reverend William Price Lewis, a younger brother. Known locally as 'The Governor', he was an outstanding example of the Georgian clergyman who combined the minimum of spiritual instruction with the maximum of material gain. Legend credits him with the incumbency of seventeen separate parishes in Glamorganshire, each one administered by a curate while William collected the income and tithes. Firmly believing that duty should never be allowed to interfere with pleasure, he devoted most of his time to hunting, and Mrs Yate in Bristol benefited by many a brace from his bag. His wife had left him after the birth of their two children, possibly because he had distributed other offspring freely about his various parishes. Mary Anne must have found him entertaining company.

The prolific Wyndham Lewis family had also produced two girls, Mary Anne and Katherine, both neighbours of Wyndham. Mary Anne Williams had two daughters, Catherine and Mary, pretty unmarried girls, of whom Mary Anne became very fond. They were not far from her own age and of gay disposition. With Catherine she went to visit some of her mother's relations, the Scropes. Emma, the Scrope daughter, had married Mr Poulett, a Swansea man, and lived near Swansea in a house delightfully named Fairy Brittain. With the lively Emma, Mary Anne and Catherine attended balls, danced, laughed and flirted. Catherine made fifteen conquests, Mary Anne reported in a letter to John, adding that her niece-in-law was 'more beautiful, more Goddess-looking than ever', and inviting him to come and see for himself. Catherine seems to have shared Mary Anne's own girlhood disposition, preferring flirtation to engagement, for of the conquests who were invited back to enliven Greenmeadow, none was successful in winning Catherine's hand.

Wyndham was often away from home, either in London or at the Dowlais works, Swansea or Bristol. Diligently he wrote home, letters which show that the marriage was a lasting success. From London in 1817, he wrote telling her that he had been to the Park and gave her an account of the fashions. Ordering some Madeira in the Borough, he had been enchanted to find that the ship which had brought the wine from Spain was called the *Mary Anne*: it put him in mind of his 'own darling', and made him even more eager to return to the Partner of his Joys. She had been ill, a rare thing with her, and the anxious husband warned her not to eat sweet things like jellies, in case they spoiled her 'genial appetite'.

There was plenty of leisure at Greenmeadow, particularly now that Wyndham's profits from Dowlais were increasing rapidly. Mary Anne occupied some of it by studying French and Italian, in which languages she soon became proficient enough to write to Wyndham. He was charmed at her enterprise and learning; they inspired him to take up Italian himself, something which would never have entered his head before he met his volatile wife. But neither studies nor business could distract his mind from 'My dear dearest Darling'. 'My spirits are not quite the thing when separated from her, but they are always elevated after reading her afftionate letters.' He went to see the celebrated Miss Eliza O'Neill play in *The Tragedy of Bellamina*, but was not so impressed with her acting as he had been at Cheltenham, perhaps because Mary Anne had been with him then. 'You cannot think how I miss my little darling. . . . I really begin to think that absence increases love, for a man does not know the value of such a prize as my darling till he has been without her society, and then he sees the loss he sustained in its true colours.' He wished he had been at the ball she attended in Neath, 'to hear them admire my little pet'.

Mary Anne was not one to mope. She filled in Wyndham's absences by entertaining. The Yates were often staying with her; Mary and Catherine Williams frequently visited and explored the pleasures of the neighbourhood. One of these expeditions was to Dowlais, founder of the family fortunes, where, regardless of pretty clothes, they went 'in tram wagons a mile and a half underground to see the mines, screaming and laughing all the way there and back and we came back looking like chimney-sweeps'. The Reverend William owned a pack of harriers, with which the girls would go hunting from New House. Mary Anne was proud of her riding. She acquired a greyhound of her own, which Wyndham implored her not to lose—it had roving ways.

When she came in from the field, there were usually guests to entertain. Her hospitality was famous among their steadily-growing circle. The châtelaine of Greenmeadow took particular pride in the personal touch. In one of the sets of verses which formed such an essential part of Regency correspondence, she addresses her friend Sir Charles Morgan of Tredegar with honeyed promises.

> The lady will try her utmost to please,
> Your bed shall be warm and made to your ease,
> But of nightcaps I own I have now got another
> To keep it and wear it and prize it for ever.
> Were I but a mouse I'd venture to peep,
> To look at my pet when he is asleep.
> Behold! deary me! oh, what do I see,
> But Charles in a nightcap given by me!
> Then come to Greenmeadow—I promise a treat,
> I will sing and I'll play the air that is sweet.
> Then come and see me again and again—
> To meet is a pleasure—to part is a pain.

It may have been Charles whose bread-and-butter letter, or Collins, as it would come to be called after Jane Austen's day, took up the following somewhat astonishing form.

To describe the great comforts I found at Green Meadow,
I commence with the pleasures of dear little bed, oh.
Such dreams I have had I shall ever remember,
It was on the night of the third of December,
Muslin curtains trimm'd with beautiful lace,
Lightly glaz'd were my sheets, you might see your face,
Pale pink were the lining, like fair Maidens' bloom,
In fact little Paradise was my whole room.
My pillow of lawn edged with elegant border,
With lavender scented and placed in nice order,
One thing only needful, without which are few charms,
But a bachelor's fate—not one in his arms . . .
Pens, paper, all colours of seals a great choice,
Books of song to amuse, had I found but a voice,
Books on religion, were my thoughts so inclined,
But I leave you to guess what took up my mind.
Silver candlesticks gilt, a most elegant pair,
Green Nangarrow or Dresden, the choicest of ware,
Gilt boxes containing most beautiful brooches,
Were I tempted to steal I defy all reproaches.
Much time would elapse before even suspicion
Would fix on the thief or day with precision.
Various the bottles with sweetest of scents
To put with my handkerchief—I shall relent.
But what was most grateful in washing my nose,
My water most strangely was tinctured with *Rose*.
From my bed to the toilet I never could pass
But my figure full length appeared in the glass.
In short all my toilet was a source of much pleasure,
But to me the attention was far greater treasure.

It is difficult not to read into this effusion a certain amount
of *double-entendre*, or to wonder precisely what Mary Anne
contributed to the pleasures of 'dear little bed, oh'. The careful
specification of date, the suggestion that the writer had more
than brooches on his mind were he to turn thief, are interesting
pointers, as is the reference to Rose. It appears from
Mary Anne's correspondence that she was known as Rose to
those who may be broadly termed her lovers. A certain 'M.A.M.'
in another piece of jocular verse, makes play with 'fairies en
couleur de Rose', adding that to do poetical justice to Greenmeadow's hostess 'would puzzle the talents of Byron and
Scott'.

Charles Morgan appears again in a brisk invitation.

No sweet guitar or lovely voice,
I think you will approve my choice.
Exhibit then your splendid foot,
To say nothing of the ankle to't,
Display thy costly gems so rare,
Rival'd alone by arms so fair,
On *Thursday* let thy blue eyes glance
With mercy on Tredegar Manse.
Champaign, they say, is good for youth,
And never fails to speak the truth,
Regale yourself with Christmas pies,
But drink to me only with thine eyes!

Evidently she added the fashionable guitar to her accomplishments, and sang to it; though it was not until 1822 that she told her brother, 'I have only just found out that I have a *very fine voice*, is it not very extraordinary that none of my family ever told me I had a fine voice?'

One cannot believe that whatever may have been the case later, Mary Anne would have been literally unfaithful to Wyndham in those early years of their marriage, in his absence and on his own territory. She was deeply fond of him and was still watched over anxiously by her highly religious mother. But she was now moving in an increasingly lively society, a preparation for the even gayer one she would find in London. A few miles away she had the Governor as a prime example of loose living. She probably knew the rumour of Wyndham's illegitimate child, but never exhibited any symptoms of jealousy throughout her correspondence. The fact remains that throughout her youth and middle age she had an outstanding reputation as a flirt, a tremendous pride in her femininity, and an unappeasable appetite for admiration. She had enjoyed Wyndham's decorous love-making before their marriage. When he was away, she may well have been unable to resist the temptation to lead her admirers on to the point when 'liberties' would inevitably be taken, and to have enjoyed the liberties without crossing the barrier into actual adultery. The amorous verses of her guests suggest coy scuffles on one side or the other of bedroom doors, kisses snatched in conservatories, possibly even closer exchanges. Simple and open though her nature might appear, and spotless her reputation, it is clear that a kind of schizophrenia existed within her. Mary Anne Wyndham Lewis was one person: 'Rose' the other. One of her adorers, 'H.L.B.', summed up his feelings on leaving her with a patent envy of his fortunately absent host.

> Farewell to Green Meadow, one ling'ring farewell,
> To Wales, where Elysium and Harmony dwell . . .
> Where happiness reigns in the zenith of power,
> *And the Rose of enjoyment* is Lewis's flower.

Among the diversions, her life was not entirely unclouded. One sorrow, which she never mentions but which certainly existed, was her failure to produce a child. There is no hint even of a miscarriage; ironically, for one so completely a woman, she was apparently barren. She loved children, compensated for their absence with pet dogs, and after her death was remembered as a favourite with the village children around Hughenden, cuddling and playing with them in a manner not usual among the ladies of great landowners. James Sykes says that she adopted a daughter, but there is no evidence that an actual adoption of the girl Eliza ever took place.[1]

Her other grief was her beloved brother John, 'the delight and torment of my life', as she called him. From the time of their separation, when he joined the Army, she wrote him long letters every other week or so. She comforted him for the many misfortunes he reported to her, praised him warmly: 'I was so pleased at your having a party to drink our healths—I fancy how well you did it all.' There was full confidence between them. It seems to have been the Williams girls of whom she wrote that 'the horror of their father . . . makes them so anxious to marry'. She recounted details of her life to him as to a diary. 'How different my journal is to yours—I rise at eleven . . . answer notes and take a lesson on the guitar, and eat luncheon, go out in the carriage, pay visits and shop. . . .' But two aspects of John disturbed her: one was his financial recklessness and the other his relationship with women. It seems as though she were trying to protect him from the wrong sort of marriage—even, at one time, from marriage itself.

> You know I never wish you to marry—if you will only keep single you may call yourself one of the Saints notwithstanding

[1] See Bibliography: *Mary Anne Disraeli*. See also Appendix.

all your wicked ways . . . do anything but fall in love, dearest. Take care that the girls do not suppose your warm manner appears more than intended as it occasions such misery.

In another, later letter, she writes:

I am gratified in finding by yr. last letter that your heart is not quite as susceptible as formerly, and hope that whenever you marry, it will be to some fair Damsel in England, who has a little money in her pocket. It is so necessary for [illegible] enduring, my dearest, and I am happy in the marriage state, and I pray to the Almighty . . . never marry an Irish woman—not that I have the smallest fear you would connect your fate with that unprincipled nation.

Some of her letters to him are strangely passionate. 'The latter part of the dear letter was so kind and *endearing*—you have no one but Mama and myself to love you in the world . . . you should never try to please any one before us, except for a wife, but God forbid you should ever have one.' Another, written from Swansea, is obscure and incoherent.

I have not the heart to scold you now you are away from me, but if you were here it were well if your wicked face got scratched. If my letter alarmed you, which you tell me was the case, I am very sorry for it. Will you forgive me if I confess you disappointed me most terribly. . . . Another time come to the scratch and tactfully and for Heavens sake do not talk *at* me. It is bad taste and what I hate. With regard to Lord Byron yr. story is not a correct one. The lady you say loved him so truly jilted him and married one of his most intimate friends whom he had himself introduced to her. . . .[1] Never forget how much I have loved you and love me for what I am doing is my last request. The time may come when our prospects may be brighter. On this, hope I shall feed while I find my John is not changed, but resigned to destroy whatever happiness you [illegible]. I always think of my dearest Viney and shall never regret what has happened between us under any circumstances.

This letter, which begins 'My dearest love', ends with a request to direct the reply to 'Mrs. Kennedy's post-office'. Its

[1] This may be a reference—inaccurate in its facts if so—to Byron's rumoured liaison with his half-sister Augusta.

final sentence reads astonishingly from a sister to a brother. But in spite of Mary Anne's curious phraseology there is no evidence of an incestuous relationship between her and John. Her love was ardent and possessive and she may have felt a responsibility for him, a character so much weaker than herself, in the absence of real strength on the part of their mother. She and he had been very close as children, only a year separating their births. He had gone from her when he was seventeen, already, perhaps, showing signs of erratic behaviour. She feared his life was going wrong, she tried to put it right by wise and frank advice. More practically, she lent him money when she could, but under protest. In 1820 she wrote commiserating on his illness, and that he had 'no one near to nurse and comfort him'.

But what makes me more unhappy, my dearest John, is that it is quite out of my power to comply with your request, for if you would give me ten thousand worlds I could not give you the £10 you ask for, as Wyndham says I should only encourage you to be extravagant, etc., etc. It makes me wretched to suppose you are now ill, in want of money, but indeed it is not in my power to give, or even lend it you.

In 1826 she was again reluctantly refusing a loan.

I think it is now proper to tell you that it was not my Uncle who gave you the £500 but your own little Whizz. I have at last determined to tell you, to convince you, of the impossibility of my supplying you with money for some years—I have borrowed the money from two people and I must pay it off.

The tale of John's debts runs like a black thread through the variegated pattern of his sister's correspondence. On every life there is a shadow; her brother was hers.

In 1818 Thomas Yate died. Like John, he was given to improvidence. In Bristol his widow drew up for the solicitors a statement of the bills she had paid for him, and mentioned 'the Loss she sustained after his death'. To John she gave some 'solemn advice', in which she strongly recommended 'his following my example in a steady example of public and private worship; having ever found through the vicissitudes of this mortal state religion and a firm truth in the Almighty has ever been my greatest comfort, which I earnestly recommend to my dearest son'. The remainder of her life, in spite of her daughter's wealth, was to be clouded with financial worries.

Changes were taking place at Greenmeadow. Wyndham, in London, was planning improvements. There was to be a new corridor, decorated in geranium and Waterloo blue, the 'prime fashion just come out' which Mary Anne had prognosticated would be all the rage. Greenmeadow was now grandly nick-named 'Pantgwynlais Castle'. When it was finished Mary Anne gave a ball in its honour, entertaining a houseful of guests—one of the many splendid routs in which she delighted, and for which she would long be remembered in Glamorgan society.

The time was coming when the house would be quiet and deserted, its hostess gone. Wyndham, who had long been involved in local politics, now moved into a wider field. Mary Anne may well have encouraged him in this. She was ideally fitted for back-seat driving: in both her marriages she was to be, like Wordsworth's Perfect Woman, 'the very pulse of the machine', with a matchless ability 'to warn, to comfort, and command'.

The year 1820 was a crucial one for England. George III was dead at last, his unpopular son promoted from Regent to King. Emboldened by his new authority, George IV decided to divorce the wife from whom he had been separated for many years. Queen Caroline, who had been travelling the Continent with a man called Bergami and a child called Willikin, arrived in London on hearing of the death of her father-in-law. She was a grotesque figure, strangely dressed, badly painted, her large, unconvincing black wig topped by a wide-brimmed hat, and she was attended by a curious retinue including a former Lord Mayor of London, an Italian count, a small girl whom she had adopted to keep Willikin company, and a turbaned attendant. A cheering crowd welcomed her at Dover. She proceeded to London amid deafening huzzas, established herself at Carlton House, and began to demand her rights to be included in the Liturgy and to be crowned. The King refused. Caroline pressed her claims, to which the King replied by bringing an action for divorce, by way of a Parliamentary Bill. For the many who supported her there were a few who did not.

Most gracious Queen, we thee implore,
Go away and sin no more;
Or, if the effort be too great,
Go away, at any rate.

The Tory party, under Wellington and Castlereagh, approved these sentiments, while the Whigs, under Brougham, were for the King. A General Election would show on which side of the fence the country stood.

The wide-sprawling constituency of Cardiff was in the hands of the Bute family, with Lord Bute at its head and Lord James Crichton-Stuart its obvious Tory candidate. Almost on the eve of the election Lord James withdrew. Surprisingly, Wyndham Lewis replaced him.

Whatever Wyndham may have lacked in dynamism, Mary Anne made up for by her energetic electioneering. She started off with an advantage as a friend of the Bute family: Lord Bute had been a guest at Greenmeadow, and was known to be solidly behind Wyndham. Her own personality was an even greater advantage. She rode into Cardiff soliciting votes with hand-shakings ('such hands!' she told John) and even with kisses, in the manner of the late Duchess of Devonshire when canvassing for Fox. She gave a goose dinner to 109 voters. 'They cheer me wherever I go,' John read. 'They are all quite charmed by my heroism. Wyndham is popular beyond what I can describe. They call him their dear little Welsh boy . . . the lower orders are mad for him.'

The result of the election was a triumphant one for the Wyndham Lewises. Wyndham defeated the Whig candidate, Ludlow, by a comfortable majority, and the people of Cardiff cheered for Mary Anne, 'the Good Lady', as she stood triumph-antly waving on the balcony of the Angel Inn, her mother so happy by her side. Ever practical, she threw into the crowd three basketsful of rich cake, ribbons and cards, earning peals of laughter and delight.

Now Greenmeadow was their home for only half the year. The rest they spent in London, first in a furnished house, 13 Burling-ton Street, now Old Burlington Street, Mayfair. Once in London, Mary Anne began to enjoy it to the full. She hardly had a moment to herself, she wrote to John in far-off Mauritius.

28

. . . having been showing off in the Riding School almost every day, with Mr. Bennett, Lucy Collet and sometimes Mrs. Bennett. I have been riding their *beautiful* colt, with his lovely long tail. . . . I think dear John would have been a little proud of a certain person had he seen her on the capering horses. . . . Mr. Bennett says he could deny me nothing when in a riding-habit and hat, with long ringlets. I have had so many compliments in the above dress that my poor head is quite giddy. . . .

For five years the Wyndham Lewises had temporary addresses, paying exorbitant rents for some of them. The Burlington Street house cost twenty-five guineas a week, and 24 Portland Square something like fifty guineas. Mary Anne was annoyed that Wyndham could spend so much on the roof over their heads but not an extra sixpence for the impecunious John. Wyndham, in fact, had taken a firm stand about John. For one thing, he was jealous of Mary Anne's devotion to her brother, and for another he thought very little of that brother. Himself a canny Welshman, 'fond of money', as Mary Anne put it, he could not bear to see anyone squandering it and expecting to live off their rich relations. John should have known better. Mary Anne was constantly upset by John's shortcomings. If he had been in England, where she could have kept a sharp eye on him, things would not have seemed so bad, but he was in Mauritius, and 'I never can bear to think of the distance between us. I never never talk of you without tears.' When John declared himself happy to hear of Wyndham gaining a majority in 1825, Mary Anne cried with joy.

He frequently provoked tears of one kind or another in his mother, who told her 'Jacky-boy' in 1828 that his sister was growing fat with a very good appetite. 'This I know will give pleasure to my own dearest son, who I dreamt of so much lately, that when I awoke I could not help crying, and oh how much I thought of you the following day!'

She felt herself a most fortunate parent in having settled her son and daughter so advantageously. But a year later Wyndham was sitting down to write frowningly to his brother-in-law: 'My dear Viney, it is now 13 months since the date of any letter recd. from you by any of your friends, so you may imagine what grief your poor mother and sister are suffering on your account. I console them by every means in my power.'

And this after John had received a handsome contribution towards his promotion to Major from his brother-in-law, and had been invited to stay with the Wyndham Lewises for a month. First it had been Thomas Yate who sponged on him, and now it was John. Like many another husband, he realized ruefully that he had married not only his wife but her family as well.

4

'A beautiful house in town'

'Wyndham has promised me a beautiful house in town, and this is to be made very pretty . . . it will be so much more comfortable to have a regular town house and country house. I shall be sorry to leave this Country for almost every person have behaved so *very* kind and handsome.'

So Mary Anne wrote to John in 1820; but it was to be seven years before a house of their own materialized.

In 1826, when another election was imminent, the Wyndham Lewises prepared to repeat their triumph of 1821. Wyndham's popularity had not decreased with time: though 'so fond of money', he had wisely given to good causes and sat diligently on charity committees. The furore stirred up by the suppression of the Irish Catholic Association the year before would, they were sure, help the Tory party and win the day. 'At least it will not be my fault if it does not,' declared Mary Anne; and rode out canvassing in a fetching Welsh costume of flannel gown and loose cape, with a black hat coquettishly perched above her ringlets. 'I put on my Welshness and give dinners to friends and poor,' said she with airy confidence.

Unfortunately for her hopes, Lord James Crichton-Stuart demanded back his seat. There was nothing for Wyndham to do, other than quarrel with the great Marquess of Bute, but concede it gracefully. Mary Anne was furious. Her vanity offended, she shook the dust of Glamorganshire from what Charles Morgan had called her 'splendid foot' and declared her intention of living in London permanently. Greenmeadow was retained and sometimes visited, but the Wyndham Lewises' permanent home was now 1 Grosvenor Gate, Park Lane.

It was as splendid a house as Mary Anne could have envisaged.[1] Park Lane was, as a Victorian visitors' guide observed,

[1] Miraculously, it still stands (1972) at the corner of Park Lane. Offices now occupy it, but the grand rooms remain to suggest the splendour they once saw, and Mary Anne's balconies still look out towards the Park.

'the most aristocratic of addresses'. A wide, handsome thorough-
fare running from the Oxford Road and leafy Bayswater to
Piccadilly, it was then undefaced by massive hotels and business
premises. Grand house succeeded grand house. Here Byron had
lived, and 'Old Q.', the rakish old Duke of Queensberry; in
Apsley House, at the Lane's southern end, still lived great
Wellington. Elgin House, Dudley House, Gloucester House,
Dorchester House, and many others were the homes of the
Mayfair élite. Opposite, in Hyde Park, where cows still grazed,
high society promenaded in Rotten Row. The Ladies' Mile, by
that elegant artificial water, the Serpentine, was a flower-bed of
colour as the rich and beautiful passed each other in open
carriages, fringed parasols twirling, elaborately bonneted heads
nodding to acquaintances, gallant escorts riding as closely as
possible by their sides. The prospect from Mary Anne's windows
was open, almost rural. There was no Marble Arch, no Byron
statue. No imposing gates commemorated Victoria and Albert
and the Great Exhibition; for Victoria was a plump little girl of
six, playing in her nursery at Kensington Palace; her cousin
Albert a beautiful, solemn little boy of the same age, dutifully
learning his lessons at Coburg in Germany. 'Uncle King', whom
the cousins shared, fat, painted, wigged and pathetic, was
amusing himself with his latest elderly mistress, Lady Conyng-
ham, and planning an addition to the grounds of Buckingham
House in the form of 'five mounds, ornamented with elegant
groups, rising into an amphitheatre above which will appear
the summit of a hill crowned with lofty pines . . . the most
remarkable of the groups to represent Neptune, surrounded by
his Court'. (Unfortunately for London, this splendid scheme,
like many other architectural visions of the King's, did not take
shape.)

Mayfair society was at its richest, most snobbish, two-faced
and backbiting. To leave a room was to leave one's reputation
behind one, more often than not. Many a lady who had risen
from very little might have been daunted. To Mary Anne her
new status came as naturally as breathing. She rejoiced in this
fine mansion, with its large, imposing rooms; a library for
Wyndham, two drawing-rooms of her own, a couple of elegant
boudoirs, and ample accommodation for servants and visitors.
Her only regret was that Wyndham's parsimony prevented her

from furnishing it as lavishly as she wished. Then 'it would be one of the prettiest houses in the world'. She planned a cheerful but imposing colour-scheme of red, gold and white for the drawing-rooms, and a special, grand, Blue Room. Sparkling with pleasure, she wrote to John:

What a lucky house this has been to me—all in the year 1827 happened—

1. A beautiful new house and furniture.
2. A seat in Parliament.
3. A living for John.
4. A grand ball.
5. My brother's promotion to a majority.
6. The lawsuit with [illegible] ended.
7. A proposal from Mr. Gibson Graham to Catherine, which she has accepted.

The seat in Parliament which Wyndham had gained after the Cardiff disappointment was Aldeburgh, a little seaside borough in Suffolk. He did not retain it long, for, by the malice of Fate, a sudden depreciation in the price of pig-iron lowered his income drastically. He took the reluctant step of applying for the Chiltern Hundreds,[1] and Mary Anne suggested that a wise move would be to sell Greenmeadow. She had turned against it, and against Wales in general, after the Lord James Crichton-Stuart debacle; and after all it was ridiculous to keep up two homes, both on a grand scale. Wyndham sadly gave in; he always did, except over John. Now, especially, he put his foot down firmly when asked for more loans. 'I begged and implored him. It is so very very hard of him and the more he sees my distress the more determined he is. He is a dreadful, dreadful fellow in his character. I can hardly bear my own feelings on this subject.'

The Grosvenor Gate establishment had, however, to be kept up in style, carriages, servants and all. Fortunately for Mary Anne, she had learnt good housekeeping economy from her mother, and like her kept strict weekly accounts. In 1818

[1] This is the traditional procedure followed by a member of the House of Commons when wishing to relinquish his seat, since by parliamentary law direct resignation is forbidden. Though no longer in existence, the stewardship of the Chiltern Hundreds is considered an 'office of profit' which no Member of Parliament may hold. By accepting the office he in fact retires.

Mrs Yate's Park Street account-book included such items as 'bunns, 2d., bunch of violets, ½d., gave a young woman in the coach 2s. 6d., milk for the dog, 7½d., soft soap for the dog, 3d.' One of the riddles in Mary Anne's Occasional Book summed up neatly her attitude to expenditure: 'When may a man be said literally to be over head and ears in debt?—When he wears a wig that's not paid for.'

While totting up household expenditure with one hand, so to speak, Mary Anne was sending out invitations with the other for the Grand Ball she had named as one of the felicities of 1827. John was favoured with a rapturous account of it.

My company were most of the first people in London. The Duke of Wellington said it was like fairy land, the best ball he had been at this season, but are you not dazzled at your little Whizzy having received the Noble Hero at her house; the Duchess appears so very kind and amiable and expressed so much admiration at all she saw . . . the balustrades of the staircases were entwined with wreaths of flowers, the whole of the balcony (which goes all round the house) was enclosed as if making part of it, a crimson carpet at the bottom, the whole lined with lampshades all the way round.

An exotic note was provided by a decoration in the supper-room—a large windmill with its sails turning merrily round with gold and silver fish swimming in the stream below.

The ball was such a success that Dukes, Duchesses and Earls came back before breakfast next morning full of congratulations, an honour which not all hostesses would have welcomed, but Mary Anne smiled as brightly at that hour as at any other. How Wyndham felt is not recorded, though in the following year Mary Anne was pleased to write to John 'Wyndham . . . has got quite fond of visiting and goes with me everywhere', and as for herself, Lord Worcester[1] got her 'all the best men about town': a curious statement in view of the fact that the young Marquess moved in *demi-mondaine* circles and was himself of dubious reputation.

The entertainments she had been giving in London had always included the two Williams sisters, 'peacocking about', as Mary Anne put it, in the gayest circles, driving in the Wyndham

[1] Marquess of Worcester (1792–1853), afterwards 7th Duke of Beaufort; M.P. for Monmouth 1813–32.

Lewis barouche in the Park, visiting and dancing with eligible partners. But the poor girls had always gone home in despair. Now, at last, the goddess-like Catherine was engaged, appropriately enough to the son of General Vernon-Graham, who had been the means of introducing Mary Anne to Wyndham. He was young, good-looking, and had excellent prospects, but Mary Anne found the constant presence of the two young people mooning about her house disagreeable (Mr Vernon-Graham she thought not very bright and such a baby) and was glad when they left. Mary Williams seems to have been left on the shelf, for in 1832 she was looking after the little school Mary Anne had started in Greenmeadow for the local children.

Useful and lively charities interested Mary Anne, but she shudderingly declined the honour of taking the chair at the Swansea Ladies' Bible Society during one of her Welsh visits. Two excessively pious people in her family were enough. She preferred to queen it at balls, race-meetings and musical evenings when she and Wyndham went back to Wales, and she was 'the Fairy Spirit of the room', as she unblushingly reported.

Nothing tired her, not even the rigours of her first holiday abroad. Typically, she had pressed Wyndham to go to France in 1830, just after the July Revolution in which Charles X had been overthrown and the Orléanist Louis Philippe elected King. Paris was a dangerous place, but Mary Anne enjoyed the spice of danger and was amused by 'the delight of the French at having turned out poor old Charles'.

They travelled to the Mecca of English tourists, Switzerland, marvelled at the Mer de Glace and Mont Blanc, journeyed on to see the sights of Italy (Mary Anne enjoyed the gaiety of Florence but found Pompeii melancholy: she did not share the fashionable 'Gothick' taste for ruins). Returning through Germany and Belgium, they were back home by May 1831.

It was a year of change for England. The long Georgian era was ended. Almost a year before, in May 1830, George IV had died, and his brother William, Duke of Clarence, was King. More popular than George, he was pineapple-headed, gauche, and what Mary Anne would have described as not quite ninepence to the shilling. But the British predilection for sailor kings was on his side, and on the whole he was felt to be a change for the better. He inherited an unruly kingdom. The

Reform Bill, dreaded by the Tory party and the aristocracy who had from time immemorial ruled England, was splitting Lords and Commons. The King, wiser than most gave him credit for, favoured it; the spirit of the times had been symbolized by the overthrow of Charles X and the establishment of Louis Philippe as a constitutional monarch. But Wellington, so great a leader in war, proved to be something of an embarrassment in peace, and remained a determined stumbling-block in the way of the Bill. He believed the whole balance of political representation would be overthrown by it, with fifty-six 'rotten boroughs' no longer sending representatives to Parliament, new M.P.s recruited from areas which so far had had none, and a £10-householder qualification for voters. It would lead to revolution; Jack would be as good as his master, said the Tories and some of the Whigs. Riots broke out, the National Union of Working Classes was formed, foreshadowing the Trades Union movement. The terrible sufferings of women and children in mines and mills was partially alleviated by the Factory Act of 1833, restricting their working day to twelve hours.

The changing climate of the times spread to all layers of society. In London, the pulse of England, the Regency rake was giving way to the dandy, the man of fashion who played at politics and flirted with principles as with ladies. It was fashionable to combine what would come to be called Bohemianism with mildly Radical tendencies. London society, once so hidebound by etiquette, called on Lady Blessington[1] and her reputed lover Count D'Orsay,[2] dandy of dandies, at Gore House, Kensington, and only ladies of strict virtue stayed away. The lovely hostess of that fine house which stood where the Albert Hall now stands became the lodestar of writers, artists and musicians. The Honourable Mrs Caroline Norton,[3] one of the three glorious granddaughters of Richard Brinsley Sheridan, held soirées in her miniature drawing-room. In Hertford Street,

[1] Marguerite, Countess of Blessington (1789–1849), née Power, m. (1) Captain Farmer, (2) Charles Gardiner, 1st Earl of Blessington. Her supposed liaison with Count D'Orsay kept her out of high society, but she was a leader of wits, artists and authors.
[2] Alfred, Count D'Orsay (1801–52), French artist, leader of fashion among London dandies. He married Lady Blessington's step-daughter.
[3] The Hon. Mrs Norton (1808–77), daughter of Thomas Sheridan. She was a noted beauty and authoress. A divorce suit citing Lord Melbourne was brought against her.

Mayfair, the Irish beauty Rosina Bulwer led a life of alternate kissing and fighting with her remarkable husband, Edward.[1]

Edward Bulwer was an author, with several successful novels behind him and a career remarkable for its versatility before him. With an income of something like £500 a year, the Bulwers lived at the rate of £30,000, a good deal of which went on entertaining. The well-born, the talented and the merely amusing were to be found night after night at 36 Hertford Street. On the evening of 28 April 1832, there was held what one particular guest described as a brilliant soirée, attended by many dames of distinction, but no 'blues'. This guest disliked 'blues', or bluestockings—lady authors who affected strange costume and learned conversation. His preference was for females who would be overpowered by his own strange costume and conversation, a blend of epigrammatic wit, erudition and rodomontade.

Unfortunately for young Benjamin Disraeli, his hostess insisted on his being introduced to a 'dame of distinction' of the type he would have run miles to avoid. The lady had particularly asked that he should be presented to her, so there was no getting out of it. 'I was introduced,' he told his sister Sarah, 'by particular desire, to Mrs. Wyndham Lewis, a pretty little woman, a flirt and a rattle; indeed, gifted with a volubility I should think unequalled, and of which I can convey no idea. She told me she liked silent, melancholy men. I answered that I had no doubt of it.'

The gentleman saw a woman who was forty and looked fifteen years younger, as pretty, as gay and as girlish as when she had married Wyndham Lewis. The lady saw a gentleman of twenty-eight, tall, slender, with a face of remarkable beauty, languorous dark eyes, a profusion of black ringlets fragrantly pomaded. He had a romantic Oriental or Spanish look: in fact he was a Jew of Hispano-Italian descent. His attire was the extreme of dandyism and blindingly colourful. On another social occasion he appeared in green velvet trousers, tightly cut and strapped beneath his silver-buckled pumps, a canary-coloured waistcoat, and lace frills at his wrists. In a drawing by his friend D'Orsay he wears an exquisitely-cut coat with wide

[1] Edward Bulwer-Lytton (1803–73), 1st Baron Lytton; novelist, politician and playwright.

revers, the collar standing up to frame his lace cravat, on whose ruffles a silk cord reclines with a dainty fob watch at the end of it. His long fingers sport huge rings, and he is manifestly very pleased with himself.

Mary Anne had an eye for a pretty fellow, and an ear for an intelligent one. She may have flirted even harder than usual in an attempt to capture Mr Disraeli's interest, and overdone the flibbertigibbet image which she enjoyed presenting: 'Oh, I'm *such* a little dunce' can be all too convincing a self-verdict to a young man who wants to talk about himself. After all, there was plenty to talk about: was he not the author of novels, *Vivian Grey* and *The Young Duke*, much praised by critics and society, a young man who might soar to any heights? A set of verses written to him by an admirer[1] that same year convey perfectly the image his worshippers (and he) entertained of his Byronic beauty and his fantastic talent.

> Merriment like Music muffled
> Lurks in thy pathetic smile,
> Youth's rich summertide unruffled
> Brooding on thy brow the while.
> Nor the dream within thy glances,
> Nor the shadow on thy brow,
> Still the pulse that proudly dances,
> Still the spirit reckless now.
>
> Desolation and distraction
> In thy footsteps flit away,
> Nor of worldly care a fraction
> Damps thy heart's elastic play.
> Springing in thy path the roses
> And the am'rous asphodel,
> And around thee daylight closes
> With a merrie elfin knell. . . .
>
> Doth the cedar-shade dream o'er thee,
> Bushy-soft and sunny dark?
> Music radiant doth restore thee
> To the City of the Ark.
> Tho' *not yet* from terraced marble
> At the deep blue fall of day,
> Virgins wild responses warble
> To thy proud persistent lay. . . .

[1] Probably his sister Sarah.

An ordinary young man would have blushed hotly to be the recipient of such outpourings. But Disraeli was not an ordinary young man.

He was quite used to virgins, and non-virgins as well, warbling wild responses to him, and Mary Anne's obvious admiration did not surprise or impress him at all. There is a story, which may be apocryphal, that at a subsequent soirée at the Rothschilds', when asked to take Mary Anne to dinner, he exclaimed peevishly, 'Oh, anything rather than that insufferable woman! but' (shrugging and hooking his thumbs under his coat-*revers*) 'Allah is great. . . .' It was a rude remark by any standards, and underneath his conceit and affectations he was a kind-hearted young man. It would seem nearer the truth that after the first meeting a flirtation sprang up between them. It was not intended to be serious, for he was looking for an unattached woman with money. A month or two later he told his sister that he was not yet married though Bulwer's brother had promised to introduce him to £7,000. Until the right rich wife turned up, the pretty little rattle would do to play romantic games with.

In the Hughenden archives a little scrap of paper survives, undated and signed with a chivalric *nom-de-plume*.

I have read your tale which I admire exceedingly. It is very poetic and Romantic, and worthy of a Troubadour. I have found out the writer, and will tell you when we meet. I hope *la belle du monde* is quite well this morn!
Your true knight,
Raymonde de Toulouse.

Accompanying it is a line of Mary Anne's dreadful handwriting:

The first note from dear Dizzy. March or April 1832.

5

'Women are delightful creatures'

The elaborately-ornamented façade of Disraeli concealed a remarkable structure. In his own way, he was as given to romancing about his own life as was Mary Anne, and according to his account of his origins, faithfully reproduced by his early biographers Monypenny and Buckle, came of a family of Spanish Jews forced out of Spain by the Inquisition in the fifteenth century, who made their home in Venice, where they 'dropped their Gothic surname, and, grateful to the God of Jacob who had sustained them through unprecedented trials and guarded them through unheard-of perils, they assumed the name of Disraeli, a name never borne before or since by any family in order that their race might be for ever recognised.'

He then reported their prosperous career as Venetian merchants for two hundred years, at the end of which, about the middle of the eighteenth century, one Benjamin D'Israeli[1] came to England, encouraged to do so by that country's appearing to be 'definitely adverse to the persecution of creed and conscience'.

In fact, later researchers[2] have shown that most of this was the product of Disraeli's fertile imagination. The earliest D'Israeli ancestors were probably Levantine immigrants to Italy, and Disraeli's grandfather Benjamin settled in England less from motives of political freedom than from a desire to 'find the best market for his knowledge of the straw bonnet trade', when he arrived from Italy in 1748. He was successful enough to end his days as a rich man, if not quite a rival of the Rothschilds, as his grandson loved to think of him; but at his death he left a fortune of some £35,000.

[1] Benjamin's father retained this spelling all his life although Benjamin dropped the apostrophe very early in life—apparently before attending school. James and Ralph adopted the spelling of Disraeli.
[2] See Bibliography: Robert Blake, *Disraeli*.

His second wife, Sarah Shiprut de Gabay Villa Real, was descended from merchants of Leghorn. Her grandson averred that her ancestors were the blue-blooded Villa Reals of Portugal, and his belief in his noble ancestry probably influenced his nature, and thereby his career, to a considerable extent. However appreciative he may have been of his grandmother Sarah's supposed nobility, he disliked her personally, as apparently did the rest of the family. It may be because of the animosity she inspired that her granddaughter, another Sarah, was invariably known as Sa—the name even appears on her portrait at Hughenden.

The first Sarah D'Israeli had an intense hatred for her own Jewish race, which she somewhat unfairly took out on her husband and the rest of the family. Her portrait shows her as a slender curly-haired woman, not of an accepted Jewish appearance, who would be attractive but for a faintly malevolent expression. Probably to annoy her husband, a member of the Sephardi congregation of Bevis Marks in the City of London, she became an informal Protestant and chose to be herself buried in Willesden Church, separated even in death from the husband who lay in the Portuguese Jews' Cemetery at Mile End. Her grandson had significant memories of how, when she came to stay with his parents in 1825, she was so nice to everybody that his mother remarked, 'Depend upon it, she is going to die.' He recalled, with horror, those Sunday journeys in his boyhood from his home in Bloomsbury Square to hers in Kensington. 'No public conveyances, no kindness, no tips—nothing.' He went so far as to call her 'a demon'.

Fortunately her son Isaac took after his sweet-natured, generous father, who had slipped small Benjamin many a present and tip when his grandmother was away. Isaac D'Israeli, born in 1766, grew up timid and melancholy in the shadow of his formidable mother, from whom he once even ran away and was brought back after having been found lying exhausted on a tombstone in Hackney Churchyard. Natural brilliance, the sympathy of his father, and a native strength that grew with his years, took him into the literary field. When he was twenty-five he published a collection of 'anecdotes, sketches and observations' under the title of *Curiosities of Literature* which became a classic, and followed this with other works, now forgotten, but in their day highly regarded. Even the hypercritical Byron said that he knew no living man's books which he took up so often or laid down so reluctantly as D'Israeli's. Admirer and author met and liked each other, as a result of which a Byronic legend was handed down in the family to influence Isaac's son Benjamin.

Benjamin's gentle, passive mother, who had been Maria Basevi, of Billiter Square, Aldgate, a Spanish Jewess by descent, seems to have been a mere background figure, 'our dear mother', 'a tender parent', and being unintellectual herself was an excellent wife for her scholarly husband. He, though something of a recluse, 'a man who passed his life in the library', was the most warm-hearted and human of men, and the idol of his son.

> The philosophic sweetness of his disposition, the serenity of his lot, and the elevating nature of his pursuits, combined to enable him to pass through life without an evil act, almost without an evil thought . . . he was fair, with a Bourbon nose, and brown eyes of extraordinary beauty and lustre . . . his white hair latterly touched his shoulders in curls almost as flowing as in his boyhood . . . everything interested him, and blind and eighty-two he was still as susceptible as a child. He had by nature a singular volatility which never deserted him.

Thus the child who was born to Isaac and Maria on Friday, 21 December 1804, at 6 King's Road, Bedford Row,[1] was to grow up in an indulgent atmosphere. Benjamin, as they called him, attended with his family the Bevis Marks synagogue, presided over by David Lindo, a relation of his mother's. Lindo, by one of those strange threads which link the lives of great men, was to become the father of Louis Lindo, who married Keats's love Fanny Brawne after the poet's death. The Lindos and the D'Israelis were for a time neighbours in Bloomsbury Square.

Benjamin's sister, Sarah, two years older than himself, adored him from the moment of his first appearance in the world. Later they were joined by three brothers, two of whom, Ralph and James, survived the perils of infancy. The third,

---

[1] Like all his homes, this elegant mid-eighteenth-century house has survived the planners, and remains, tenanted by solicitors, at the eastern end of Theobalds Road, surrounded by similar dignified neighbours. Even the Mews have escaped, and the coach-house and stables. The Bevis Marks synagogue also survives.

Major-General Sir James
Viney, C.B., Mary
Anne's uncle.

Major John Viney Evans,
Mary Anne's brother.

Isaac D'Israeli,
Benjamin's father.

Benjamin Disraeli as an
infant.

Sarah ('Sa') D'Israeli, Benjamin's sister.

'If there is any merit in writing illegibly, you shine.' A page of Mary Anne's handwriting.

'Disraeli's golden youth'
by Daniel Maclise, R.A.

Henrietta, Lady Sykes,
by A. E. Chalon, R.A.

Naphtali, did not. A miniature by Cosway shows Benjamin as a heavenward-gazing cherub with fair hair, clasping a cluster of fruit. He was a happy child, fortunate in receiving a tolerant education at three private schools[1] where Jews were not only allowed but encouraged, and where Benjamin was remembered as having been conspicuous in school dramatics, as author and actor. In the holidays, his brother Ralph recalled, he 'played at Parliament', always keeping for himself the role of Government leader and spokesman, while his annoyed brothers were relegated to the Opposition. If Ralph's memory was reliable, no child can ever have been more truly father of the man.

When he was nine a quarrel grew up between his father, who had never taken his Judaism seriously, and the Elders of the Bevis Marks synagogue, leading to a final split the year after the elder Benjamin's death. Isaac and Maria resigned, without themselves becoming Christians; but on 11 July 1817 the two younger boys were taken to St Andrew's, Holborn, to be baptized, and on 31 July Benjamin and Sarah were baptized into the Anglican Church by the Rev. J. Thimbleby. The change was to have a profound effect on his career, for Jews were not to be admitted into Parliament until 1858.

In 1817 the D'Israelis moved to 6 Bloomsbury Square; Isaac was now practically next door to the British Museum, where from his youth he had spent a large part of his time buried among books. They were living in much higher style than in Bedford Row. This huge magnificent house, on the corner of the Square and Great Russell Street, has been preserved and is still most handsome and imposing (in spite of office furniture and strip lighting) with its great hall still adorned with antlers, its sweeping staircase and bold Greek key frieze, and servants' area which is almost a miniature street.

Benjamin followed his father into individualism and into literature. He read voraciously, retained information and quotations like a photographic plate, studied intensively at home, toyed with the law and abandoned it after eating dinners at Lincoln's Inn, and suddenly emerged as a novelist. He was twenty-two when *Vivian Grey* was published in 1826, by the

[1] His brothers both went to Winchester, but Benjamin (possibly at his mother's behest, as he hints in *Vivian Grey*) was spared the rigours of public-school life.

family's lifelong friend, John Murray. Under Murray's banner he marched into the world of *littérateurs*, wits and poets. Like his hero Vivian Grey he was an elegant, reckless lad with 'a devil of a tongue' and just enough of dandyism to preserve him from committing gaucheries. Such he was when Mary Anne met him, laughing at himself for his 'confounded puppyism; but then, mine is the puppy age, and that will wear off'. By the year of their meeting he had written and published another, not very good, novel, *The Young Duke* (1831), and revealed in it his growing Parliamentary interests, in which his political originality first emerges.

> Am I a Whig or a Tory? I forget. As for the Tories, I admire antiquity, particularly a ruin; even the relics of the Temple of Intolerance have a charm. I think I am a Tory. But then the Whigs give such good dinners, and are the most amusing. I think I am a Whig; but then the Tories are so moral, and morality is my forte; I must be a Tory. But the Whigs dress so much better; and an ill-dressed party, like an ill-dressed man, must be wrong. Yes! I am a decided Whig. And yet—I feel like Garrick between Tragedy and Comedy. I think I will be a Whig and Tory alternate nights. . . .

He had travelled widely abroad during the years of his young manhood, thanks to the friendship and patronage of a solicitor, Benjamin Austen, and his brilliant, beautiful wife Sara, herself an author *manquée*. Her portrait shows her as strongly resembling Sa D'Israeli. She was only a few years older than Disraeli, and many years younger than her husband. It would not have been extraordinary if an *affaire* had developed between them, but their relationship never seems to have gone beyond a warm friendship. Perhaps she had rather too many brains for Disraeli's taste. He was certainly susceptible to feminine charm, writing to Austen, 'Women are delightful creatures, particularly if they be pretty, which they always are; but then they chatter—they can't help it. . . .'

His love, at this time, was reserved solely for his sister. Sa, as her family called her, was beautiful, gentle, intelligent, a true daughter of her father. She worshipped Benjamin, and he her, with a passionate warmth expressed in the letters between them. In 1831, while on a grand tour of the East which was to be important to him in giving him the vision that marked his subsequent career, he had the terrible task of writing to her from Cairo that her fiancé, his travelling-companion William Meredith, had died of smallpox.

Oh! my sister, in this hour of overwhelming affliction my thoughts are only for you. Alas! my beloved, if you are lost to me, where, where am I to fly for refuge? I have no wife, I have no betrothed; nor since I have been better acquainted with my own mind and temper have I sought them. Live, then, my heart's treasure, for one who has ever loved you with a surpassing love, and who would cheerfully have yielded his own existence to have saved you the bitterness of this letter. Yes, my beloved, be my genius, my solace, my companion, my joy . . . we will feel that life can never be a blank while gilded by the perfect love of a sister and a brother.

Strange that Mary Anne, then unknown to him, cherished just such a passionate love for her brother; and that she, the epitome of pretty women who 'can't help' chattering, would one day come to be his genius, his solace, his companion, his joy. But in 1832 their union was far away. Disraeli plunged into politics in the by-election at High Wycombe, Buckinghamshire, canvassing with his slogan 'I am neither Whig nor Tory. My politics are described by one word, and that word is England'. High Wycombe was suspicious of his point of view, and disapproving of his standing as a Radical; even when he literally stood, magnificent in dandy attire with his ringlets streaming in the breeze, on the porch of the Red Lion Inn, his hand nonchalantly laid on the heraldic plaster beast. Indicating its head, he told the crowd, 'When the poll is declared I shall be there, and my opponent', pointing to its tail, 'will be there.' He was to be proved wrong. Only thirty-two votes were recorded, and of these only twelve were for him.

He had had a very slender chance to begin with. In opposition to the 'high Radical interest' he proclaimed, there were at High Wycombe two sitting Whig members, Sir Thomas Baring and Robert Smith, both supporters of the Reform Bill, passed by Parliament in June 1832, which to High Tories seemed to be the death-knell of the aristocracy. It gave the vote to the increasingly wealthy middle class, created new constituencies, ended many others, and was devised 'to take effectual measures for correcting divers abuses that have long prevailed in the choice of members to serve in the Commons house of parliament, to deprive many inconsiderable places of the right of returning members, to grant such privilege to large, populous and wealthy towns, to increase the franchise of many knights of the shire, to extend the electors' franchise to many of His Majesty's subjects who have not heretofore enjoyed the same, and to diminish the expense of elections.'

Disraeli had no real superiority of argument over the two sitting members, and it was not surprising that he lost, despite his gift of oratory. In December of the same year he was again defeated at High Wycombe's main election; in a much increased electorate, he won only 119 votes out of 298. It was particularly disappointing, for with his flair for symbolism he had had a chair made in pink and white, his favourite colours, in which to be 'shouldered' by his triumphant supporters. So ended his second attempt to get into Parliament. A year later he stood for, and lost, the London constituency of Marylebone. His time was yet to come.

High Wycombe was home ground to him by 1832, for his family was now living at Bradenham Manor,[1] just outside the town. A large, handsome house of Tudor origins, it stands at the foot of the Chilterns, with fine gardens and the remains of a beautiful beech forest behind it. Adjoining is the village church, and around were meadows, woods, and a few scattered cottages. Here, in Buckinghamshire peace, all the D'Israelis could live happily, Isaac wrapped in his studies, Sa assisting him and struggling to overcome her grief for Meredith, and Benjamin brooding on a new novel, *Contarini Fleming* (published in 1832). During the Parliamentary session he would stay in London, visiting the House to hear speeches and study statesmen. His friend Bulwer had now entered as Member for St Ives, Huntingdonshire, and was active for Reform.

Disraeli's career was still in the chrysalis stage, his refusal to identify himself with either of the great Parties alienating him from both. In his private life the suppressed passion which can be felt behind his emotional declaration to Sa was finding another outlet. He continued to meet Mary Anne and her husband socially, but apart from frivolities between 'La Belle du

---

[1] The Manor and its surroundings are little changed today (1972), but it now houses International Computers Ltd.

Monde' and her true knight 'Raymonde de Toulouse', their relationship remained merely social. In January 1833 he recorded that he went to Covent Garden in a private box with the Wyndham Lewises and others, but very soon afterwards he was attending the theatre with the lovely Mrs Caroline Norton, remarking slyly that 'public amusements are tedious, but in a private box, with a fair companion, less so.' In April there was an epidemic, probably influenza, going round London. Disraeli escaped it, and paid a round of visits to his suffering friends: 'both Mr. and Mrs. Bulwer still indisposed, Mrs. Windham [sic] a ghost.'

In May 1833 Mary Anne had recovered sufficiently to give one of their splendid déjeuners, which Disraeli attended, but with his attention not on his hostess. 'Dearest Sa' was asked

> . . . would you like Lady Z . . .[1] for a sister-in-law, very clever, 2500l and domestic? As for 'love' and beauty, all my friends who married for love and beauty either beat their wives or live apart from them. This is literally the case. I may commit many follies in life, but I never intend to marry for 'love', which I am sure is a guarantee of infelicity.

This cynical viewpoint was obviously induced by observation of the marriage of Bulwer and Rosina, who by now were not merely fighting but biting. Sa had suggested to her brother that companionship might be as good a basis for marriage as love, to which he replied irritably, 'As for companionship, the phrase is vague, I don't know what it means. I shall always be with my wife at the proper times and in proper places.'

He was seriously considering marriage, on this rather un-inspiring basis. The clever, domestic, and dowered Lady Charlotte admired Disraeli's brilliance, but married someone else—ironically enough partly at the instigation of Mary Anne, for Lady Charlotte's suitor, Josiah John Guest, was a business partner of Wyndham. Disraeli had earlier in May been refused by Ellen Meredith, who might have been his sister-in-law, had William Meredith lived.

A man unable to do without women, yet curiously unsuccessful with them at this time, Disraeli had in 1832 found an

[1] Lady Charlotte Bertie (1812–95), daughter of the Earl of Lindsey. Her remarkable career touched the lives of Disraeli and Mary Anne at many points. See Bibliography: Lucille Iremonger, *And His Charming Lady*.

accommodating one. Clara Bolton was the wife of one Dr Buckley Bolton, who had at one time treated Disraeli. She was older than Disraeli, a vivacious socialite, politically involved, a great giver of parties and collector of literary and political 'lions'. Sir Philip Rose,[1] Disraeli's executor, who knew the D'Israelis well in his youth, prefaced the letters she wrote to Disraeli which were found among his papers with the comment 'By his family she was looked on as D's mistress.'

One would hardly guess it. Clara was evidently expert at writing only what might be read by other people if a letter were carelessly left lying about—not that her husband would have been in the least disturbed, judging by his later conduct. Among the outpouring of political comment and general gossip there was little to suggest a passionate attachment. Now and then her obvious admiration for Disraeli shows: '. . . civility bores you to death so pray do not wed one of them [conventional women]. You must have a brilliant star like your own self. Keep your heart quiet.'

With strange detachment, for a mistress, she was recommending marriage to him, with a Miss Trotter, a brilliant, rich, but lonely creature, as her candidate. Miss Trotter did not appeal, and the Bolton liaison continued. In July 1832 Clara was writing to him less guardedly than usual: 'I long to hear you thunder forth against that weak and sordid faction [his opponents in the High Wycombe by-election]. I know I shall blush when I ask for *their* opinion of your speaking, all I hope is that they are totally ignorant as to its meaning. *I wish you were here.* . . .'

One phrase shows a glimpse of Clara which may explain why she attracted Disraeli and others: a shaft of poetic comparison, one flashing fiery legendary figure seen in another. 'Your rushing up to town on Sunday last appears like a dream. You are like *Hotspur's Ghost.*'

But even when the veil of conventionality slipped for a moment, she was his 'Sincerely', or even his 'Faithfully', and he was 'My Dear Sir'. And if she was literally such a Cautious Clara on paper she was probably equally so in her salons in King Street, St James's, so that few people knew of the real relationship; her young lover was allowed to make useful and

[1] Sir Philip Rose, 1st baronet, High Sheriff of Buckinghamshire 1878.

entertaining connections through her agency without the traditional fetters of a jealous mistress clanking round him. She certainly taught him something, and gave him material for the youthful philosophizings of his diaries, so often concerned with women. A plot outline called *Fate* concerns 'a Man always accompanied thro' life by his destiny—a conqueror for instance always accompanied by a beautiful mistress, the daughter of some monarch he has slain. This woman shares his bed and his confidence, but watches for an opportunity for ample revenge.' Clara's revenge was to come.

Disappointed as Disraeli was in 1832 by his Wycombe defeat, it may have been Clara who inspired him to such soothing couplets as:

> Easy it is to appease the stormy Wind
> Of malice in the calm of pleasant womankind.

and the waning of emotion between them may be reflected in the melancholy:

> Love is like the shadow seen
> When the sun first lights the skies,
> Stretching then o'er all things seen,
> But dwindling as each moment flies.

Clara's reign was short. There seems to have been something not entirely likeable about her; Sa did not approve of her after entertaining her at Bradenham, and left her brother in no doubt of her feelings. Disraeli afterwards referred to Clara in his diary as a 'decoy duck', for reasons which will emerge later. Before the end of the year he had finished with her, and was again searching for his ideal, rationalizing his search in his diary. 'The search after Happiness is the Alchemy of life.' 'In the human mind everything finally resolves itself into passion—learning, religion, a philosophical theory, a religious creed, finally lead to passionate fact.'

In a box at the Opera on 18 May 1833, he was talking poetry and travel with young Lady Charlotte Bertie, and even toying with the idea of marrying her. She was impressed with him: 'noise and light are his fondest dreams, and nothing could compensate him for an obscure youth—not even glorious old age.' But some of his sparkle that night was for the lady in whose box he was sitting. She was a married woman—married to a baronet, at that, and the mother of four, so that she did not qualify for the matrimonial offer Disraeli was determined to make to somebody. Yet his search had again led him to a 'passionate fact'. He fell madly in love with Lady Henrietta Sykes.

She came of a good Norfolk family of French extraction, the Villebois of Marham Hall; her father's wealth came from brewing (he was a partner in Truman and Hanbury), and her husband, Sir Francis Sykes, was the owner of Basildon, a Berkshire mansion whose grandeur impressed Disraeli. She had the maturity Disraeli preferred in his women, and was beautiful in a plump, sumptuous fashion, with the round dimpled cheeks, white sloping shoulders, languishing eyes and glossy swathes of dark hair so admired in the charmers who featured in Lady Blessington's *Books of Beauty*, though, curiously, her portrait in the *Book* for 1837 is far from flattering, giving her the appearance of a fat and hungry diner eyeing a succulent joint, and at the same time absent-mindedly strangling the terrier on her lap. One can only assume it to be a bad likeness, for in a portrait painted in 1837 by Daniel Maclise[1] she looks wonderful *en grande toilette* draped in furs and hung with jewels, and probably looked even better *en robe de nuit* with her rich hair romantically loose about the white shoulders. Her nature was as passionate as Disraeli's, and as unfulfilled, in spite of Sir Francis and four children (but Sir Francis had delicate health and lacked fire of any kind). She was deeply sensual and perfectly frank about it.

In the novel based on their amour, *Henrietta Temple* (published in 1836), Disraeli poured out his first impressions of his lady, in a burst of lyrical fireworks. His hero, Ferdinand Armine,

> gazed with rapture on the dazzling brilliancy of her complexion, the delicate regularity of her features, and the large violet-tinted eyes, fringed with the longest and the darkest lashes that he had ever beheld . . . her lofty and pellucid brow, and the dark and lustrous locks that were braided over her temples. . . . Amid the gloom and travail of existence suddenly to behold a beautiful being, and as instantaneously to feel an overwhelming conviction

[1] Daniel Maclise (1806–70), Irish portraitist and historical painter.

that with that fair form for ever our destiny must be entwined
. . . to be prepared at once, for this great object, to forfeit and
fling away all former hopes, ties, schemes, views; to violate in
her favour every duty of society; this is a lover, and this is love!
Magnificent, sublime, divine sentiment!

Ferdinand Armine, pale and trembling, 'leant against a tree
in a chaos of emotion'. Benjamin Disraeli, more realistically,
paid a social call on his divinity and made his feelings plain to
her. Within a matter of weeks they were in the throes of a
passionate *affaire*, and Disraeli was writing to Austen to say
that he was sorry not to have seen him as arranged, but that he
had been only 'nominally' in London for the last ten weeks.
'The engrossing nature of my pursuits I leave to your imagination.'

As always, his first filial concern was to introduce her to his
family. Sa was terrified that Lady Sykes would be bored to
tears by the quiet life of Bradenham, and urged Benjamin to
'send the claret directly as we want that at any rate'—presumably to enliven the evenings. But Henrietta was not bored; she,
too, was violently in love and everything and everyone connected with her lover was enchanted. She gave young James
(usually called Jem) a present of stag's antlers. The visit passed
happily. Disraeli, in return, was invited to the Sykes's holiday
home at Southend, where he had to leave Henrietta in August.[1]
She, who also had a natural gift for purple passages, wrote him
long, passionate letters.

My Soul—and is it the day? the first of many that are to pass
away without my seeing you. . . . I do not complain, far from it,
Love. I feel I have been the cause of your wasting much time.
. . . It is the night Dearest the night that we used to pass so
happily together. I cannot sleep and the sad reality that we are
parted presses heavily upon me—very very heavily . . . the
returning to *our* House and seeing the solitary chair and knife
and fork and the bright fire blazing as if from cheerfulness spoke
more forcibly to me than any language could do. . . .
    Best Beloved, do you love me? Do you indeed? How often
I asked you that question, how often have I been soothed by
your assurance of devotion to me. I do not doubt you, oh no,

[1] Porters Grange, Southend, now the Mayor's Parlour, is a handsome Tudor
manor of red brick, surrounded by pleasant gardens. Henrietta and Disraeli
called it 'Brick House'.

I dare not. It would drive me mad. I have faith, the most implicate [*sic*] in all you have said and sworn . . . my best blessing is with you, Darling of my Heart, Adieu, think of me.

In her loneliness she was comforted to think of him asleep in bed, to remember that she knew his room, and the white couch which held happy memories for her. She called herself his Mother, and wished she might kiss his headaches away. She begged him not to work too hard, to take care of his health—'for your own Henrietta's sake *do do* . . . do not let me disturb my Ammin's dreams, but let me rest on that faithful bosom softly pillowed by those gentle sighs.'

'Ammin' was her pet-name version of Armine. She, who wished herself clever for his sake, was clever enough to pick up the rhythm of his prose and his Byronism and reproduce it in her letters.

Your pale face is before me my Beloved and the tears gush . . . when I feel I may not be with you and another person usurps the privileges of your own wife, and pays you those little attentions which it would be the study of my life to offer you and oh! the watchful eye of a lover can so easily discover. Say, dearest, would not the tempted [illegible] happiness upon my bosom and the eyes oftener close, if I were with you ever? think of the happy ten moments on the Sopha. It is balm to feel you had repose, and so will not suffer from over-excitement. . . . I have sometimes beautiful imagery in my heart of what I could do, and would do for my Ammin, and then I am almost sorry I have not power to prove my love, but whatever my Ammin wishes me to do I shall never be found wanting.

Evidently she loved him enough to contemplate divorce from Sir Francis, looking fearfully into the future when another woman should legally take her place with 'Ammin'. Her hold on him, unmarried, was tenuous. After every bout of love-making she feared he might be tired of her.

My pensive love did the deep feeling of last night banish all thoughts but those of rapture and love and is there no reaction? . . . *Love me* my Soul *love me* and be assured that the measure of my idolatry for you is full to the brim. Every breath I draw is yours, even *now* your kisses live on my lips and face and I feel the passion of your embrace.

Only a month after their separation she was still suffering keenly: 'For my Soul's Treasure. I have the darling letter and have covered it with kisses . . . and one tiny precious spot, how I do love it . . . to my dying day I will never be separated from you again.'

Disraeli's letters to her have disappeared, probably destroyed by her family in later years; but it seems that he had held out to her some hope that they might one day marry, for she looked forward to 'the happy happy future I trust when my Love is to finish the book that is to be the Glory of his life as well as mine[1] . . . all happiness will be ours yet.'

She certainly made him happy at the time. In his diary for 1 September 1833 he wrote:

> I have passed the whole of this year in uninterrupted lounging and pleasure—with the exception of offering myself for Marylebone and writing a pamphlet, but the expected vacancy, thank God, did not occur; and one incident has indeed made this year the happiest of my life. How long will these feelings last? They have stood a great test, and now absence, perhaps the most fatal of all.
>
> My life has not been a happy one. Nature has given me an awful ambition and fiery passions. My life has been a struggle, with moments of rapture—a storm with dashes of moonlight—Love, Poetry.

The two pages which should follow are missing, and the next words are: '. . . achieve the difficult undertaking. With fair health I have no doubt of success, but the result will probably be fatal to my life.'

Confusedly he rambled on about his wish to be idle and enjoy himself, and yet be more energetic than ever in his career, prompted by Pride. 'They shall not say I have failed. It is not Love that makes me say this. . . .' Had he been truthful with himself, Love was not his ruler; Henrietta for all her ardour was not enough for him. He forgot, as he scribbled on, alone at midnight, all about Armine's oath to forfeit all former hopes, ties, schemes and views, and began to analyse himself. 'I am only truly great in action. If ever I am placed in a truly great

---

[1] *The Revolutionary Epick.* An epic poem on the French Revolution, which fell completely flat, possibly because of Henrietta's distracting charms and the fact that Disraeli was living 'solely on snipes'. But poetry was not his forte.

position, I shall prove this. I could rule the House of Commons, altho' there wd. be great prejudice against me at first.'

During Disraeli's absence from Henrietta in August 1833 something happened which would prove to be the death of their *affaire*. Her husband had been away, grouse-shooting, while they had been enjoying the pleasures of love by the bright fire at 'Brick House'. Henrietta returned to London, and was suddenly called on by none other than Clara Bolton, angry and jealous, soon followed by Sir Francis, demanding to know what his wife had been up to with Disraeli in his absence. A violent scene followed. Sir Francis forbade Henrietta to see Disraeli again. Determined to find out why Clara had revealed their affair to Sir Francis, she went round to the Boltons', saw her husband's carriage at the door, marched in without knocking, and confronted the pair, not *in flagrante delicto* but obviously shocked to be discovered.

Henrietta uninhibitedly informed Mrs Bolton how uncommonly she disliked her, how she knew about her liaison with Sir Francis just as they knew about hers with Disraeli, and extracted a promise that they would not interfere with her if she did not interfere with them. Clara attempted a tirade, but was vanquished by the now confident Henrietta, who had the satisfaction of leaving them both in tears, feeling that 'the fracas did good'.

A year followed in which there existed in the ancient house at Southend a French-farcical situation, with Clara and Henrietta spitting venom at each other over Disraeli, Sir Francis and Dr Bolton proclaiming the greatest fondness for him, and Disraeli himself distractedly trying to get on with his epic poem. When he was away Henrietta consoled herself by kissing his bed and washing his brushes. When Sir Francis left for a European tour, and Clara also disappeared from the scene, Disraeli and Henrietta lived more or less openly together at her London house in Upper Grosvenor Street, a few doors away from the Wyndham Lewises'. Sometimes Henrietta panicked, a little belatedly, about the possible consequences of their constant intimacy.

I suffered last night from a fit of horror. I will hide my head in the dear bosom and ask you a question. Do you think any misery can occur to us *now* from all the loved embraces? I fear we are very rash people and when I think I shake—answer please a little yes or no and I beseech you not to be angry with me . . . remember yes or no. . . .

Disraeli must have found this a hard one to answer. Presumably he was 'careful' in their love-making, taking the responsibility as a gentleman, in those days, had to do. Henrietta was obviously far from barren, and he had so far been successful in preventing any 'Little Consequences'.[1] In any case, their agreement with Sir Francis must have ensured that if any 'occurred' they could be passed off as little Sykeses, however strongly they looked like little Disraelis. But the occasion never arose. Disraeli, deeply fond of children, never had any, so far as is recorded. At Southend he played for hours with Henrietta's little Eva, 'who with her golden locks and rosy cheeks is a most beautiful child, and prattles without ceasing'.

During the summer at Bradenham in 1834 he was describing to his diary his eventful year. 'The end of '33 and spring of '34 passed with Henrietta in Essex, writing the first three books of ye Revd. Epick. Returned to Bradenham before Easter, then to town and remained there until this moment. A season of unparalleled success and gaiety.' In his letters to Sa (censored in publication) the name of Lady Sykes frequently cropped up, without comment, and there is mentioned a very dull dinner-party at the Wyndham Lewises'. His diary records that in the spring Henrietta had moved to Park Lane, to a house which she furnished with lavish and enchanting taste. 'What a happy or rather amusing society Henrietta and myself commanded this year. What delicious little suppers after the Opera . . . we make a point always to have some very pretty women.' This was perhaps unwise on Henrietta's part, for her lover was not unaware of the attractions of the pretty women, and to his diary he gave himself away in his mention of renewing his acquaintance with the 'three matchless sisters', the former Sheridans, 'with whom

---

[1] Information on contraception was available at this time: Francis Place had published his leaflet, *To the Married of Both Sexes*, in 1823, and in 1832 Dr Charles Knowlton, an American, published his sophisticated *Fruits of Philosophy, or the Private Companion of Young Married People*. Intended to help the working classes limit the numbers in their families, these were certainly read by more literate people who could be bothered to take such precautions.

I was so intimate last year, but shall I ever be forgiven. Methinks the fair Helen[1] wd. be merciful if—but never, never!'

Then comes a significant entry. 'I became acquainted with Lord L. [Lyndhurst] at the latter end of the summer of 1834. We took to each other instantly. I sat next to him at dinner at Henrietta's.'

Lyndhurst was sixty-two, American-born and brought up by his artist father. Well-preserved and handsome in a slightly sinister style, brilliant and capable, he was a notorious womanizer and had a general reputation for lack of principle. He and Disraeli liked each other on first acquaintance, and he perhaps saw the promising young man, half his age, as a sort of Faust to his Mephistopheles. Their lifelong friendship and political association began at that memorable dinner. Henrietta furthered it enthusiastically. Disraeli assured his diary that the perfect confidence of Lyndhurst was responsible for his growing success in his career.

Between him and Henrietta the atmosphere was changing. Her influence with Lyndhurst was strong, and it was not merely the influence of a society hostess. That autumn she travelled abroad with him, not alone, but leaving behind her whispers that she had become his mistress. To Disraeli she admitted that she liked him very much; no more. The Continental journey came as a shock to Disraeli it appears, even though he had been asked to join the party. He wrote to Lady Blessington, ever sympathetic, that he had been very unwell, and was glad of her friendship. 'The change of life was too sad and sudden. Indeed I am quite at a loss how to manage affairs in future as I find separation more irksome than even my bitterest imagination predicted. God however is great, and the future must regulate itself, for I can't.'

It sounds like the beginning of the end of the *affaire*. The golden autumn he loved, particularly golden that year, did not cure an illness, a combination of pain and languor and probably psychosomatic, to which he was prone and which kept him in bed.[2] He was writing out his regrets and longings in *her* novel,

[1] Helen Selina (1807–67), one of the 'three beautiful Sheridans', poetess and playwright, married Commander Blackwood and became Countess of Dufferin and Countess of Gifford.

[2] In the 1820s he had had a serious breakdown and was always subject to nervous illnesses.

Henrietta Temple. The fictional Henrietta's letters echoed almost word for word those of the real one; and for all his sufferings the author could not help relapsing into moments of bathos, as when Henrietta Temple is told that Armine, after becoming a temporary maniac through disappointed love, was the victim of a profound melancholy. Henrietta, naturally enough, fainted.

> Lord Montford rushed forward just in time to seize her cold hand.
> 'The room is too hot,' said one sister.
> 'The coffee is too strong,' said the other.

Henrietta Temple ends with the lovers reconciled and everybody in a general state of bliss, the Armine nursery enriched with young Sir Glastonbury and his brothers Temple and Digby, while still in arms is 'the most charming sister in the world, with large violet eyes and long dark lashes . . . who bears the hallowed name of Henrietta'.

But the real-life lovers remained on ambiguous, semi-friendly, semi-amorous terms for almost two years more, with Lyndhurst playing Pig in the Middle. The details of the triple alliance will never be known: the Hughenden papers give nothing away, Disraeli's letters to Henrietta have disappeared, and Lyndhurst burnt all his correspondence in his last days. An invitation to Henrietta and Lyndhurst to come to Bradenham together did Disraeli's reputation no good politically. He and she continued in the social whirl with Henrietta attending on 19 July 1835 a great fancy-dress ball at the house of the queen of Tory hostesses, Lady Londonderry. Henrietta went as a Reynolds portrait, with powdered hair, two of the Sheridan sisters were beautiful Grecian women, and Disraeli told Sa complacently that his own dress was 'very good, with some additions, such as a silken shirt with long sleeves'. Amid all the gaiety, Disraeli was pressing on towards fame, driven by pride and ambition. Passion, for the moment, was behind him. In autumn 1836 he wrote laconically in his diary: 'Parted for ever from Henrietta.'

It was not Lyndhurst who separated them, but a personage new in the story; the Irish artist Daniel Maclise, a cheerful, handsome womanizer, one of Disraeli's personal circle and a close friend of Charles Dickens. Of her unfaithfulness with

Maclise Disraeli wrote to his lawyer Pyne[1] that it was one of those domestic convulsions which strike one to the centre. It had the same effect on the previously complaisant Sir Francis when in the summer of 1837 he caught Henrietta and Maclise in bed together at Park Lane, perhaps 'sipping coffee and kisses at the same time', as she had done with Disraeli, and took legal proceedings against her. Because of his own doubtful reputation these were dropped, but Henrietta's good name was ruined for ever. In 1837 Disraeli was recalling 'the terrible catastrophe of Henrietta . . . exactly one year after we had parted'. Nine years later she was dead.

---

[1] William Pyne of Pyne and Richards had met Disraeli through Sir Francis Sykes.

6

'The Rose of enjoyment is Lewis's flower'

On 19 June 1837, King William IV died. 'The King dies like an old lion!' Disraeli wrote to Sa. The next day the new Queen, eighteen-year-old Victoria, received her Peers and Privy Councillors at Kensington Palace. With Lord Lyndhurst went Disraeli, and stored up memories of the affecting scene for the novel he would write one day, *Sybil*. He felt himself near the throne in more senses than one. He had been steadily climbing the Parliamentary ladder for the last five years. After three election defeats he had given up his independent position between the two fires of Whiggery and Toryism, and settled for the Tories. He belonged to the Carlton Club, that Tory stronghold. He dined at great Tory houses. When he had been sent to fight the Taunton by-election in 1835 he was described as 'a gentleman for whom all the Conservative Party are most anxious to obtain a seat in the House of Commons'. His powers of oratory, his newspaper quarrel with the unpopular Irishman Daniel O'Connell, which gained him wide publicity,[1] had brought him into the public eye. He was heavily in debt. He liked to live well, and Henrietta had been expensive. He owed money not only to his worried father but to professional money-lenders and to his old friend Benjamin Austen, a debt which ended the friendship. His new novel *Venetia*, which was published in May 1837, brought in some money; but novels were neither lucrative enough nor fulfilling to his wide ambitions. The 1837 Maidstone election proved his chance.

When Parliament was dissolved after the King's death, and a General Election impended, an interesting situation arose at

---

[1] During the Taunton by-election, Disraeli was reported in the Press as calling O'Connell 'an incendiary and a traitor'. In fact he was quoting what the Whigs, who had now concluded a parliamentary alliance with O'Connell, had said of him. O'Connell, enraged at the report, aimed a vicious diatribe at Disraeli.

Maidstone, whose Tory seat Wyndham Lewis had won in 1835. The old Whig member, Roberts, retired, leaving a straight contest between Tory and Radical. Wyndham Lewis's seat was safe, but as Maidstone was entitled to return two Members, another was vacant; and Maidstone chose Disraeli. Whether Mary Anne had the slightest backstairs influence on the choice is unknown; but it seems reasonable to presume that Wyndham recommended the brilliant young man who had sat so often at his dinner-table, and that Mary Anne spoke for him. She was certainly known to admire Disraeli. After the election, one jealous admirer wrote peevishly to her:

> The people are ignorant of the full extent of your partiality for your friend, which urges you to quarrel with all who won't believe him a Martyr, they will naturally infer from your warmth that there is more truth in the accusation than you are pleased to acknowledge. So that instead of convincing the world that nothing but Mr. D.'s superior acquirements, and the good people of Maidstone's pure patriotism, are the levers by which that gentleman was forced into his Parliamentary seat, you will but the more induce them to believe that it was nothing but Mr. Wyndham Lewis's sufferance and money.

Disraeli, however, was far from being a Martyr at Maidstone. Gorgeous in peacock attire, strings of golden chains across his waistcoat, and flowing curls, sublimely ignoring jeers of 'Old Clo'!' and 'Shylock!', he sailed to victory with a majority of 200 votes over the Radical Colonel Perronet Thompson. The Whigs under Melbourne, however, kept their majority and remained in power.

'I think I made the best speech I ever made yet,' he wrote to Sa on 4 July. Mary Anne was in London that day, and Wyndham reported to her, 'Disraeli was on his legs more than an hour: he is a splendid orator and astonished the people.' Indeed he had. He had inveighed against the cruel Poor Law Act; he had been passionate and funny and tireless. They had never seen or heard anything like him before at Maidstone. Mary Anne rushed down to witness his triumph—and, of course, Wyndham's—wearing a dress of electric blue, both dazzling and symbolic[1]—taking her mother with her to see the fun. She wrote exuberantly to John.

[1] 'The purple light of love', the poetess 'L.E.L.' called it.

60

I cannot explain to you the tumult of joy we have all been in, Wyndham's great popularity in giving so largely to the poor &, Mr. Disraeli being so fine a speaker joined to my humble worth carried everything before us. . . . My head is so dizzy with the noise I have been in and I am so tired, cannot you fancy me driving about the Town? Some of the women fell down to me in the streets. Many of them clasped Wyndham in their arms and kissed him again and again in spite of his struggles which sent Mr. Disraeli and your Whizzy into fits of laughter, our colours all purple. . . . Mark what I say—mark what I prophesy, Mr. Disraeli will in a very few years be one of the greatest men of his day. His great talents, backed by his friends Lord Lyndhurst and Lord Chandos, with Wyndham's power to keep him in Parliament, will insure his success. They call him my Parliamentary protégé.

Disraeli's first known letter to her after the election was warm but formal. He had gone home to Bradenham, had been astonished to find the walls of every town plastered with pink placards (his own colour at the Wycombe election) coupling the names of Wyndham Lewis and Disraeli. At Wycombe he had found great rejoicing, church bells ringing, illuminations at night, the town band blaring out long after midnight, and all in his honour and that of Mary Anne's husband. He and his family all wished very much that the Wyndham Lewises would pay them a visit among their 'beechen groves' and enjoy 'simple pleasures and a sylvan scene and an affectionate hearth'.

They went; Mary Anne liked the D'Israeli family on sight, particularly old Isaac and gentle, clever Sa, so like yet unlike her brother, and 'Tita', Battista Falcieri, Disraeli's manservant. He had been Byron's gondolier and devoted attendant—had, indeed, held him as he died—and Disraeli, encountering Tita on his early travels, took him home as a living souvenir of his hero.

After the Wyndham Lewises had left, Disraeli sat down at once to write to Mary Anne. 'After you went, everything and everybody were most dull and triste.' Before their visit he had sent her flowers from Bradenham's orange groves, fearing 'the showers have robbed the orange groves of their fragrance, & therefore I will not say in sending them to Mrs. Wyndham Lewis, like the Queen in *Hamlet*, "Sweets to the Sweet!"'

Already they were on very friendly terms; Maidstone had

sealed the bond of friendship. The 'orange groves' letter is signed 'Dis', his signature always to her until it became merely 'D'.

It would have surprised Disraeli, battered from Love's wars, to know that the gay, serene Mrs Wyndham Lewis had herself spent a not uneventful few years. Without suffering from such passionate cravings as his, she needed something that was not in her life. Wyndham was in his fifties, a delicate, not markedly virile man. In spite of his ardours at Clifton, the first edge of his infatuation for 'Mary Anne, beauteous, true and just' must have worn off long ago, and any physical charms he may have possessed had not improved with time. His attractive oddities, too, must have become rather tiresomely familiar to her. There is no doubt that he continued to love his wife, but by the time she and Disraeli first met he must have taken her very much for granted. When he had stood for Maidstone as Tory candidate in the autumn of 1832, and went there to begin his campaign in the following December, he had not been accompanied by Mary Anne, who was wintering at Brighton with her mother. This time he did his canvassing unaided by the vote-catcher with the fetching Welsh hat and short petticoats. She was increasingly irritated by his parsimony, particularly towards her brother. 'I grieve that Wyndham should write you so angry a letter,' she wrote to John, 'but his fondness for money is to me unaccountable.' Her heart was still John's. 'My own dear brother, we have so few relations that we must love each other the more. If I had children I suppose my affections were more divided.' This does not sound as though Wyndham shared a great part of them. Yet his lack of generosity did not extend to her, for she told John, 'I long to show you all my diamonds. I get more given me than almost any wife in London and a lovely brooch, emeralds, rubies, yellow diamonds, pearls and bracelets', and her mother was proud to see her attending a Court Drawing-room glittering with diamonds in great profusion.

She flirted. At a ball she met Prince Poniatowski, and bet him a ring that she would make him love her. Apparently she lost and was a shade disappointed, for when he went back to Poland she missed him. He was soon replaced by more susceptible gentlemen. Mary Anne, who could not bear to throw away a scrap of paper, kept all their notes and letters, which tell a story very different from the usual picture of Mary Anne's life in the last years of her marriage to Wyndham Lewis, which, but for her political activities, are practically unchronicled. Writers about her and Disraeli have ignored these letters, either from chivalry or ignorance that they existed, but she filed them amongst her immense store of correspondence, and they lie in the Hughenden Archives.

Several are unsigned, notably one written in elegant copperplate.

A Gentleman who has long deeply admired Mrs. Wyndham Lewis and who yesterday presumed to follow her carriage home from the Park, aspires to the honor of her acquaintance, but fears to seek an introduction to her through any friend who might be so happy as to be known to her, lest a motive should be suspected, or an enquiry made, which might defeat his hopes.

If Mrs. Lewis should be in the Park today at her usual hour, and would condescend to express her forgiveness of this liberty by waving her handkerchief out of her carriage, or by dropping a flower, with or without a line inside, she would make him the happiest of Beings. Or if she would walk for a moment in Portman Square at half-past six or seven, he might have an opportunity of addressing her—he is unable to make any apology for this presumption, but by pleading an impulse too strong for resistance; but if he is fortunate enough to obtain her forgiveness, he will prove by his respectful devotion that he would rather die than offend her delicacy, and that he would guard her purity with his Life rather than allow a breath to tarnish it.

The reference to Portman Square dates this letter to the early 1820s, when the Wyndham Lewises were living in furnished houses before settling at Grosvenor Gate. About 1833 she was being pursued by an ardent Spaniard.

Illustrious Madam,
I am oblig'd to go to the country, that is the reason I could not have the pleasure to see you a fortnight ago, and when I arrived in town I got the order, which oblig'd me to go to Spain, in that consequence my departure shall be next week.

My honour oblige me to go against my will, that is the fate of my profession. I am extremely sorry of it, because I must go to kill the peable of my country, or to be killed by them, that and the consequences of the horror of civil war [the Carlist war]. I deplore the fate of my beautiful but unfortunate country, and of my terrible situation too: that is dreadful to my feelings, but I cannot help it, and that is my great sorrow and grief. I wish you happiness, notwithstanding of your cruelty. If you don't hear from me, you would say: the person adored me 13 months is no more. . . . Adieu, perhaps for ever.

In September the susceptible Latin was still waiting for a steam packet to Santander, and begging her for another interview before sailing, hoping she would not be so cruel as to refuse him her address, and to 'drop it down, at time your carriage will pass before me in the dusk of the evening'.

Perhaps Wyndham was a *mari complaisant*, shrugging his shoulders at the extraordinary behaviour of his wife, which was taking the form of the use of accommodation addresses and secret meetings (the 'Regent Street Lords' was one).

> August 22nd 1836
>
> Your letter reached me in safety—your dear, dear letter. Need I say how it has been treasur'd? It should have been answered, but I have been out of town on a tour to the Menai Bridge. Our carriage broke down and your poor Unknown nearly killed. Do not think me capricious, then. I tell you I almost repented having written to you, and felt I had escaped some dreadful, some dangerous happiness in your not being able to meet me.
>
> I do not think—altho' love I have so long time—you would have given me courage to support myself when actually in thy dear presence. You ask me to come to your house. Oh! do not think so very ill of me—indeed, indeed, my only crime is loving you.
>
> I hope with all my love that you are happy and enjoying yourself with your friends—is there any chance of your coming to town? at all events write, tell me if you have a heart capable of love, in all its beauty. Will you accept and believe a heart, which is yours and yours only—direct always to Charles Shanklin, Esq. to the care of F. Thompson Esq., No. 11 Waterloo Place, Regent Street.
>
> As you are a man of honor I implore, I charge you not to try to discover my name—or you will bring down certain destruction on me. When we meet you shall know all.

The recipient of this letter remains nameless, but he seems to have been in political circles, promising in one letter to 'get this posted by the first M.P. I meet'. The three letters from him

64

which she kept are polite and amiable but far from fiery. He is at a loss to conjecture why his Incognita should reproach him for trying to find out her address. He is afraid she is unhappy, and would enjoy alleviating her grief. He invites her to come and see him at six o'clock at the house he has mentioned to her.

She was certainly keeping doubtful company during her early years in London; such company as the raffish Lord Worcester introduced to her. Did she in fact bestow on her admirers anything more than coquetry, leading them on and dropping them when they became too pressingly ardent?

Mary Anne had at least two passionate affairs during the years of her marriage to Wyndham. She maintained for something like three years an ambiguous relationship with George Beauclerk, a man whom society considered to be her lover in the fullest sense.

George was descended from the Duke of St Albans, the direct result of the liaison between Charles II and Nell Gwyn. Born in 1803, he appears to have chosen the army as a career. He had a home in Ireland, at Ardglass, County Down, and rooms at 23A Grosvenor Street West, where he was living in the early 1830s, very near the Wyndham Lewises. Though nominally serving in the Royal Welch Fusiliers, George seems to have spent more time in drawing-rooms than in the field, or the mess, in diligent pursuit of a wife with a fortune. Rosina Bulwer, writing to Chalon[1] in 1856, told him that George had succeeded in getting out of Lady Hotham a legacy of £2,000. How unjust it was, Rosina cried, that disgusting brute succeeding in his designs to such a tune

> ... a wretch who so recently figured in a police court for so villainous a crime; but being a sexagenarian legacy hunter it's satisfactory (to himself) that he should have succeeded at last. Some sixteen years ago, during the life of her first husband, he was playing precisely the same game with that old ass, Mrs. Disraeli, little dreaming that she used to show me all his letters and roar over them.

Rosina goes on to suggest that Beauclerk's aim in Mary Anne's case was marriage—not the implication conveyed by his

---

[1] Alfred Edward Chalon, R.A. (1780–1860), portraitist, born in Geneva, came to England in 1789. He painted many beauties of the day including Mary Anne and Rosina.

own letters; and embarks upon a caricature of Beauclerk, whose manly beauty Chalon evidently admired.

> Now I am going to fly in the face of the whole Royal Academy ... I cannot agree with you as to the superior physique of that beast Beauclerk to Dizzy. Whether it is knowing what I do of the brute, but he always gives me the idea of a Brummagen Brigand as manufactured at the Surrey Theatre of Richardson's Show: whereas there is both character (I don't, of course, mean moral character) and uniqueness in Dizzy's grotesque ugliness, as he is a facsimile of 'The Black Princely Devil' in a book of Chinese superstitions. . . . as for Gorge's flourish of penny trumpets about *his* character . . . there is only *one* man in England who *could* do it justice, and that was Calcraft the Hangman. The wretch's disgusting vanity, too: he one evening, at Brighton, entertained Lady Hotham for three hours with all the women in London who had been in love with, and made set at, him. . . .

Rosina's picture of Beauclerk is at variance with his letters which read more like the products of a prosy father chiding a misbehaving daughter than anything else. The first is of immense length, rambling and peevish. It refers to the precious petulances of her last three letters 'which I can only attribute to that spoilt child humour'. She has reproached him for not spending more time with her, an accusation which he repudiates; she has had about four times as much of his time as any others of her sex for a very long period. There is no extent to which his intimacy with any woman gives her the right to tyrannize him. 'Had our intimacy passed the boundary of matrimonial rights you had doubtless a right to call me arbitrator of my liberty. . . .' Then follows a long scolding about her frivolity as contrasted with his own habits and thoughts 'all of a grave sombre cast'.

> Had you not gone then out to play the Coquette with me . . . I fancied that I might reclaim you from such society. . . . I told you the truth about my regard for you: hitherto I have no attachment, but my circumstances are such that I unite myself I infallibly must to someone with money. This being the case, I cannot . . . allow the world the slightest reasons for supposing that I have a dearer interest in you than you as a married woman ought to sanction. . . . I do not see why I should not visit you as others do from time to time. I highly respect your husband, and I cannot bear that he should see your inconstancy.

Beauclerk had been attracted to her by her 'kindness with an air of romantick feeling', but his own nature, 'romantick to the last degree', has been chilled by her occasional sharp cold manner and avoidance of the touch of his hand. Then follows what suggests strongly that Mary Anne's coquetry went beyond the bounds of propriety, if not quite to the last fence. The sharp cold manner and stand-offishness

made me think you were coquettish, naturally of that sort of icy disposition (phisically). . . . Miss Gore and others had frequently declared their conviction that you were quite a safe person to flirt with, that your natural feelings were not at all those that placed you under temptation, that would injure you.

The next reason was, that in conversation, you frequently made use of the terms *disgusting, filthy, beastly,* etc., when referring to *others'* intrigues . . . now the consummation of an intrigue is only thus designated by people who are not capable of appreciating such delight because what is not for an instant considered as disgusting between a young married couple cannot be essentially more so between two other people who love each other, but between whom some bar interposes to allow of gratification being lawful.

In view of this, Beauclerk had abandoned all idea of ever going beyond Platonism:

Then it was by your own account that you felt piqued at my unsupportable selfishness of heart, and then, as you say, you proceeded to cast all your powers upon me to the end of making me a suitor at your feet. So it was that you at last began to feel in earnest what you commenced in sport. [Four lines heavily scratched out.]

Now you know what I meant when I told you that I could never condescend to see and not *have*. . . . I told you the plain truth when I stated that my intimacy with you had, in many instances, been the cause of my not visiting at houses where I used to visit, and who don't visit you . . . you must be very shortsighted and determined to avoid seeing, if you cannot understand the conclusion which the world *must* have drawn from seeing as it does my cab or stanhope standing at least 3 times a week at your door for a whole hour together, and for which notoriety your door is more aptly situated than any in London, facing, as it does, the most common egress and ingress to the Park.

. . . [your] whole conduct to me for 2 years was an unceasing mystification of your feelings. . . . The *end* of all love with me is *gratification.*

67

How much gratification he received can never be known. But she visited him alone, as he says in another note, and took risks with her reputation which suggest a reckless involvement. Their affair appears to have dragged on for a few years, and when Wyndham died he was a suitor for the widow's hand. His last letter was written as a jealous admirer, criticizing Mary Anne's delight on Disraeli's Maidstone election.

It was a good thing for Mary Anne that George Beauclerk's letters to her never reached the publicity of print. Evidently, after their liaison had ended, she became alarmed at what George might do with her correspondence, and persuaded his brother Charles to return the letters. His reply greatly relieved her.

27th July [no date]

Dear Mrs. Wyndham Lewis,

I return you the letters all safe—they entirely remove from your intimacy with my Brother all grounds for any ill-natured scandal that the world may have cast upon it—and they prove you a most good-natured person and not half or a quarter so [illegible] a one as the world takes you to be. Otherwise you could not have put up goodnaturedly for so long, with such very uncomplimentary epistles, just a series of [illegible] I am informed, from a preux chevalier to a fair lady. I am not surprized indeed at your dropping a correspondence so fraught with lectures and disagreeable advice that never was asked. . . .

Very truly yrs,
Charles Beauclerk.

George remained a bachelor until 1861, when he was 58. Then he became the husband of Maria Sarah Lonsdale, who survived until 1923. She bore him five children, and he died after ten years of marriage.

Even more astonishing than the Beauclerk connection was Mary Anne's liaison with Augustus Fitzhardinge Berkeley, who had been one of the 'swains' of Clifton. Their first relationship seemed to have ended with her engagement to Wyndham, when Augustus himself married. His family, even more than the Beauclerks, had earned an unenviable notoriety.[1] The Berkeley Peerage Case involved Augustus, third son of the fifth Earl of Berkeley to be born out of wedlock, in the problem of the succession to the title.

[1] See Bibliography: Bernard Falk, *The Berkeleys of Berkeley Square.*

68

Augustus, as well as his eldest brother William, had long records of profligacy and seduction. He was one of the Worcester Set, mixing with actors and singers of dubious repute, with demi-reps such as Harriette Wilson;[1] and Mary Anne was there too. Mary Anne's cousin, Walsh Porter, a song-writer, held out the bait to her that if she would persuade Madame Vestris, who had been a mistress of the Prince Regent, to sing one of his songs, she might get a walk-on at the theatre, and beforehand he would personally give her 'a glass or two of brandy and water, good and strong, then you will sing out like Miss Tiddy. I hope you may be able to make me laugh . . . and now adieu my merry cousin.'

They all frequented Lady Blessington's salon; and Caroline or Carline, one of the pleasanter members of the Berkeley family, who married James Maxse, was a friend of Disraeli and Mary Anne. During their married life she entertained them at her beautiful home, Woolbeding.

Augustus Berkeley's first letter bearing a date was written soon after Wyndham Lewis's death in March 1838 and makes it clear what his relations with Mary Anne Evans had once been.

April 6th [1838]
I hardly know how to address you. Time has done its office, and what perhaps might formerly please may now create disgust. Be that as it may, I claim the knowledge of sorrow. Bowed down with grief, this heart naturally flies for succour to those it best loves; and thy name, Rose, flourishes still in the only green spot of my memory, and there will exist

> 'Fram'd in my heart,
> Shrin'd in my treasur'd thoughts'

till life becomes extinct. . . .

Thus much for myself. But a new era opens upon you. Free, unshackled, your *imprisoned* passions let loose. Oh! beware the glare of those passions do not deceive you, and light you to wedded misery. The babbling world already gives you to the Tory novelist; my forebodings point another way, and for your happiness, I trust I am mistaken.

O that I were untrammelled like thyself, I would enter the lists, win and wear thee.

[1] Harriette Wilson (1789–1846), born Dubouchet, courtesan, mistress of many noblemen including Lord Worcester, and author of the celebrated *Memoirs* published in 1825.

But enough of this, the aim and end of this letter is to beg assurance of your continued—Love it must not be, Friendship is far, far too cold.

'Imagine something keener far, more free from stain of clay
Than Friendship, Love or Passion are, yet human still as they.
And if thy lip, for Love like this, no mortal word can frame,
Go ask of Angels what it is, and call it by that name.'

Thine, Augustus.

His next letter makes it even clearer he was interested in her new availability.

14th July, 1838

It gave me great delight, dear Rose, to find from my friend that you appeared still to take some interest in my fate, And fancy not because I do not seek your society I value it less than ever. The truth is I have not spirits or energy to encounter strangers. I am unequal to society, and the fear of finding you surrounded by those who can contribute to your amusement deters me from seeking your door.

I have little to interest me now, and *nothing* but what is connected with the past. And even now when I dwell in thought upon that brief and rapturous period when we were *all in all to each other*, my heart throbs with emotion.

Of course time has done its work and the agony I felt for months after our separation has long since subsided.

Yet never can the recollection of that dear dream of my existence become a subject of indifference to me. I leave, I own, on Monday, & I could not depart without addressing to you these few lines. On my return I shall like to see you, unless indeed my courage fails me as yesterday. Three times did I advance to your door and three times did I as hastily retreat, overcome by a nervous sensation. I should blush to confess to any one *but you*.

Every blessing and happiness attend you is the prayer of
Augustus.

His line was now a hopeful Platonism, blissfully unaware that Mary Anne was seeing and corresponding with Disraeli on a far from platonic level.

27 July, 1838

. . . Oh! Rose, now that love is tempered by time, I feel we could be *very dear* friends. Since our first meeting you have lived in the world, while I have been in comparative solitude, and in solitude it is that love reigns triumphant.

But I have done with Love. I shall look upon you as the *dearest* friend I have upon earth. . . .

Farewell then, dear Rose. Thoughts of thee will be

'Like flowers within the cold rock found
Alive, where All's congealed around.'

By November Mary Anne had obviously encouraged Augustus by the granting of compromising meetings: 'I shall be in town tomorrow, dear Rose. Send a line to meet me at the Albion in Cockspur Street, to say when and where you are to be seen.' He is 'affectionately thine, Augustus'. Soon afterwards he writes, 'If I can see you anywhere this evening do not fail to acquaint me.' Any communication she may honour him with 'will be received privately and safe by directing it to this Hotel'.

After Christmas a curious letter arrived at Grosvenor Gate.

If my dear Rose, and *dear* she must be in every sense of the word, as she cost me £40,000 (well worth the money!)—if, I say, my dear Rose is at home and alone on Monday next let her leave word at the Albion Hotel for me to attend her at dinner.

How had Mary Anne cost him £40,000? The only conjecture to suggest itself readily is that he had once sacrificed a rich marriage for her sake and at her demand. In a later letter to Disraeli she bursts out to him that she hates married men; it would not be unlike her to have insisted on bachelorhood in a lover. But in his second attempt Augustus got nothing like his money's-worth. An envelope inscribed 'For Rose' is a cry for mercy: 'O! D.D.D.[1] Forgive, dear Rose, forgive. Henceforward I will prove myself worthy of your lenity. Coach just leaving. Once more I cry forgive—.'

She led him on, then shut him out. 'I returned to town last night, and called at your house today. After your kind note I was surprised and annoyed at being refused admittance, unkind Rose.'

On another occasion he was allowed in.

'You were glad to see me' and oh! wonderful condescension, deigned to smile.

[1] This was a catch-phrase among the Gore House Set (Lady Blessington's salon) and meant 'Dear delightful damned!', or 'Darling detestable devil', or any other combination of words beginning with D.

71

I would rather have your frowns, or at least something that others do not partake of. Your smiles indeed—ask every witless Fop, every gaudy insect that flutters his buzzing nonsense in your ears—ask them I say if your smiles are withheld.

No, Rose, you inflicted a deadly wrong upon my tender Love in withdrawing your *Hand*. As a reparation, I *demand your lips*.

You can easily arrange a meeting through the Regent Street Lords, your vow of silence shall be respected. Words 'given us to conceal our thoughts' are not necessary.

Delay not but hasten to make the only atonement in your power and do justice to my moderation in not asserting my long-abused *rights* to greater and more tender favours.

These were evidently not granted, very likely because of the more serious turn her relationship with Disraeli had taken.

Farewell Rose then for ever. Tho' I confess your power un-diminished. Enjoy your triumph, it is your *greatest* and your *last*. I am now hopeless as you are heartless. Henceforth my sole aim will be to emancipate myself from your thraldom, and even try to *hate* you . . . you are no more worthy of affection than I of Heaven. He who can best play the Fool to amuse the present hour becomes for that hour the God of your idolatry. Continue to play your fantastic tricks; 'till Angels seem to weep.'

'To a Nunnery, go'—you know the rest.

Disraeli evidently did not regard Augustus with any particular suspicion, for while he listed him among the vultures who appeared round his dove when the eagle departed, he did not single him out for special jealousy.

Twice more Augustus Fitzhardinge Berkeley crops up in 'Rose's' correspondence. His farewell note may have summed her up shrewdly enough in her coquettish role; but he was emphatically wrong that her triumph over him would be her greatest and her last.

7

'Seventeen years of unbroken happiness'

Just as 1827 had been a lucky year for Mary Anne, so 1837 was a momentous one for Disraeli. Henrietta was permanently removed from his path. He was, at last, in Parliament. 'What fun, and how lucky I should esteem myself!' he wrote to Sa; and in his diary, 'I am now as one leaving a secure haven for an unknown sea. What will the next twelve months produce?' One result he hoped for was relief from the heavy debts which encumbered him, which did not stop him from making a bid for Chequers Court—'not under £40,000,' he nonchalantly told his solicitor; 'perhaps £10,000 more, as there is timber.' The letter ends with a postscript: 'I enclose the blasted bills.'

His maiden speech, on 7 December, concerning the much-disputed Irish elections, was far from a success, more because of his manner than his matter. The House was unused to flamboyant, glittering, long-haired young men, and Disraeli resembled Dickens's strolling actor Alfred Jingle rather than a modest young political novice [1] Unlike his Maidstone opponents, and the caricaturists of *Punch*, they refrained from mentioning 'Old Clo', but their howls, meows and hisses of derision completely drowned the end of his carefully prepared, affected speech. But if he did nothing else, he made an impression on the House and his first mark on history, as he shouted before he sat down, 'I will sit down now, but the time will come when you will hear me!' Sir Robert Peel cheered him; Lyndhurst wrote to congratulate him. He wrote to Mary Anne:

> I made my maiden debut last night. . . . I can give you no idea of the unfairness with which the Rads and Repealers met me, but I fought my way with good humour and I hope not altogether

[1] Ellen Terry, who met him during her calamitous and brief marriage to G. F. Watts, thought him remarkably like Henry Irving, and Jingle was one of Irving's most successful roles.

without spirit thro' tremendous clamour and uproar. . . . I am not in the least dispirited by all this friction.

When he came back to London from Bradenham in January 1838 he expressed himself delighted to go to *Hamlet* with Mary Anne, after dining with her 'at half-past five'. It was a bitterly cold night, but Mary Anne had procured a good warm box, with a fire[1] in it from Lord Chesterfield. Tea was served to counteract the frost outside, and Disraeli thought it was really very amusing, though he considered the young Charles Kean mediocre. Mary Anne had been complaining that Disraeli had been dull and dispirited and was doing her best to cheer him up. Wyndham was not there.

Notes were flying between Grosvenor Gate and Disraeli's lodgings in Duke Street, St James's. Delivered by hand, they show an easy intimacy and something more than social acquaintance. He is 'very disappointed'. Her letter has made him, or perhaps finds him, very melancholy. There has been some sort of flirtatious joke about a flower. 'Women are too quick; you are quite wrong about the bouquet. I therefore send you back the flower, which has served since its return for the mark of the book which I am now reading.' She is not 'Dear Mrs Wyndham Lewis' any more—his notes are unprefaced, and he is a squiggled 'D' or 'Dis'. (Others, in the House and elsewhere, called him Dizzy so often that his real name was almost forgotten.)

On 14 March 1838 both their lives were drastically changed when Wyndham Lewis, in his sixtieth year, died suddenly of heart failure at Grosvenor Gate, in Mary Anne's presence. Upset as she was, she sent word to Disraeli. He came to her at once, and found her full of real grief as well as shock. For years she had been leading a frivolous life in which Wyndham's solid presence had been taken for granted. She had been unfaithful to him with various men, to various degrees; if he had known, he had not reproached her, even about the latest admirer, his own political colleague. Full of tears, she searched her over-brimming correspondence cabinets for his last tender letters. On New Year's day he had written:

[1] Fires in the ante-rooms of boxes were frequently the cause of the burning-down of London theatres.

My own darling, I was delighted to receive your letter last night, it made the old year run out in happiness. I now wish you a happy New Year that we may live together many more years with equal solace to each other as heretofore. . . .

A note of three days later she endorsed 'the last letter I ever received from dear Wyndham'. It ended 'God bless you my affectionate kind dear, and believe me your own devoted and faithful husband, W.L. Make my regards to the D'Israelis and tell them how grateful I feel for their attention to you.'

She looked through a pile of other letters from him. One began 'My little guardian angel', another 'My own Toutou'. Among the pile there was an envelope containing a lock of his hair cut off in 1828. She had a sentimental obsession with locks of hair. Before his coffin was closed she snipped off a grey wisp and laid it with 'another taken only a minute before he dropped down dead at my side'.

It was probably Mary Anne, forgetting all the squabbles about John's extravagances, who composed the epitaph for his tombstone in Kensal Green.

He was renowned for his charity, which in him did not cover a multitude of sins, but only heightened many virtues. This tablet was erected to his memory, by his widow Mary Anne Lewis, who was united to him for seventeen[1] years of unbroken happiness.

Everybody who had known Wyndham seems to have liked him, and tributes poured in, some in sincere if indifferent verse.

> Cold is the hand which comfort could bestow,
> Dim that mild eye which wept o'er others' woe,
> Hush'd that kind voice which bade the hungry eat,
> And still that heart which could experience beat.
> O Death insatiate! why must Lewis go?
> On such a gen'man's heart, why deal thy blow?

distractedly enquired a poet of Maidstone. Mary Anne copied into her Occasional Book some lines which epitomized Wyndham for her; perhaps he had written them in the long-past days at Clifton.

[1] This is the first recorded evidence of Mary Anne's falsification of her age. They had in fact been married twenty-three years and she was now forty-five. She thought, doubtless, that her chances of remarriage would have been less had her true age been known.

Though all the world should bid me tear
Thy long-lov'd image from my heart,
Though every voice should whisper near
That thou and I must ever part—
Fear not, my love can ne'er decline,
My soul still hopes and prays for thine.

She wrote sadly beside them: 'How I miss Whm. I feel like a body without a soul now that he is gone.'

Her mother was at Grosvenor Gate to comfort her. A fortnight after Wyndham's death she was able to write to John that his dear sister was more composed, and that they must hope time would restore her to better spirits. That day (28 March 1838) she had been out in the carriage for the first time, with Lady Strafford and her daughter. John was expected home soon; his mother warned him to write a line before appearing on the doorstep, as Mary Anne was too 'sadly reduced' to be equal to any sudden surprise.

Disraeli wrote her affectionate notes reminding her that he was with her in spirit though his Parliamentary duties might take him away from London. The first of them ends 'God bless you, dearest'. Already the rumours were circulating; and had been, perhaps, even before she was widowed. One of the most active scandal-mongers was Mary Anne's 'friend', Rosina Bulwer, who, nearly twenty years later, was to tell Chalon about the Beauclerk affair, and that Beauclerk intended to marry Mary Anne for her money:

but Dizzy, who had also entered the lists with him, being the cleverer rascal of the two, was in at the death and so married the lean widow, or rather her fat jointure, for which he proposed the *very* day poor Wyndham Lewis died, as the Coroner's Inquest were tramping up the stairs (for he died suddenly of a heart complaint). *This* I know for a *fact* from having been in the house at the time, and Mrs. Dizzy owning—or rather *proclaiming* —the 'soft impeachment' to me herself.

This was a malicious lie. Rosina was so embittered by her matrimonial miseries that she would say anything about anyone; and 1838 was the year in which she worked up a major grievance against Mary Anne. When Wyndham died Rosina was in Bath, staying in Queen Square with her friend Miss

Bagot. A week after his death Miss Bagot wrote to Mary Anne apologizing for Rosina herself not sending her commiserations, but she was in sad grief—her poor little faithful dog Fairy died yesterday. Mary Anne, who knew how fondly Fairy had loved darling Mrs Bulwer, would, of course, be able to judge the severity of the blow. Mrs Bulwer was very, very unwell. Nevertheless, she had roused herself sufficiently to thank Mary Anne for sending her a copy of a tribute to Wyndham, and to add that the widow would be welcome to Bath for a change of air and scene whenever she felt like it.

A little later, Rosina managed to write to her friend personally. The letter did not, as one might expect, begin with condolences about Wyndham, but with the cry: 'My heart literally feels torn up by the roots—for everything is continually reminding me of that poor little darling faithful creature, which seemed the only thing in the wide world that *never* turned on me or against me, and that did not ill-use me for loving it. . . .'

Mary Anne, good-natured though she was, not unnaturally thought this a little unfeeling, and said so to various people. One of them mentioned her remark to a friend in a London club, who in turn passed it on to Rosina. In July she received a diatribe from that lady, attacking her on several counts. Over the last three years, she said, people had been telling her that Mary Anne had 'insatiably' spoken of her in an unkind and deprecating manner, despite the fact that when *she* had heard Mary Anne's name smirched with falsehood and slander she had defended her, and had been told it was a pity Mary Anne was not so sincere towards her, for there was nothing lowering and slighting she did not say about Rosina.

Then came her account of the club incident, and a defence of her own sorrow for Fairy—'the only faithful, true, and disinterested heart I possessed, even tho' it belonged to a poor little dog. The next thing I heard was that it was "publicly announced" that you were to be married the moment you threw off your weeds; this, I confess, surpriz'd and disappointed me in you all the more.' The letter ended in frozen politeness and a veiled threat—'This old world is a strange Diorama, and in its various chances and changes it sometimes happens that the last become first'—and the return of twenty pounds Mary Anne had lent her a year before.

To this Mary Anne immediately replied with admirable control, refuting Rosina's charges of unkindness, but admitting that she certainly thought Miss Bagot mad to write to her at such a time about a *dog* in such strong language . . . how could she but feel such ungracious remarks? 'I have been a widow not five months,' she went on:

> The first month you refused to stay with me—the second I was in Wales, quite as miserable. The third month (but then I only wanted gentleness and kindness) I might have been useful to you for the Drawing Room and Lord Devonshire's parties . . . in the last 6 weeks my house has been fill'd by those who have charm'd me in every way. Again I repeat—I have not yet been a widow five months—no one has had the indelicacy of even hinting marriage, and you are the only person whom I could forgive for having believed such a report.

Finally, she begged Rosina not to let her 'heart be embitter'd towards one who had never injured you . . . we have known each other too many years for either of us to alter, and we must be perfectly aware of each other's respective faults and virtues.'

To this eminently kind and sensible letter Rosina replied with more vituperation, dragging in the name of the 'Monster', Bulwer, and remarking that in the old days one of his chief quarrels with her was for being so fond of Mary Anne, whom he was wont to classify with Lady Stepney[1] 'and other disreputables'. She professed herself delighted to hear that the rumours of Mary Anne's forthcoming marriage were unfounded, and lapsed into a plea that Mary Anne should 'pull me down, as you please, it will only be as I have seen an old tree uprooted, or an old column pulled down—the ivy that twined round it in better days clung to it still'.

Mary Anne's exasperation was probably tempered by the thought that poor Rosina very frequently drowned her sorrows, and was apt to write letters Under the Influence. Even so it was annoying to find the old Beauclerk and Berkeley scandals raked up, and to know that Rosina obviously did not believe the lie she had been obliged to tell about no proposal having been made to her.

---

[1] Catherine, Lady Stepney, novelist, m. (1) Russell Manners, (2) Sir Thomas Stepney, groom of the bedchamber to the Duke of York. She was a popular hostess, 'pretty, accomplished and fashionable'.

It cannot have pleased her particularly to receive later a burst
of poetic reproach from Rosina under the title *False Heart,
Beware!*

> Is it well to pay me back with insult and with wrong,
> For all thy wayward madness, I had endur'd so long,
> For all the anxious nights that I had o'er thee wept,
> In sickness and in sorrow, with a loss that never slept.
> We hoped and feared together, when fame and race you first
> begun,
> Was it well to trample on me, when the golden prize was won?
> If the purchased loss you sought to deck a wanton's shrine
> Could no less oblation serve, than this poor heart of mine?

Concluding with the threat:

> But for thee, false heart, beware, fate aye in a circle moves,
> And the chalice she gives back, oft tenfold more bitter proves.
> But for thee, false heart, beware, for thee, false heart, beware!

Most women would have torn this up; but Mary Anne could
not bear to part with anything in the way of correspondence. It
lay there, among her papers, when she died.

The tenuous friendship between Mary Anne and Rosina may
have been strengthened by an episode in the previous year,
when Rosina's marriage with Bulwer had broken up. By
Rosina's account, she had been living apart from her husband,
but had called one evening at his rooms, just in time to see his
current mistress vanishing by another door. This useful evidence
she immediately passed on to Mary Anne, who advised her to
settle for a Deed of Separation. This was done (and signed, in
fact, at Grosvenor Gate, in the presence of Mary Anne and
Wyndham); but Mary Anne, somewhat discreditably, chattered
about it to other friends and it got back to the ears of Bulwer.
He wrote her a warning letter.

My dear Madam,
 You must permit me to place thoroughly before you what I
venture to consider grounds for a certain caution on your part
relative to the situation of Mrs. Bulwer and myself. Paragraphs
have appeared in more than one newspaper containing a very
grave calumny upon me, namely that Mrs. Bulwer found some
person in my rooms and that our separation is in consequence of
that discovery.

These rumours, he went on to say, had quite obviously emanated from Mary Anne. He denied that they were true.

> The real grounds of my separation are these: violent provocation on her part, over a series of years, frequently forgiven by me; the last act of coming to my rooms and without the smallest excuse making a scene, going then to your house and writing me from thence a letter which if I published it would justify fifty separations.

He adjured Mary Anne in future to be cautious in the statements she made on his affairs; but nothing would ever silence her tongue when she got hold of an entertaining story.

8

'*Thy Hand, fair Lewis*'

Marriage had certainly not been discussed between Mary Anne and Disraeli in April, when she was in Wales settling Wyndham's affairs. 'I do not know where to turn for love,' she wrote to her 'dear kind friend Dizzy', adding that John did not love her as he used. She begged him to go on passing plenty of 'time with Lady L. [Londonderry] . . . because the more you go there or to any other married lady, the less likely you are to think of marrying yourself . . . I hate married men . . . I would much sooner you were dead. . . . Selfish, yes I am.'

Even allowing for her sorrow and loneliness for Wyndham, this sounds just a little like a widow fishing for a new husband. Disraeli, however, was wiser than he had been. Mistresses were all very well, but he had not been particularly successful with the last two. Clara had caused him embarrassment; Henrietta had gone near to trapping him into an ugly divorce suit. Whether or not he had literally made love to Mary Anne during Wyndham's lifetime, as she once rashly told Rosina, he had taken her home to Bradenham very soon after starting up a warm relationship with her. But to commit himself to marriage was a very different thing. He had said to Sa four years earlier that 'I may commit many follies in life, but I never intend to marry for love, which I am sure is a guarantee of infelicity.' It was a principle that permitted no easy rejection. Among his notebook jottings is a significant passage:

There is in unhappy marriages a power of misery which surpasses all the other sorrows of the world. The entire soul of a woman reposes upon conjugal attachment. To struggle alone against her lot, to advance towards the grave without a friend to regret you, is an isolation of which the deserts of Arabia give but a slight idea; and when all the treasures of your young years has [*sic*] been given in vain, when you cannot dare even to hope for the end of your life . . . the heart revolts, it seems that you are deprived of the gifts of God upon this earth.

It is unhappy marriage seen from the woman's point of view, but Disraeli, who liked women so much, could feel a deep sympathy for them. He might well make Mary Anne unhappy. He had only known her as merry and charming, before Wyndham's death; now, after this, her first real grief, he saw that she could suffer. If he married her, and they were as incompatible as Rosina and Bulwer (who had started their marriage perfectly well on a tide of passion) he would make her most unhappy and do no good to the career which meant so much to him. And so he wrote her a cool diplomatic letter. He was pained, he told her, to note the tone of depression which had marked her last letter from Wales. Of course her feeling was natural, but she must get over it and not despair.

> The future for you may yet be full of happiness and hope. You are too young to feel that life has not yet a fresh spring of felicity in store. Altho' you have few near relatives, they are such as are dear to you; a mother whom you love, and a brother to whose return you look forward not only with affection, but with the charm and excitement of novelty.

His own family had loved and appreciated her from the first, he assured her.

> As for myself, I can truly say, that the severe affliction which you have undergone, and the excellent, and to me unexpected, qualities with which you have met them, the latent firmness and sweet temper, will always make me your faithful friend, and as far as my advice and assistance and society can contribute to your welfare or solace you under these severe trials, you may count upon them. For as you will know, I am one of those persons who feel much more deeply than I ever express.

She must put up with the 'miserable circle of narrow-minded people' at Greenmeadow, and keep her temper. 'W.L. [Wyndham's brother, the Governor] is annoyed because he finds that though a woman, he cannot take you in. You have more wit in your little finger than circulates through his gross body.'

This is brotherly, even avuncular, advice. In his previous letter he had considered that circumstances had in some degree placed her under his charge, and as her brother was not there, and she was a lone lamb in this world, he thought it proper to bestow such advice upon her. It was as good a justification for coolness as any.

He, like Rosina, had heard rumours linking his name and Mary Anne's. Even as early as April 1838, Augustus Berkeley reared his melancholy head with his own peculiarly egotistic brand of sympathy, and mentioned that rumour gave her to the Tory novelist.

Mary Anne's reputation certainly needed watching, in this year of her widowhood, and not only because of re-marriage rumours at such an indecently early date. A very strange case appeared in the papers[1] early in 1839 about a Mr Robert William Jackson, a barrister and former candidate for the Parliamentary seat for Armagh. One day in public, probably in a club frequented by M.P.s, he began to make derogatory remarks about Mary Anne's morals, claiming her to be well known to him. He then broke into a tirade about an incident in Regent Street when he, on horseback, drew up alongside Mrs Wyndham Lewis's carriage and was about to address her when she stopped the carriage, got out, and went into a shop to avoid him. Further comments on her character brought down upon him the wrath of a Mr William John O'Connell, who spoke sharply about the impropriety of using the lady's name as he had done, and affirming that he had always heard her spoken of in terms of the highest respect at the house of a neighbour of hers, the Honourable Mrs Mackenzie.

A brawl broke out, as a result of which Mr O'Connell challenged Mr Jackson to a duel. They met next morning on the green at Battersea Fields at the chilly traditional hour of six, and, says the report, 'but for the interference of the police the tongue of the calumniator would have been silenced for ever, who would have been taught a lesson that he should carry with him to his tomb.' Mr Jackson and his friends were arrested, and Mary Anne's reputation vindicated.

Among the headaches and irritations of settling up Wyndham's affairs in the company of the Governor, her fellow-executor, and travelling to Bristol and Gloucester in connection with the Viney properties which the now impecunious Sir James

[1] The news-cutting is unidentified.

83

Viney had mortgaged to Wyndham, it was very pleasant to get Disraeli's cheerful letters about the pleasant happenings in London; the soft warm May weather, the married bliss of Lord and Lady Hardwicke,[1] she a sweet singer, he 'so frank and gay . . . I never met persons who seemed to enjoy life more, or who seemed fonder of each other, than the Hardwickes. . . .' He told her with pride that he had been invited to a grand banquet given by Lord Chandos, with a guest list including Wellington, the Peels, and Lyndhurst. She promptly sent him a present to wear on the occasion: a set of gold chains to drape across his waistcoat. He had a tremendous weakness for these fashionable ornaments; Sir William Fraser[2] recalled that in his earlier days he was absolutely 'hung in them'. A lady whom he was taking down to dinner asked him, 'What *is* the meaning, Ben, of all these chains? Are you practising for Lord Mayor, or what?'

He was delighted by Mary Anne's 'exquisite offering', which had arrived just in time for the banquet, and assured her that 'with unaffected delight I felt that for the first time in public I wore *your chains*. I hope you are not ashamed of your slave.' It was a symbolic gift. He ended his letter, 'I am happy if you are.'

He was able to give her a present in return before long. As a Member of Parliament, he attended Queen Victoria's Coronation (Mary Anne, as the widow of a late M.P., could not), discovering to his pleasure that court dress, with its elegant knee-breeches, revealed that he had a very fine leg, which, he told Sa, he had never known before. A commemorative gold medal was presented to him, which in turn he presented to Mary Anne. Gold for gold; it was like an exchange of rings. In the next month he was the only guest at Grosvenor Gate, except for old Lord Rolle, privileged to watch the splendid review in Hyde Park from Mary Anne's drawing-room window; more guests would have made it look like a party, unseemly in her widowed circumstances. What a bore she must have found them by now: perhaps this was one of the deciding factors in her acceptance of Disraeli as her future husband. For by the middle of July he was frankly avowing his love. Wyndham's will had left

[1] Charles Philip Yorke (1799–1873), 4th Earl of Hardwicke, admiral and politician; became Postmaster-General and a member of the Cabinet, 1852.
[2] Sir William Fraser (1826–98), 4th baronet, politician and author; Tory M.P. for Barnstaple, 1857–9, Ludlow, 1862–5, Kidderminster, 1874–80. See Bibliography.

Mary Anne rich, to the tune of something like £4,000 a year, although this was only a life-interest. It would die with her, and the entail, together with the house, would then go back to the Wyndham Lewis relatives in Wales. Disraeli was not aware of this, he said later. If he had been, it would surely have made no difference, though he still needed fortune in a wife. By now he was head over ears in love, and the lady's money and fine house were but added attractions.

Did he know how old she was? Did he ever know? Her death certificate makes it clear that he did not, giving her age as eighty, four years less than was the truth. That she was a little older than himself he counted an advantage—she could play the mother as well as wife and mistress, as her predecessors had done; but that the 'little older' was twelve years is unlikely to have occurred to him, or to anyone who had neither enquired into dates nor listened to Rosina's catty comments. At the time of her second marriage she was forty-six, an age when most women would have looked every day of it, without twentieth-century aids to skin care and other preservatives of beauty; but she seemed almost untouched by time. Hardly any descriptions of her at this time have survived, but one is by a woman, her friend Letitia Landon, 'L.E.L.',[1] the poetess, who wrote her a thank-you letter for a morning on the Grosvenor Gate balcony watching a review in the Park.

> I have . . . visions of white plumes, military music, with a back-ground of pretty faces, and all the colours of the rainbow. As for yourself, you looked perfect, from your mignon feet, just like Thetis, if instead of silver she wore silk slippers,[2] to the prettiest of caps. I now understand why you wore blue, it is in such excellent contrast to your drawing-room draperies [they were yellow damask].

When her portrait as Mrs Disraeli later appeared in Lady Blessington's annual *Book of Beauty*, her friend George Dawson eulogized her thus:

[1] Letitia Elizabeth Landon (1802–38), published poems between 1820–9, novels, 1831–7, her best known being *Ethel Churchill*. She was a friend of Mary Anne and moved in the Gore House set; her name was connected with several men, but in 1838 she married George Maclean, governor of Cape Coast Castle, and died mysteriously, probably from poison, in the same year. Some evidence points to suicide.

[2] Thetis, queen of nymphs in Roman mythology; 'Thetis' tinsel-slippered feet' were mentioned by Milton in *Comus*.

When to his view the *Rose* uprears its head,
All other beauties are forgotten, fled . . .
Bewildered with the beauteous rivalry,
The choice, unfettered, fondly turns to thee.
Still to thee turns, all confident to find
The features but the index of the mind
Glowing with truth, sincerity and ease,
Stamped with the surest attributes to please,
Intelligent and gay—the joyous smile
Speaking a bosom free from art and guile . . .
This feeble strain, sprung purely from the heart,
Has dared to paint thee simply as thou art.

Tiny, glowing of complexion and forget-me-not blue of eye, she was still irresistible to men. One of her admirers (we do not know who because she copied his farewell verses in her own hand), who seems to have been banished about this time, was exasperated into writing:

Since you, fair lady, deign to ask
The reason why I stay from you,
I'll e'en discard my wonted mask
And give for once my reasons true.
Then I learn—despite what now I seem—
That I have known the thrilling touch
Of passion in its wildest stream,
Have known, and felt it, *far too much* . . .
O were you but less kind and tender,
Or were you less serene and fair,
Or had your radiant eye less splendour,
And less of gloss your silken hair . . .
Or were you but more lightly gay,
Or were you e'en but more severe,
I then had never staid away,
For nought I then had had to fear.

To which Mary Anne had pertly appended a quotation peculiarly appropriate to herself:

Quit, quit, for shame, this will not move,
This cannot take her.
If of herself she will not love,
Nothing can make her—
The Devil take her!

Though condemned to mourning dress instead of the bright colours she loved (too bright for good taste, other ladies were apt to say) she no doubt made capital out of even that gloomy garb. A bereaved lady whose portrait appears in the same *Book of Beauty* as Mary Anne's wears a delightful black watered-silk gown, close-fitting to reveal the 'shape', as bosom and waist were called, the bodice cut higher than it would have been in happier days, the shoulders draped in a 'bertha', the elaborate lace shawl-collar which set off so well a pair of white shoulders and a long neck, while vandyke lace cuffs emphasized the fragility of the delicate wrists. The lady of the picture wears a suitably lachrymose expression, which we may be sure did not often appear on Mary Anne's face.

Later in her life she wrote off for an analysis of her character to a Miss Richardson, having heard much of the lady's fame. From what evidence this was to be drawn is not clear; if from handwriting, it is astonishing that the Character contains anything complimentary. As it is, Miss Richardson seems to have summed up her subject with some accuracy.

> Accustomed to every comfort and indulged in all her wishes, she has never learnt how to conceal her feelings or moderate their violence. Hence proceeds a certain degree of excitability at the slightest annoyance and in extravagant mirth in the moment of amusement. Naturally gifted with a warm heart and ardent disposition, she is capable of sincere affection and even of extraordinary devotion, but from the circumstance of having been constantly in the society of (soi-disant) literary people, and adopting a strong language they sometimes employ, she gives to the expression of a sorrow a harshness which destroys the attractive softness of one in affliction, and often diminishes the full force of a natural thought by the over-strained language in which it is clothed.
>
> Quick, clever—too fond of a jest—and too apt to ask a puzzling question, she makes society gay and her own house particularly agreeable.
>
> She is lively in her manner and so amused with anything ludicrous that on first acquaintance she leaves the impression of a gay, thoroughly witty person, but not of one capable either of strong passion or acute feeling.
>
> On better acquaintance, the character becomes softened and her manner assumes more gentleness and less frivolity.
>
> Her features are regular, her figure graceful and her feet and hands particularly well formed. Her countenance lights up as she speaks, but from the want of repose in her general conversation it is difficult to judge how far the face really expresses the feelings.

> She is conscious not vain of her attractions, and inclined to discover the merits of others rather than dwell on their faults.

It is amusing to compare this shrewd portrait with the twin Characters which Mary Anne drew up of herself and Disraeli, after their marriage (see pp. 114–15).

Mary Anne lost little time in taking up the Disraeli family's invitation to Bradenham, where she was a more than welcome visitor, guaranteed to raise everybody's spirits rather than depress them with memories of the Dear Departed. Dizzy was annoyed that the arrival of Wyndham's brother in town on family business delayed her coming, but the following weekend she was able to join him there and be reunited with her love's family. She had written of them to her brother so enthusiastically when she had first visited Bradenham, that large homely place brimming with servants, horses, dogs, and books. Old Isaac D'Israeli she thought 'the most loveable perfect old gentleman I ever met—a sort of modern Dominie Sampson[1] and his manners are so high-bred and natural. Miss Disraeli is handsome and talented, and [there are] two brothers.' The brothers, Jem and Ralph, were as charmed by Mary Anne as was their father, who delighted in writing her little tributary verses. This habit had begun as early as the first visit she paid to Bradenham, with Wyndham, after the Maidstone elections, when she replied to one of his poems: 'Accept my delighted thanks for the most perfect lines ever penn'd by mortal man . . . how gratified and charm'd must I feel for so much wit and kindness all mine.'

After the spring visit Sa was begging her, if she really preferred country rambles to London strolls, to come back and enjoy them at Bradenham, where there were still some beautiful hours left in every day. No friends, Sa assured her, had thought more of her in her affliction than they had done, and none had more devotedly prayed for her happiness, 'dearer to all here than their own. May God bless you both.'

So the truth was out—not that it had ever been very carefully concealed from the D'Israeli family. By August she was at Bradenham again, invited by a love-crazed Disraeli. The sun was shining, he had told her, Bradenham looked beautiful, green and fresh, even bright—but She was not there, and the

[1] An old-fashioned, pedantic character in Scott's novel *Guy Mannering*.

talk of the kind, good, only moderately amusing people about him was 'insipid after all that bright play of fancy and affection which welcomes me daily with such vivacious sweetness'. On her arrival he presented her with a sonnet of welcome: not, to be exact, spontaneous, but adapted with significantly optimistic changes from one written for the visit of some earlier divinity, disguised under the name Myrrha, which he had copied into his notebooks and kept.

> Her step sounds in my father's hall: her voice
> Echoes within the chambers of my youth,
> And for a moment if my heart rejoice,
> Lonely so long, and where I deemed, in sooth,
> The sunshine of soft thoughts no more should dwell.
> Have I not cause? For is there not a spell
> Of rare enchantment on my raptured life,
> Tingeing all things with its immortal light,
> While images of sorrow and of strife
> Before it fade, and all is sweet and bright
> As her own face? Ah! sweet one, once to sigh
> That such a face might love me, was a dream
> Might well become a poet's fantasy:
> And on me now, say, can it deign to beam?

Obviously it could, and had done through the glowing hours of that summer. While in Rochester, Kent, in July, he had had all his resources of energy strained by having to make a speech to 107 people after a grand breakfast, a grand *déjeuner* barely over by 3.30, and a grand dinner at 5.30. Even allowing for the gastronomic capacities of the times, imagination boggles at the digestive consequences. Disraeli went out in an attempt to walk them off, but came back very little better, and rose to make his speech in a despairing state ('a funk' was his description), never beginning a sentence with the slightest idea of how it would end. His guardian angel came to his rescue, however, he reported, aided perhaps by the fact that he was wearing Mary Anne's present of a locket with her picture in it, the ribbon carefully arranged so that the locket itself (probably the one she had given Wyndham) lay over his heart. 'God bless you my own, most sweet and faithful Mary Anne and love me as I love you, more you cannot', he wrote to her in gratitude.

Her autumn visit to Bradenham lasted until 7 October. As well as walking in the beech groves with Disraeli, she was enlivening Sa's lonely life and delighting the male members of the family with her varied and generously-bestowed talents. Accompanied by piano, she sang the popular ballads of the time, Tom Moore's Irish Melodies and lyrics from the works of the recently-dead Sir Walter Scott. One of her particular favourites was the Ballad of Alice Brand, a romantic piece of pseudo-medievalism from *The Lady of the Lake*. This was from the repertoire of Madame Vestris, and another was the less cheerful Coffin Song, based on the legend of the lady who was buried alive but managed to extricate herself—alas, too late. ('How the Devil,' Walsh Porter had asked Mary Anne, 'did the lady find strength to break out of her two or three coffins, so as to be found on her knees in the vault?')

And, of course, there were parlour-games round the library fire of beech-logs. These simple games were dear to people without recourse even to entertaining reading matter. Riddles were high favourites, and Mary Anne had an endless stock of them, from those she remembered from her youth and recorded in her Occasional Book ('Why is Tishen's fat daughter Polly like Mr Pitt?—Because she's a great Polly-Tishen') to more recent examples. 'Why is a pretty woman like a muffin?—Because she is toasted.' 'What single word will ask this question, have I strength?—Am-I-able.' Conjuring tricks, too, were one of Mary Anne's specialities. She did tricks with cards. 'Place six parcels, counting from each card eleven. Example, take four of diamonds. . . .' Old Isaac, whose sight was failing rapidly and painfully, so that his beloved books were no longer what they had been to him, rejoiced in her accomplishment, and loved to try to out-trick her and detect the secrets behind her mysteries. To one, which she sent him by post, he replied in a charming verse.

Thy Hand, fair Lewis, by the Graces taught,
Folds empty letters, but with meaning fraught;
I found my Match! my honour and my shame!
Oh skilled to snare me in thy witty game!
Beneath those coloured Veils the feat was done,
A hundred billets all enclosed in one!
A hundred Lovers or a hundred friends
These might have blest!—all mine, these Odds and Ends!
Each poignant scroll so delicately writ,
Th' unwounding arrow of each pleasant Hit.

Wyndham Lewis.

Mary Anne Wyndham
Lewis. From a miniature
by Rochard, 1829.

'The new boy.' Mr Punch as headmaster receives
Disraeli into Parliament, 1837.

Benjamin Disraeli.

Selina, Countess of
Bradford, in youth,
after Sir Francis Grant,
P.R.A.

Mary Anne in 1840,
after her marriage to
Disraeli, by A. E.
Chalon, R.A.

Benjamin Disraeli in
1840 by A. E. Chalon,
R.A.

> Some write four leaves, and thrice will cross their lines,
> But all their Nonsense not a Jest refines;
> 'Tis yours to show, with Humour's playful ease,
> That Trifles are not Trifles—when they please.

A sparkling addition to the family was just what the D'Israelis needed. Isaac could seldom go out, Sa had not mixed in society since the death of William Meredith; Ralph and James were the only ones who could escape from Bradenham. As for their mother, her reactions are not recorded, and it can only be presumed that her relations with her future daughter-in-law were pleasant. She seems to have been less fond of Benjamin than of her other children, and less appreciative of his brilliance than he felt was necessary. It was not until 1847, after a particularly dazzling speech of his, that Sa told Mary Anne that her mother had confessed at last that she had never before thought him equal to Pitt, but that now she did. In the year of his courtship, 1838, he wrote a sonnet 'To My Mother nursing me on her birthday', but otherwise he kept singularly quiet about her.

Mary Anne's vivacity must have been something of a relief in a household where an atmosphere of scholarly calm had so long reigned. One gets some impression of it from one of Disraeli's little love-verses to her after their marriage.

> Though November brings no roses,
>   No garlands for the fair,
> Though November brings no posies,
>   To deck a lady's hair;
> Yet it brings us all together,
>   Who've been parted for a while,
> And through its gloomy weather,
>   It brings your sunny smile,
>   My Marianne!

Not only was she entertaining, but there was about her a certain earthiness which her society rivals did not hesitate to call vulgarity. She had been brought up in the country, on a farm, in the uninhibited eighteenth century. On the more refined level, she revelled in what would later be called Spoonerisms, such as the one about the Welshman who, when asked 'Where did your horse get that wound?' replied 'At the Wattle of Butterloo', and in repeating Letty Landon's story about the pastry-cook of Leeds who was so distressed about the political state of that town that she complained that 'when it comes to Annual Ballads, and Universal Suffering, Leeds will be too hot to hold us'. On a lower plane, she regaled the company with a curious story concerning a visit ostensibly paid by her to Cheltenham, where, staying at an inn, she 'perceiv'd an interesting-looking man in the passage, but it was his companion who mostly attracted my attention—he had the most beautiful black eyes I ever saw in my life. And what made their sparkle beautiful, they were fix'd on me, having put up my glass to ascertain this fact.'

Her tale continued. On the fourth day of her stay, as she sat waiting for her carriage, the door opened, the gentleman entered and approached her, and before she could move, his leg was on her lap! 'Of course I ordered him out of the room—he made no answer but look'd hard at me (Oh those beautiful eyes!) and stood at a great distance. He had no hat on a beautifully shaped head with dark hair. I got into a most sincere rage and at last he left the room, leaving something behind him, but more of this anon.'

Later that night, she continued, having dismissed her maid and lost herself in an exciting novel, out walked the handsome stranger from behind a turn-up bedstead.

> I could not breathe or move for terror. He threw himself on the bed—I ran to ring the bell. . . . I then scream'd, half-frantic, 'Waiters, chambermaids, come to my assistance!' and a beautiful girl appeared. She threw her arms round his neck, crying 'Dearest Graham, why do I find you here?' but oh, the brute, the horrid horrid brute, what do you think he did? Why, he began to bark like any other dog, and began to eat my supper. Shall I tell you what he left me in the room?

What the romantic Disraeli thought about this remarkable adventure, recorded in her Occasional Book and obviously a favourite party piece, is beyond conjecture; but the odds are heavily in favour of his preferring it to the raptures of Henrietta, and when Mary Anne called for 'a glass of brandy and water, good and strong', before singing one of her ballads to the hypnotized D'Israelis, she was not given a thimbleful of ladylike ratafia instead.

An impromptu invitation issued to her that winter by Ralph, who had inherited the family fondness for versifying, gives a pleasant picture of her visits to the quiet house at Bradenham.

Dear Lady! leave the foggy town,
   At Bradenham find a peaceful rest,
Now all thy tender cares are o'er,
   Oh hasten here our loving guest.

What though no sun illumines our groves,
   Our Beechen paths are strewed with mire,
As night falls on, a wond'rous tale
   Come tell us round the Library fire.

As lightly tread thy fairy feet,
   While warbling forth some favourite tune,
How 'Young St. Kevin stole to sleep',
   'Past twelve o'clock', 'Rise gentle morn.'

Come wreathed with smiles, fair Queen of Grace!
   Here kindness and affection sure
Await the lively Mary Anne,
   The beauteous Madame Pompadour!

9

'Dear Dizzy became my husband'

After such a successful visit from the merry widow, it was hardly surprising that Disraeli's spirits fell with an alarming bump on her departure. The day after she had left, on 6 October, he had not recovered from the 'stupefaction' of parting from her, had scarcely left his room or spoken to his family. All was dull, silent, spiritless, the charm was broken, the magic fled. He believed it might end well, but something had happened between them before she left which had thrown him into a fever of doubt. 'The course of true love never did run smooth. Alas! Alas! mine I fear will be wild and turbulent. May it not terminate in a fatal cataract! Remember!' Then came the mystical mark which was presumably meant to signify love, kisses, and passionate embraces, a shape varying between an ellipse, a triangle and a turnip.

'Our last hours should be passed in peace, if not in pleasantness. Pray let us meet, and look happy, even if we be not.'

Probably what had happened was nothing worse than Mary Anne's insisting that her full term of widowhood should be complete before she married him. Knowing her melancholy Dizzy, she was kind enough to write to him as soon as she got back to Grosvenor Gate a letter which cheered him up and sent him rushing off, after an energetic morning working at his poetic tragedy *Count Alarcos* (published in 1839), to spend a day or two with her in London. But back at Bradenham doubts and fears again overcame him, and he could hardly believe that their love was not a romantic dream. He poured his passionate feelings into *Alarcos*, promising her that she would not read it without emotion, for it came from his heart, and her name was before him, 'the name of her who is my inspiration, my hope, perhaps my despair.'

> Dark doubt my breast invades,
> Darkly as twilight fades
> Over our woods and glades,
>   I have no hope!

This gloomy poem ended with an assurance that his spirit hovered over her, and as he drew the Mystical Mark 'my hand trembles . . . and my lips grow pale'. The repeated 'bless you' before the scrawled 'D' looks tear-blotted. One cannot help feeling that his long-suffering family had never found him more difficult to live with.

Jealousy, of course, was consuming him. Berkeley was still around, lurking at the Albion in Cockspur Street, and so was another Augustus—Stapleton[1]—and Neale, the opera-singer. He feared 'fading emotion and final estrangement' because of these people, though she protested that there was no one in London who interested her enough to keep her from him: this because she had mentioned a few trivialities about the gentlemen who surrounded her. Disraeli, now in a state of hysterical jealousy,

> conjured up Stapleton like the Serpent in Paradise—whispering in the ear of Eve, familiar toad! reading to you his damned tragedy . . . and you, charmed, interested, and forgetting your captive victim. . . . Fortunate Berkeley, thrice happy Stapleton, cursed Neale! what is it to you whether he takes snuff or not.

What, indeed? Poor Mary Anne received one postal tirade after another.

---

[1] Augustus Granville Stapleton (1800–80), private secretary to George Canning; author of *Political Life of George Canning* and *George Canning and his Time*.

I cannot reconcile Love and Separation—I wish to be with you, to live with you, never to be away from you . . . in a sparry grot, with the Nereids singing to us from their shells of pearl—but then they wd. not be half as sweet as your own sweet voice . . . in Fame as well as Love, my motto is 'All or Nothing'.

He was even jealous of her women friends, and objected particularly to Rosina Bulwer:

that woman. She is thoroughly vulgar & I think quite heartless. You must not mistake her jolly good nature as an evidence of feeling: it is merely the impulse of the Irish blood. Indeed she is so thoroughly a daughter of Erin that I never see her without thinking of a hod of mortar and a potatoe.

Towards the end of 1838 it seems that she had given him sufficient assurance of her love to calm him. Indeed, one note suggests that she had given herself, and that he feared somebody in her household might have noticed traces of his presence in her bedroom. 'I hope you were fortunate this morning: my heart misgives me. He left his chain & seal as well as his watch in Grosvenor St.' It was his occasional habit to refer to himself in the third person.

In December, beset by influenza, he told his 'Dearest Love': 'I have been obliged to betake myself to bed again, and wish you were with me there.' By now she was his 'Dove', his 'Little Dove', and he her 'Eagle'. 'Your little dove loves you so much', she wrote to him. 'Believe me, dearest, I am yours faithfully now and for ever.' She even admitted her faults of temper. 'Dear, dear Dizzy. . . . How I love to think of you and all your tenderness and forbearance towards your little dove when she is in a passion with you. You know not how grateful this often makes me.' In spite of which she assured him 'Dizzy, I deserve your love so give me all you possess. Me and only me mind.' (He had been spending rather too much time, she thought, with the attractive Lady Londonderry.) He reassured her. 'I think if a woman be faithful and amiable she will never lose the heart she has once gained, at least judging from my own feelings and my own life.' Henrietta's escapades with Lyndhurst and Maclise had left their mark.

He was worried in case her new portrait by Chalon would not do justice to 'the fair face of Mary Anne', probably basing his fears on a miniature of her painted in 1829 by Rochard,[1] which certainly does not flatter her, being stiffly posed and giving her an unbecoming hairstyle of corkscrew curls and an expression of pert inquisitiveness rather than of vivacity. Fortunately, Chalon achieved a much more pleasing portrait (now hanging in the Hughenden drawing-room), in which she looks quite ten years younger than in Rochard's, shows off her neck and shoulders and not a little of her bosom in a delicious bodice of lace, with pink bows, and her broad intelligent brow beneath a plain centre-parted hairstyle, enormous bunches of ringlets framing her face rather in the manner of Elizabeth Barrett's spaniel Flush. Her expression is elusive, neither gay nor grave, as though she refused to give anything of herself away. But in the candid eyes there is a warmth not to be hidden, and the full sweet mouth curves up in the beginnings of a smile. As in the much later painting by Middleton,[2] which now reigns over the Hughenden drawing-room, she wears the same expression of suppressed gaiety.

So she must have looked, somewhere about that time, when she inspired Disraeli to a set of verses more frivolous, if no less heartfelt, than his usual outpourings.

> Would I were that flea
> That is biting your knee,
> (And if I were there
> My bite would be sair)
> Or at least a young fly
> That is near your bright eye!
>
> Or were I a dove,
> This I tell you, my love,
> That I should make my nest
> In that exquisite breast.
>
> Or were I even Pol
> As proud as the Sol,
> I think I should tip
> A kiss on that lip.

---

[1] François Theodore Rochard (1798–1858), French portraitist. He exhibited at the Royal Academy 1820–57. His miniature of Mary Anne is in the Disraeli room at Hughenden.

[2] J. G. Middleton, the English genre and portrait painter. He exhibited in London 1826–72.

But I am poor Dis,
With a secondrate Phiz,
And all I can do
Is to love you most true.
My Mary Anne.

And five times more, in a scroll, he distractedly scribbled 'My Mary Anne!'

Disraeli and Mary Anne were certainly engaged by Christmas, for she had given him a ring, the sight of which kept him assured that the romance was not a dream; and the locket was still on his heart. She was coming, with her mother, to Bradenham for Christmas, which threw him into a trance of strange and fascinating rapture, as he put it:

> Till I embrace you I shall not know what calmness is. I write this to beg you to have your hand *ungloved*, when you arrive, so that you may stand by me, & I may clasp & feel your soft delicious hand as I help your mother out of the carriage; now mind this, or I shall be more insane with disappointment . . . a thousand and 1000 kisses. More, more, come, come, come. . . .

On the first of January 1839, he was noting that the year had come in with rain. 'I hope it will end with sunshine.' She was back in London. He wished her the happiest of New Years, 'and indeed I hope and believe it will be the happiest of our lives'. And she replied:

> Dearest, dearest Dizzy, I must write to you the first person this year. A few hours after you have received this I shall be clasped to your ever faithful heart. Keep yourself warm and well and do not go out in the cold except to take some delightful walks with your devoted Mary Anne.

But the hope was marred by her persistent refusal to name an early date for their wedding. It was not merely a question of the conventional year's widowhood, but something else. In December he had written 'you told me once that you required a year to study a character; one year has nearly elapsed'. (So they had been close friends, if not more, before Wyndham's death.) The atmosphere at Grosvenor Gate was stormy, for other reasons, it seems. Disraeli wrote to Sa on 28 February:

> I am very busy—in domestic affairs the broils between mother, brother and daughter rage as terribly and continuously, that I

hardly know what it will end in. I cannot venture to ask Ralph to dine in the present state of affairs, as I suppose my constant presence, tho' 'not confessed', is at the bottom of it on their side; for they begin—I of course never open my mouth, and am always scrupulously polite, but what avails the utmost frigidity of civilisation against a brother in hysterics and a mother who menaces with a prayer-book!

Today we dine at Scropes [Mary Anne's Devonshire cousins], but the old sinner has only asked M.A. and myself and '*not John*'. The mother is of course frenzied.

It is difficult to conjecture what the family strife can have been about, other than the fact that Disraeli and Mary Anne were not officially engaged, and perhaps her mother and brother 'raged' at her for compromising herself by entertaining Disraeli so often. There was another painful subject, raised, and settled, a few weeks before: money.

In the early summer of 1837 Mary Anne had lent Disraeli enough to tide him over some trouble with the Maidstone electors, who were suing him for 'considerations' he had been unable to pay. People, of whom Rosina was doubtless foremost, were constantly warning Mary Anne that her suitor was 'only after her money', and when, perhaps in the dark hours between night and morning, she thought of his political ambitions, his extravagance and his debts ('the Mess of Benjamin', Rosina called them) and his violent insistence upon marriage, she wondered whether she was wise to encourage him, or whether she would be laughed at for taking on a fortune-hunter— particularly one twelve years younger than herself (whether he knew it or not). Disraeli, on the other hand, was seriously worried that she would not fix a date for their wedding—would not, perhaps, marry him at all. Was he beginning to look like a gigolo to London society—an ambitious young man who was paid by a rich woman to make love to her? He knew from gossip that he was not the first man whom she had entertained outside the bonds of matrimony. On 7 February 1839, he determined to put her to the test and settle the matter for good. Had he not told her it was all or nothing with him, and meant it? On the impulse, he dashed round to her house. A conversation followed in which she managed to tell him her fears, and he told her his in no uncertain fashion. From the long letter he wrote to her afterwards it seems that he stood over her and demanded that she should marry him to save his reputation; that she lost her temper, called him a selfish bully, and ordered him never to darken her doorstep again.

He went back to Duke Street and sat down to write one of those letters which may well be written to relieve the feelings but which should never be sent. It was very long,[1] very rhetorical, and eminently harsh. Their affair, he told her, was approaching ing absurdity. Everybody expected to hear of their wedding-date, and one friend had even offered them a honeymoon home. She was a woman of the world—she must realize that if things remained as they were she would look disreputable and he infamous, and, incidentally, ridiculous. He was determined to save 'that honor which is the breath of my existence', over-looking the fact that it had been in some jeopardy in the Clara–Henrietta imbroglios.

He then avowed, most curiously, that 'when I first made my advances to you I was influenced by no romantic feelings' but that his father wished him to marry, he himself needed the solace of a home, and 'shrunk from all the torturing passions of intrigue'. Then he coldly summarized Mary Anne's advantages as a wife—'rich, pathetically widowed, amiable tender, & yet acute & gifted with no ordinary mind'. One, in fact, eminently suited to be the partner of such as he.

Her fortune, in fact, had proved to be much less than he had thought, and so could not possibly have been the tie that bound him to her. 'Had we married, not one shilling of your income shd ever have been seen by me. . . .' Little did he think ('weak, wretched fool!') that when he had actually wept in her presence about the Maidstone debacle, and she had so unexpectedly and generously poured her 'treasured savings' upon his bosom, that he was receiving the wages of his degradation.

As a final insult, he said he had been warned by everybody about her character. 'Coxcomb to suppose that you wd conduct yourself to me in a manner different to that in which you have behaved to fifty others! . . . Was there no ignoble prey at hand that you must degrade a bird of heaven? Why not have let your Captain Neil[2] have been the minion of your gamesome hours witht humiliating and debasing me.'

[1] It is quoted in full in Robert Blake, *Disraeli*, Appendix 1.
[2] This may have been the Neale of an earlier reference.

A final burst of melodramatic self-pity and a warning that when she was past attracting men she would recall to her memory the passionate heart that she had forfeited, and the genius she had betrayed. The signature was 'D'.

It is a terrible letter, for the writing of which the bird of heaven deserved at the least a fusillade of small-shot and the loss of some feathers. But Mary Anne was a woman above the rage, sulks, or public vilification of the writer; few would have been, but she loved him. For a few days she let him simmer. Then she wrote:

> For God's sake come to me. I am ill and almost distracted. I will answer all you wish. I never desired you to leave the house, or implied or thought a word about money. I received a most distressing letter, and you left me at the moment not knowing. . . .

And the next day:

> My darling, my love can be of no value to you dear Dizzy after all the harsh and unkind thoughts you have expressed and, of course, feel towards me. . . . I beg you to be explicit and answer this, also my letter of yesterday. In the meantime I will believe all that's kind and fond of you whatever your feelings may be towards your poor Mary Anne.

He had been suffering very much, and had thought himself rejected—deservedly, as of course he knew. He went to Grosvenor Gate more humbly than he had ever gone anywhere before, poor drooping Eagle, and his Dove took him in her arms and comforted him and named the day.

There is among her papers a set of verses 'To Mary Anne', written perhaps at Bradenham after their marriage, which is a full, deeply felt, most tender apologia for the whole unhappy episode.

> 'Tis not alone the glittering eye
>   Nor the flushed cheek,
> Nor the wild heart's impassioned sigh
>   My love shall speak.
>
> In hours as sweet and not less tender
>   I bless thy name,
> And tho' not bright with passion's splendor
>   I love the same.

I love thee in the gentle hours
　　We tender roam,
Amid our glades and sylvan bowers
　　That grace our home.

When in the unrestrained tide
　　Of our true hearts,
In past and future, as they glide,
　　We play our parts.

I love thee when the moonbeams rest
　　On thy soft brow,
And when thou leanest on the breast
　　Thou lovest now.

Oh! love it ever! In that love
　　Alone I live.
And tho' my faults thou well may prove,
　　Love—and forgive!

The D'Israelis rejoiced. They had put up with a great deal from the eldest son of the family in the last months, and they had been afraid that Mary Anne, that enchanting acquisition to such a sombre family, might slip through their fingers. When at last the glad news was announced, Isaac expressed with his usual warm lucidity his own feelings and his family's.

My dear Daughter! for I fondly respond to the endearing title you have invested me with—I learn of your approaching union with my son with great pleasure and satisfaction, in which all here participate.

You have both been so long intimately acquainted with each other's habits and tastes, that 'your Papa' may confidently augur every domestic enjoyment—and their permanency for now you are more than Friends—and your Happiness can no longer be separated.

You make me quite in love with you, when your truthful language so deeply appreciated the susceptibility of my son's character—at least you know him!—and it is delightful to me that he will be united to one who can respond to his feelings.

Many thanks for the caricature—but we long to see Dizzy with a prettier, a more graceful and a more congenial 'Pair' than H.B.[1] has bestowed on him.

---

[1] John Doyle (1797–1868), portrait-painter and political caricaturist under the signature H.B. Grandfather of Sir Arthur Conan Doyle. He drew Disraeli and Bulwer Lytton as 'A Pair' in 1839.

My wife and myself are anxiously awaiting the pleasure of seeing you here—tell this to Dizzy—and my love, and believe me most affectionately yours.

I. D'ISRAELI.

The little presents she sent her new 'Papa' delighted him, charmingly as they were bestowed. 'Papa begs to acknowledge the silver Groat—a groatsworth of kindness has its value—but the accompanying Kiss is so precious, that he cannot think of bestowing it even on Majesty herself—he therefore shall keep it to be returned—on demand!'

Following an illness that summer, Isaac 'rejoiced' to hear that she was better, and longed to see her happy and tranquil and to listen to her chorus of 'Good Night! Good Night! Many! Many! Many!'

Though Disraeli had told Mary Anne in his impassioned letter that everybody expected to hear of their engagement, it seems that this was not entirely true. Constance, Lady Battersea,[1] remembered when writing her *Reminiscences* that both were guests at a party given by her grandmother, Mrs Montefiore,[2] in Great Stanhope Street, that spring.

Their engagement had not yet been announced, and my mother and her sister were quick to remark the little intimate nods and smiles interchanged by the two friends sitting on opposite sides of the table, and the way they drank to one another's health as they raised their wine glasses to their lips. To these young girls Mr. Disraeli had been a joyous, fantastic, captivating acquaintance, whilst to them Mrs. Wyndham Lewis looked and seemed very much older than the man to whom she was about to give the unquestioning devotion of her life; quite elderly, in fact, and quite unfit for the post she was about to fill. They thought they were merely witnessing an amusing flirtation. When they were told of the engagement on the morrow their surprise was boundless. Can we not hear them saying 'What! that old woman and our brilliant friend? Impossible!'

To girls as young as the young Rothschilds no doubt any woman of forty-six would seem to have one foot in the grave, ringlets and bare shoulders notwithstanding. And it may be that

[1] Constance Rothschild (1843–1931), married Cyril Flower, later Lord Battersea, in 1877.
[2] Henrietta Rothschild (1791–1866), widow of Abraham Montefiore.

this was one of the evenings on which a forty-six-year-old beauty under strong candlelight could not quite 'keep her lustrous eyes' as bright as usual, or her skin as smooth.

She had, besides, a trouble on her mind which doubtless showed in her face. For a long time her brother John had been ailing. The climate of Mauritius had not suited him. His temperament was neurotic: the newspaper reports of an influenza epidemic in 1837 had thrown him into 'a constant state of nervous excitement' in case his 'Whizzy dear' or his 'Angel Mother' should catch it, and in spite of his apparently shameless sponging on Wyndham his debts had worried him. 'I am like a horse with a large stone untied from his neck, having paid Wyndham £500 which I got his receipt for this morning. . . . I feel my star rapidly rising, as Napoleon used to say.' It rose high enough to make him a Lieutenant-Colonel in June 1839; then, in his sister's house, he fell ill and died on 2 July.

Disraeli reported to Sa:

> The sufferings of our friend terminated yesterday about seven o'clock in the evening. He was in a state of stupor from the preceding midnight until that time when he expired without a murmur in complete exhaustion.
>
> We were endeavouring to prepare Mrs. Yate for the catastrophe by some intimation of his dangerous illness at Bristol, when the sad event occurred. Of this she is aware, but remains ignorant that his body is under this roof. She has borne the announcement with more serenity than we cd. have hoped for, but it is impossible at present to form any opinion of its effects upon her.

Obviously John's death was a blow to Mary Anne, tiresome though he seems to have been, and far from a favourite with Disraeli, who usually referred to him as 'the brother'.

Mary Anne had him buried in the fashionable cemetery of Kensal Green, beside Wyndham, and composed an epitaph for him commemorating his service 'throughout the Peninsular War with great gallantry', and his death 'deeply lamented by his brother officers'. His age was wrongly given as forty-four; he was, in fact, forty-eight.

His death was not only saddening to the Grosvenor Gate household but inconvenient in the extreme. Strict etiquette demanded that Mary Anne should go straight back into the mourning she had not long, and under criticism, left—modified by purples and whites, perhaps, but mourning nevertheless. And worse, her wedding was fixed for 28 August, after the prorogation of Parliament. Some ladies would have postponed it, and there was doubtless criticism of her for not doing so. But the Disraeli motto, soon to be hers, was 'Forte nihil difficile'— to the strong nothing is difficult—and in her notebooks there is a jotting of a significant verse.

> Time *was* is past—thou canst not it recall,
> Time *is* thou hast—employ the portion small;
> Time *future* is not—and may never be,
> Time *present* is the only time for me.

Disraeli told Sa: 'Mrs. Wyndham seems to have rallied and all is very good. We shall not postpone the marriage but for about a month from this time—she herself suggested the propriety of going down to Bradenham before it, and is extremely amiable to the family since I have ceased to battle on the subject.'

He had not been well himself, subject to one of those mysterious attacks which beset him throughout his life. 'Had it not been for fomentations of poppies and camomile every two or three hours during the night I cd. not have endured it. Nothing but the most devoted nursing carried me thro'!' The nursing, obviously, was Mary Anne's.

Disraeli went to John's funeral; Mary Anne comforted her mother as best she could and went on steadfastly with the wedding preparations. And on the date planned they were married, very quietly, at the fashionable church of St George's, Hanover Square. Mrs Yate was there, and Bulwer and a representative of the Scropes, and Lyndhurst; very few others. *The Times* mentioned it in the briefest of announcements in the Marriages column, and the same issue contained a poem by the bridegroom on a completely non-matrimonial subject.

He had written to Mary Anne, not long before:

I look forward to the day of our union as that epoch in my life which will seal my career: for whatever occurs afterwards will, I am sure, never shake my soul, as I shall always have the refuge of your sweet heart in sorrow or disappointment, and your quick and accurate sense to guide me in prosperity and triumph.

Unlike most pre-marital forecasts, this one was to prove completely accurate.

In characteristic fashion, Mary Anne recorded the events and circumstances of her wedding-day. 'Gloves 2s. 6d. In hand £300. Married 28.8.1839. Dear Dizzy became my husband.'

10

'A mother and a mistress and a friend,
A Phoenix, captain, and an enemy'

It is far from clear why none of the D'Israelis attended the wedding. Sa was of a retiring nature, Isaac was nearly blind, but the whole family accepted later invitations to stay at Grosvenor Gate. Leaving it as an unsolved mystery, one can at least conclude that it was not out of ill-will. Afterwards Sa wrote to thank her brother on their mother's behalf for his letter telling them that the couple were safely away on their honeymoon and very happy. The event, she said, had been celebrated most joyously at Bradenham, with bells ringing all day, and a grand dinner for all, followed by dancing and feasting. She goes on to say that their wedding-day, a splendid one, was celebrated by a curiosity of Nature. On their last visit Disraeli and Mary Anne had been shown a beautiful, ephemeral flower, one of the specialities of the Bradenham garden. On that wedding morning, as if to do honour to the day, one flower alone opened, 'in every part completely double, bearing six leaves instead of three, and very large and splendid. Was it not a most curious circumstance? We accepted it as a happy augury.'

In her next letter Sa enquired whether Nash[1] still reigned on the Pantiles: in spirit, presumably, as that celebrated Beau had been dead almost seventy years. The Disraelis were beginning their honeymoon at Tunbridge Wells, and could have replied that the ghost of Nash had been banished long ago from that graceful precinct. Like all the spas which had flourished in the eighteenth century, the Wells was not what it had been. Out-rivalled by the growth of seaside resorts, it had declined from the days of its glory, when all the beauty and fashion of London came to walk in the Pantiles and take the waters, creating a

---

[1] Richard 'Beau' Nash (1674–1762), arbiter of fashion, known as the King of Bath.

garden of colour in wide-spreading skirts and high-piled powdered wigs. It had, like so many spas, attracted gamblers and disreputables; the Bible-inspired names of its several mounts were the only holy things about them, and before long elegant Georgian houses would be knocked down and replaced by massive, hideous hotels and ugly cottage terraces.

Their own honeymoon haven, the Kentish Hotel, was to be one of these victims. At the time a pleasant Georgian inn, its site is now covered by unattractive rococo brick buildings with shops below. They were unlucky in their weather—it rained incessantly, so that Disraeli only walked on the Pantiles once. There was scarcely anybody there they knew, or cared to know, he wrote to Sa. Only Lord Monteagle[1] was staying there. Twice they braved the rain to visit friends: Lord Camden[2] at Bayham, and Lord De L'Isle[3] at Penshurst. Lord De L'Isle was unfortunately out shooting, and missed their visit, but they met and played with his children, and found them quite charming. Mary Anne wrote to her 'only dear Papa' at Bradenham:

> I wish you could see your happy children—we simplify life—first to talk—to eat—to drink—to sleep—love and be loved. I never saw Dizzy looking so well, and I would say happy, only it is not for me to say so. We leave this place tomorrow for Dover, to which place our letters will be forwarded.
>
> Dizzy is so lost in astonishment at finding himself a husband, that the first time he had to introduce me to some of his friends he called me Mrs. Wyndham Lewis!—and at the ceremony he was going to put the ring on the wrong finger! Is not his conduct most atrocious, considering we all know him to be so great a character, that naughty man!

She signed herself 'with an affectionate embrace your truly happy daughter, Mary Anne Disraeli.'

To this Isaac promptly replied.

> My dear Mary Anne,
> I am delighted to receive from my new daughter in her new

[1] Thomas Spring-Rice (1790–1866), 1st Baron Monteagle, politician. His posts included that of Secretary to the Treasury and Chancellor of the Exchequer. He introduced the penny-postage scheme.

[2] Sir John Jeffreys Pratt (1759–1840), 2nd Earl and 1st Marquess of Camden. In his time he was Lord-Lieutenant of Ireland, Lord of the Admiralty, and Secretary of State for War at the time of Trafalgar.

[3] Philip Charles Sidney (1800–51), married Sophia Fitzclarence, natural daughter of William IV; created Baron De L'Isle and Dudley 1835.

name, her affectionate remembrances—with an assurance of the happiness that she is at once receiving and imparting, and I pray that the Stalk which now bears two-flowered may long wanton in sunshine.

If Dizzy in his first emotion of introducing his Lady Consort to his friends could not at once forget the late Mr. Wyndham probably he is not the first married man in that embarrassment —recent from his Bridegroomship—the name is changed in a minute, but the tongue will for some time keep to its old custom. The mischief if any soon cures itself, for a husband will be so perpetually reminded of his wife's name that there is no chance of his forgetting it—the Happy only will love its frequency. I think Adam was the only man who never miscalled his Dame, she never having to change her name, which she got when the good man contrived to name all the animals about him.

As for the marital incident concerning 'the right finger', who would not have confided in your own quick adroitness? But what signifies the finger even holding the magic circle? the hand moved with the heart.

So 'brown' harmonises with 'silver' rather than with 'gold' [she had told him that their liveries were 'silver, brown and yellow']. Of this I was not aware, but as contrasts are effective, the light will look best on the dark, rather than the dark on the dark. Therefore, as you say, they are 'quite perfect'. I hope Dizzy has arranged as we agreed about the carriage. If you proceed to the Continent, I hope you will find some fragment of a lost Summer. . . .

What Disraeli had arranged about the carriage was unimportant, as it happened, for Isaac had arranged to present his new daughter-in-law with a very special one. 'I have been thinking how much I wish to be remembered by you—you are now a favourite Jewel, and ought to be inclosed in a case, fit for a safe conveyance—and if you will permit me to build you a new Carriage, it will be my Jewel-case. . . .'

From Tunbridge Wells they drove to Ashford, spent the night at an inn, thence through Hythe to Dover, where they stayed at the Ship Inn before crossing to Calais. The passage was rough but rapid, taking only two hours and twenty minutes, during which poor Mary Anne suffered dreadfully, as did everybody save her husband, he reported complacently. Baden-Baden was reached after a long, complicated, but on the whole comfortable journey ('such are the revolutions of modern travel!' commented Disraeli after they had journeyed from

Cologne to Pforzheim with their own carriage, transported by steamer).

Their three-month honeymoon must have been just what they needed after the long, stormy courtship. Mary Anne seems never to have felt tired. Baden she dismissed as not much better than Cheltenham—public dinners, balls, promenades, pumps, music and gambling, while Disraeli appreciated the melodramatic scenery, the bright little river, the white sparkling town of some dozen palaces called hotels, and a couple of old ruined castles. He was equally charmed by the dramatic vistas of the Black Forest, and by the fête at Stuttgart where King Frederick William, surrounded by a brilliant court, sat in a pavilion in the midst of a beautiful mead and distributed prizes to richly-dressed peasants who must have looked like the *corps de ballet* for *Coppélia* and *Giselle* combined. Munich provided a round of sightseeing, and so did Ratisbon, Nuremberg, and Frankfurt. One suspects, however, that Mary Anne may have been rather glad to settle down in the Hotel de l'Europe in Paris early in November, and begin a series of gay parties of English visitors. Disraeli reported delightedly to Sa that at one of these gatherings the host had called up his son to be introduced by the curious name of Chidiock Tichborne Nangle, thus christened after one of the essays in Isaac's *Curiosities of Literature*.

'Mary Anne is particularly well, and in her new costumes looks like Madame de Pompadour, who is at present the model of Paris—at least in dress.' The silks used for evening wear at this time were often brocaded, richly embroidered with flowers, in the manner of the eighteenth century, and the fashionable low neckline gave every opportunity for Mary Anne to show off the pearls Wyndham had given her. Disraeli noticed that the shops of Paris, even in less illustrious quarters, rivalled those of Regent Street. The theatres were lively, too: they went to the Opera to see Auber's *Fairy Lake*. It was all gay and delightful, but Disraeli had been busy catching up with the political news from home, and was anxious to be back in England. Besides, it was all costing money, though no doubt much of it was Mary Anne's. He was in debt, as usual, and since the scene in February money had been a touchy subject between him and Mary Anne. She disliked his extravagance, and disliked even more the idea of borrowing. He wrote to his lawyer, Pyne, on his honeymoon: 'Mrs. D. is aware that I am about raising a sum of money but is ignorant of the method.' Now that he was married to a wealthy wife his credit was better than it had been, and he seems to have been inclined to make rather free use of it. They had congratulated themselves that they had not been given to lovers' quarrels during their courtship; the only marital quarrels between them of any significance were to be about finance. Though he confided every other detail of his life to Mary Anne, Disraeli kept extremely quiet about his money troubles.

His debts were virtually his only worry now, but for the failing sight of his father. Sa's account of this perturbed him, and he wrote to her that both he and Mary Anne were uneasy and unhappy about Isaac, and would look after him if he would come up to stay with them and take medical advice. They were feeling flat after the gaieties of the honeymoon, and London was smothered in fog, but Isaac made the journey and declared that he 'never was in such excellent quarters, or so kindly treated in his life, except by yourselves'. Disraeli was relieved to have the doctor's opinion that the 'spectres' before his father's eyes had no organic cause, and were merely the result of a morbid nervous system. He remarked jokingly that his father thought him looking very well, which made him fear he was *really* blind. Alas, before very long the old man whose whole life had been books was to be totally sightless.

With the long conquest of Mary Anne over, and her permanently beside him, Disraeli was at last able to concentrate upon his career and prove the truth of his prophecy made to her before marriage: 'Health, my clear brain, and your fond love; and I feel that I can conquer the world.'

A more exciting world politically, or one fuller of opportunities for an ambitious man, would have been hard to find. The Reform Bill of 1832, forced through the Lords by King William IV's agreement to create peerages, thus ensuring that the will of the Commons prevailed, appeared to have made social conditions worse than ever. The Chartists[1] were inveighing against

[1] The 'People's Charter' was published in May 1838. It called for extension of the franchise to those who were not landowners, voting by ballot, equal electoral districts, salaries for Members of Parliament and annual parliaments. Its supporters were called Chartists.

the Whigs, and the Liberal Ministry was in trouble. True, they had passed the Poor Law, by which the wretched homeless could find shelter, but workhouses were universally loathed. Disraeli, although living in luxury in the house with the gold-curtained drawing-room, was far from unaware of the unhappy condition of the poor, and saw in their plight an opportunity to benefit mankind and do himself some good simultaneously. In the last weeks of the 1839 session, just before his marriage, he had made a celebrated speech on Chartism. Its principles appealed to him. It was the descendant of the old Radicalism, but with vast differences.

> The time will come when the Chartists will discover that in a country so aristocratic as England even treason, to be successful, must be patrician. They will discover that great truth, and when they find some desperate noble to lead them, they may perhaps achieve greater results. Where Wat Tyler failed, Henry Bolingbroke changed a dynasty, and although Jack Straw was hanged, a Lord John Straw may become a Secretary of State.

Long ago he had disputed frivolously with himself about the relative merits of Whig and Tory: the Whigs gave such good dinners and dressed better, but the Tories were so moral, and morality was his forte. Then, fighting for High Wycombe, he had made a more serious statement of his position: 'I am neither Whig nor Tory. My politics can be described in one word, and that word is England.'

He stood in an excellent, even a unique position politically. By his Party label he was of the Tory Opposition. But even in days when Party discipline was far less strict than now, he was markedly an individualist to the highest degree; a man sufficiently exotic to see the condition of England with detachment, sufficiently gifted with imagination to appreciate her wrongs; an orator dramatically eloquent enough to plead for them; and a new and rare species of politician, a man of the intellectual middle class. In 1845 he would speak out for the miseries of the agricultural and industrial workers in his novel *Sybil, or The Two Nations* with a force and reality which had never appeared in any novel of his before, for at last he was free from the introversion and outdated Romanticism which had marked his earlier books. As a novelist he had two great faults—a lack of self-criticism and a complete inability to recognize when he was being ridiculous. He could be as epigrammatically witty as Wilde would be:

I rather like bad wine. One gets so bored with good wine.
You should treat a cigar like a mistress; put it away before you are sick of it.
A Protestant, if he wants aid or advice on any matter, can only go to his solicitor.
I have always thought that every woman should marry—and no man.

Or he could, like his hero Contarini Fleming, grow intoxicated with his own eloquence. But in *Sybil* he had found a theme which involved him, roused his feelings, and gave him the kind of eloquence which is not verbosity. And with the same enthusiasm and integrity he threw himself into the struggle for social reform of 1840. He wrote to Sa on 15 January: 'The other night all the town was terrified with expected risings of the Chartists. The troops ordered to be ready, the police in all directions, and the fire-engines all full, as incendiarism was to break out in several quarters.'

And a few days later: 'The Parliamentary campaign begins fiercely—war to the knife.'

Mary Anne, in the background, prepared her husband for the fray in the cleverest ways possible. He had always been a hypochondriac, even allowing for a nervous disposition, and so she sent for the distinguished Dr William Chambers,[1] a neighbour and an eminent consultant, to give him a thorough examination. The result delighted Disraeli, as the doctor satisfied them both 'that I am, or ought to be, never unwell again'. He also felt a certain importance in being on the list of a physician so great that he could only spare the Disraelis one visit a week.

She also provided him with something a public figure needed: a hostess. For the first time he could entertain at home in state, with forty covers laid and the brilliance of candlepower he loved. And for the first time he could attend other people's entertainments with a beautiful, amusing and legitimate companion. They dined at Mrs Montefiore's, with great Jewish names around the table—Rothschilds, Montefiores, Alberts and

---

[1] William Chambers (1786–1855), physician to St George's Hospital.

Disraelis—not a Christian name there, Disraeli remarked, 'but Mary Anne bore it like a philosopher'. They went to the great house of Stowe, to the Buckingham Ball, to all the London houses that counted, except perhaps those whose hostesses had made a pet of Disraeli before he married: Lady Londonderry was one of these. At home, Mary Anne would sit up till all hours talking politics, about which she modestly professed to know nothing and to hate, or giving him frank criticisms of his writing, which nobody had ever dared to do before in his home circle. In her he had found what Shakespeare's Helena de Rousillon declared a wife should be:

> A mother and a mistress and a friend,
> A Phoenix, captain, and an enemy.

Mary Anne, who did not go in for flights of Shakespearean metaphor, devised, soon after they were married, a 'Character' of herself and her husband. She was more unkind to herself than the perceptive Miss Richardson had been, and completely kind to him.

It had to begin with a verse, of course.

> His eyes they are as black as Sloes,
> But oh! so beautiful his nose.

Then came the contrasting qualities, his on the left, hers on the right. In the light of his subsequent career, it may be concluded that she knew less of her husband at this stage than she would in time to come. Thus the list ran:

HE	SHE
Very calm	Very effervescent
Manners grave and almost sad	Gay and happy-looking when speaking
Never irritable	Very irritable
Bad-humoured	Good-humoured
Warm in love but cold in friendship	Cold in love but warm in friendship
Very patient	No patience
Very studious	Very idle
Very generous	Only generous to those she loves

Often says what he does not think	Never says anything she does not think
It is impossible to find out who he likes or dislikes from his manner. He does not show his feelings	Her manner is quite different, and to those she likes she shows her feelings
No vanity	Much vanity
Conceited	No conceit
No self-love	Much self-love
He is seldom amused	Everything amuses her
He is a genius	She is a dunce
He is to be depended on to a certain degree	She is not to be depended on
His whole soul is devoted to politics and ambition	She has no ambition and hates politics

So it is evident they sympathize only on one subject; Maidstone like most husbands & wives about their Children.

From the day of their return from honeymoon, life was better for Disraeli than ever before. For the first time he was formally introduced by Lyndhurst to the great Wellington, leader of the Tory Party, who gave him a gracious and friendly reception and looked 'right hearty'. On 17 February 1840, with the rest of the House, he went to the Palace to deliver a congratulatory address to Queen Victoria on the occasion of her marriage,[1] rejoicing in the splendour of the deputation's appearance— especially his own. 'It was generally agreed that *I* am never to wear any other but a Court costume; being, according to Ossulston, a very Charles II.' The little Queen, he noted, looked well, Prince Albert on her left was in 'high military fig'. After their marriage, Disraeli had reflected, with pleasant retrospection of his own honeymoon, that they must be enjoying themselves on the slopes of Windsor.

The year 1840 in Parliament was marked by the beginning of its new home, a 'sumptuous pile of buildings' along the banks of the Thames at Westminster. Designed by Sir Charles Barry,[2] it was to soar skywards in majesty, a coronet of pinnacles above its 1,100 rooms and two miles of passages, its south-west aspect dominating London with the great Victoria Tower. The old

[1] She had been married to Prince Albert of Saxe-Coburg on 10 February 1840.
[2] In 1836 he won the competition for the design of the new Houses. The building was completed by his son, Edward M. Barry.

Houses of Parliament had burnt down in 1834, to the gratification of young Charles Dickens, whose views on class, privilege and Reform were very much those of Disraeli. Yet these two great contemporaries were never to be associated in any cause. The two men met about 1836, at the Gore House salon of Lady Blessington, where the lovely Countess was giving a house-warming and a party for the venerable Walter Savage Landor, visiting from Bath. She had scoured London for 'young lions' for him to meet, and Dickens, though still 'Boz' of the *Sketches* to the world in general, was becoming a celebrity through the early numbers of *Pickwick*, then three months old. Dickens fancied himself as a dandy and modelled his own costume on that of the elegant Frenchman, D'Orsay, with variations to suit his own florid taste. It would be pleasant to know his reactions to that other young lion, Disraeli, in that sumptuous drawing-room with its walls hung in green damask, white and gold furniture on the green carpet, and the smiling hostess, half-buried in an armchair covered with yellow satin. No less colourful, there sat at the window a striking figure, 'lividly pale, eye black as Erebus, ringlets falling over left cheek . . . his gold-flowered waistcoat reflecting the rays of the setting sun'.

Was Dickens there on the night when Disraeli, his beautiful voice controlled to drawing-room dimensions, talked 'like a race-horse approaching a winning-post' about the fantastic Beckford, living at Bath in two houses joined by a bridge, one occupied by himself and his servants and the other by a Spanish dwarf who was under the illusion that he was a Duke? It may be that such wild anecdotes put Dickens off the teller, and caused him to mistrust him as a politician, and to fail to realize that their sympathies lay in the same direction.

The Disraelis and the Dickenses would have made excellent neighbours, and Mary Anne would have been particularly good for poor baby-ridden Catherine; but, though there are in the Hughenden papers scraps which suggest that the ladies met through their mutual friends the Milner-Gibsons,[1] the men obviously had no use for each other, until their last meeting of

[1] Thomas Milner-Gibson, statesman, had been at school with Disraeli. His wife was a charming society leader who embarrassed the Government by supporting the Italian Risorgimento, and entertaining Garibaldi and Mazzini. She was a leading Spiritualist, holding seances with the celebrated Scottish medium William Douglas Hume.

all, when Disraeli was old and Dickens dying. Disraeli went so far as to caricature Dickens in his last novel, *Endymion*, as the popular novelist, Gushy.

> 'I tell you what,' said St. Barbe, as they were watching one day together the humours of the world in the crowded tea-garden and bustling bowling-green of Canonbury Tavern; 'a fellow might get a good chapter out of this scene. I could do it, but I will not. Why, if that fellow Gushy were to write a description of this place, which he would do like a penny-a-liner drunk with ginger beer, every countess in Mayfair would be reading him, not knowing, the idiot, whether she ought to smile or shed tears, and sending him cards with "at home" upon them as large as life. Oh! it is disgusting! absolutely disgusting. It is a nefarious world, sir. You will find it out some day. I am as much robbed by that fellow Gushy as men are on the highway. He is appropriating my income, and the income of thousands of honest fellows. And then he pretends he is writing for the people! The people! What does he know about the people? Annals of the New Cut and Saffron Hill. He thinks he will frighten some lord, who will ask him to dinner. And that he calls Progress.'

Yet each, unappreciated by the other, stood for Progress in this year of 1840, when the Old England of the Age of Reason was on its death-bed, soon to be buried beneath loads of brick and railroads. Disraeli was travelling the country, speaking for the Tories at meetings at the public halls which the growing industrial towns were building for themselves and posterity. The Disraelis went to Brighton for a visit; Disraeli ate a great many shrimps and Mary Anne found almost as many people of her acquaintance to gossip with. Her mother was at Grosvenor Gate, supervising the improvements and alterations which would finally banish the ghost of Wyndham from his old home, and writing respectfully to her daughter: 'You will find the house exactly what you could wish, the carpeting down, and everything else well cleaned. I am partial to Mary, she is such an excellent servant. I agree with you, the Cook is a very good one for her station in life.'

In September, when the Disraelis were staying with Sir Edward and Lady Sugden,[1] Mrs Yate was gratified to note that they had gone to church with their hosts,

[1] Edward Sugden (1781–1875), lawyer and statesman. Created Baron St Leonards 1852.

. . . knowing how much it would enter into my feelings where I wish my own Darling Daughter would constantly attend, how happy it would make me, being in possession of so many amiable and endearing qualities as your dear self, how many could I number, so anxious for the happiness of others, and my Dearest Maryanne I thank you a thousand times for the many comforts you have bestowed upon myself.

Her 'Dearest Maryanne' was somewhat deficient in piety, but her mother could not remonstrate too strongly, for she depended too much on her son-in-law. 'Many thanks to Mr. Disraeli for managing the business for me.' Disraeli had inherited from Wyndham a scatter-brained mother-in-law with a string of complicated troubles about shares and properties, which the future Chancellor of the Exchequer, himself still heavily in debt, managed for her with courtesy and patience, though one has the impression that she bored him dreadfully. The old lady's pension was a constant source of anxiety, as even she realized: 'I hope Darling will excuse my dwelling so long upon one subject.' She was indeed fortunate in her second son-in-law, obviously a little in awe of him, and quite contented to glide between Bradenham (where she was treated with 'domestic kindness'), her old haunts in Bristol, and Grosvenor Gate, making herself useful to her daughter when she could by such little aids as telling the cook to get some cutlets of mutton with cucumbers in for their return from a visit, her reward being Mary Anne's assurance that they would be delighted to see her 'dear face and affectionate smile' again. Disraeli's ever-pale face obviously worried her; she needed to be constantly told by Mary Anne that 'Dizzy is so strong and well now, and ever so happy . . . he is got so fat, & in such fine health and spirits. . . . I have dear darling Dizzy so jovial, bless him.' And from a holiday in Caen Mary Anne begged her, 'Pray take care that you dress yourself warm, *very*, and put your washing-stand by the fireplace as it used to be, and take care of your caudle-cap.'

Mrs Yate's health was slowly failing throughout the first two years of her daughter's marriage, and in April 1842 Disraeli went to the Middlesex Hospital to get an invalid carriage of a special kind for her—there were only two in London—and sent her a picture of it. It was supplied by Marks & Co. of Cavendish Square, and using it 'Invalids how severely afflicted may be conveyed any distance with perfect security'. It was her last means of transport. Nursed to the end by Mary Anne, she died at Bradenham in the spring of 1842, after a life which had held more brightness than sorrow.

However busy a life the Disraelis were leading, they always found time to write to those who needed news, particularly to Sa, tied to the house with her ageing mother and blind father. She was the first in remote Bradenham to hear that the Queen had been safely if rather suddenly delivered of a princess at ten minutes to two in the afternoon of 21 November; and that, on a more frivolous level, Mary Anne had served up a perfect Spanish pudding at one of their dinner-parties, and had firmly refused to part with the recipe; and that they had spent a happy Christmas at Deepdene, the country house of the M.P. for Gloucester, Henry Hope,[1] and had been very merry and agreeable, with 'many Christmas gambols, charades, and ghosts'. Mary Anne's Christmas present was a pair of pretty Dresden figures, a little gentleman in a cocked hat and a most charming little lady, very like herself, covered with lace. They both wished those at Bradenham a very happy Christmas and New Year. And, Disraeli might have added, an exciting one.

---

[1] A supporter of Young England. The Disraelis were frequent visitors to him at his country seat, Deepdene. He was a millionaire, having inherited fortunes from his uncle and his father. Disraeli dedicated *Coningsby* to him.

'My dear Mrs Dizzy'

In May 1841, the by now unpopular Whig Government of Lord Melbourne[1] received its death-blow. Like the proverbial creaking gate, it had hung on and on, to the rage of the Tories, and Disraeli, under the name 'Atticus', published a strong letter to the Duke of Wellington in which he urged him to act with 'a happy audacity' and get rid of his opponents. He even went to the length of flattering the Duke on having an appearance perfectly fitted for leadership. But it was the Budget of that year, with its ill-judged reduction of the duties on foreign sugar and timber, that turned the scale. Sir Robert Peel moved a vote of want of confidence, which was carried by the derisory majority of one. Melbourne asked for a dissolution of Parliament and the Queen gave her consent.

A general election followed. Disraeli was no longer popular with his Maidstone constituents; disputes with them over money had lost him their support. But, always lucky, he had a good friend, Lord Forester,[2] who helped him to stand for Shrewsbury. Thither he went, with Mary Anne, and she threw herself into the frenzy of canvassing with the vigour of her earlier efforts at Maidstone on behalf of Wyndham Lewis. Shrewsbury was a comparatively small town, remote from London, and Mary Anne set out to dazzle it. She had to work hard, for Disraeli's opponents had taken the trouble to put up posters all over the town, giving the 'Judgment Debts of Benjamin Disraeli, Tory Candidate for Shrewsbury', and listing his creditors and the sums owed to each one. Mary Anne was furious; but Disraeli, calmly surveying them

---

[1] William Lamb (1779–1848), 2nd Viscount Melbourne, statesman; entered Parliament as a Whig M.P. for Leominster 1806. Irish Secretary under Canning and Wellington; Home Secretary under Grey 1830–4; Prime Minister 1834 and 1835–41; adviser to the young Queen Victoria.
[2] John George Weld, 2nd Baron; M.P. for Wenlock 1826–8, Captain of Corps of Gentlemen at Arms 1841–6.

through his eyeglass, merely remarked, 'How accurate they are. Now let us go on.' Goaded into putting on her best performance, Mary Anne knocked at house-doors, introduced herself to shop-keepers, hobnobbed with high and low, and helped carry the day for her husband on a tide of charm. When he went back to Shrewsbury the following August, he wrote to her that wherever he went he heard nothing but 'Mrs. Disraeli—why does she not come, and when will she come?' The shopkeepers in particular had fond memories of her. 'Such a gay lady, Sir. You never can have a dull moment, Sir!' And Disraeli told them proudly that she was a perfect wife as well as a perfect companion, that she and he were separated for the first time in five years (his arithmetic was not entirely accurate) and that 'we are alas, parted on our wedding day. The women shed tears, which indeed I can hardly myself restrain. . . . Our wedding feast must be on Thursday, but, if I die for it, I will write you some verses tomorrow.' Which of the many sets of verses he wrote to her is not known, but on their first anniversary he had written:

> The seasons change, sweet wife, but not our love,
> And the revolving year, that all its moons
> Hath counted since thy bridal hand I pressed
> Brings us yet moons of honey. Blessed day!
> That gave me one so faithful, & so fair,
> To glad and guard my life! A graceful sprite
> Hovering o'er all my fortunes; ever prompt
> With sweet suggestions; and with dulcet tones
> To cheer and counsel. O! most perfect wife!
> Portia were not thy rival! May thy cheek
> Dwell on my heart for ever, thy quick brain
> As ever my Egeria! Weal or woe,
> Each accident of fortune—welcome all—
> So thou art by my side, & thy fond glance
> My star of inspiration. On this day,
> That made thee mine, I bless thee.

All of which was perfectly true, if a trifle flowery. She had set herself up as his adviser, guide and agent, without ever exerting domination. That she was faithful does not seem to be in question. No more notes from disappointed lovers appear amongst her correspondence. Her natural flirtatiousness would never be subdued, but Disraeli was all in all to her, as she to him. Not that temptation did not still come her way, even at the age of fifty-one. There survives at Hughenden a strange letter in French, with a note in her writing on the envelope, 'From a great Rogue, answered by a threatening letter'. The postmark is Paris, and the letter a rambling account of how, in one of the most grand and sumptuous streets of Munich (presumably while the Disraelis were on their honeymoon), the writer had been overcome by the sight of a lady of noble appearance, whom he had followed, but who eluded him. He had then come to England, and while strolling in Grosvenor Square 'in search of the sun' he had seen the same lady, on the arm of a gentleman.

> Now they tell me it was you, Madame . . . is it possible to entertain the thought of your speaking with me? of receiving me for a moment? Alas! I think not. But I suffer so much that the cold proprieties and common laws of my life are useless to me . . . tomorrow at noon I will come, Madame, to your door, if you will deign to bend on me your gracious regard.
> Your very humble servant, G. DE LAGRANGECHANCEL.

Then follows a dejected note dated 11 December 1840.

> You have not been kind, Madame. It is the common law, 'tis true. I accept it, for I don't know what dream of the mind. . . . I have said to a woman that I suffer—I am unhappy—help me! She has done—'comme les hommes'. This will be a black page in the chapter of my life. *You* draw that page, Madame, you will see two portraits the features of which will reproach you.

M. de Lagrangechancel had evidently found the door of 1 Grosvenor Gate firmly slammed in his face, and had received the 'threatening letter'. As long as her beauty lasted Mary Anne would attract men, but she knew better now than to beckon them on.

With Shrewsbury in his pocket, Disraeli thoroughly enjoyed the traditional chairing of the successful candidate—'gorgeous and fatiguing'—after a monumental visit to forty Salopian pubs ('quaffing the triumphal cup', he called it). Then came a great dinner, after which he and Mary Anne were glad to retire to the comparative peace of Loton Park, the home of that fine old English gentleman Sir Baldwin Leighton,[1] whom Disraeli had met during his early travels in the East. The visit was made

[1] M.P. for Shropshire 1877–85.

even more delightful by Sir Baldwin's agreeable wife and 'children lovelier than the dawn'. Then, after some more lionizing, they returned to London and the congratulations of their friends.

Disraeli was back in Parliament; the Tories formed the Government but he did not get office. On 30 August 1841, Sir Robert Peel,[1] the new Prime Minister, went to Windsor and kissed hands. Then he began to form his Cabinet. Lord Lyndhurst became Lord Chancellor and the aged Wellington was comfortably accommodated as leader of the Lords. But nowhere appeared the name of Disraeli. He waited for a week, then in desperation wrote to Peel, pressing his claims and pointing out what a storm of political hate and malice he had endured in the name of the Tory Party. He implored the Prime Minister, out of his well-known justice and magnanimity, to save him from intolerable humiliation.

The night before, Mary Anne had also written a letter to Peel. She had a certain personal influence with him in that his sister, wife of her admirer the poetical Mr George Dawson, was a close friend of hers. But she was clever enough not to lean on this fact when she set down her plea for her husband.

Dear Sir Robert Peel,
I beg you not to be angry with me for my intrusion, but I am overwhelmed with anxiety. My husband's political career is for ever crushed, if you do not appreciate him.
Mr. Disraeli's exertions are not unknown to you, but there is much he has done that you cannot be aware of, though they have had no other aim but to do you honour, no wish for recompense but your approbation. He has gone farther than most to make your opponents his personal enemies. He has stood four most expensive elections since 1834, and gained seats from Whigs in two, and I pledge myself as far as one seat, that it shall always be at your command.
Literature he has abandoned for politics. Do not destroy all his hopes, and make him feel his life has been a mistake.
May I venture to name my own humble but enthusiastic exertions in times gone by for the party, or rather for your own splendid self? They will tell you at Maidstone that more than £40,000 was spent through my influence only.

[1] Sir Robert Peel (1788–1850), 2nd baronet, statesman. In his long and illustrious political career he established the police force (called 'peelers' and later 'bobbies' after him) and founded a centrally organized 'Conservative Party' from the loose coalitions of the Tories.

Be pleased not to answer this, as I do not wish any human
being to know I have written to you this humble petition.
I am now, as ever, dear Sir Robert,
Your most faithful servant,
MARY ANNE DISRAELI.

Whether Disraeli knew of her letter is doubtful. She may well
have kept it from him, to save his pride in the event of her plea
being successful not because of his personal merit, but by her
lobbying for him. In any case, both letters failed to move Peel.
He replied coolly to Disraeli, denying that any member of his
Cabinet had received authority to encourage the idea that he
might be in the running. Disraeli had not said anything of the
kind, and Peel had obviously not troubled to read his letter
carefully. Suavely he thanked Disraeli for his application, but
regretted that he was unable to take into account any of the
claims Disraeli had pressed.

It was a bitter disappointment. Apart from the humiliation,
Disraeli badly needed the salary an office would have brought
with it. The anniversary of his marriage had been marked by
something much less agreeable than his poetic eulogy of his wife.
A writ for one of the debts which lay so heavily on him was
delivered to Mary Anne by mistake, and she flew into a temper
which made him 'very unwell', he told his solicitor. To make
matters worse, Pyne, for some unknown reason, ceased to act
for him about this time, and he was forced to attend to his own
financial affairs. He seems to have lacked entirely the traditional
Jewish flair for finance, and another 'Mess of Benjamin' ensued.
By now he owed something like £20,000. He lived in constant
apprehension that Mary Anne would open his mail while he was
away from home and discover yet more bad news.

She disapproved, but she got him out of his difficulties by one
means or another, paying off something like £13,000. She would
always watch his bank account with a sharp eye, as she watched
his health and his career. He knew it, and was grateful from the
first. All was over, he wrote to Sa after the failure of his application to Peel, and the crash would have been overwhelming but
for the heroic virtues of Mary Anne, whose ineffable tenderness
and unwearied devotion never for a moment slackened. 'I must
and ought to console myself for any worldly mortification in the
possession of such a wife—but it was principally to honour her

that I aspired to this dignity.' They were thinking of 'vagabonding abroad' to get over the disappointment, and in their absence Grosvenor Gate was to be the home of Sa and the rest of the family, if they wanted a London holiday. 'I can't affect to be in good spirits,' wrote Disraeli, who before his marriage would have been weeping and tearing his hair at such a catastrophe, 'but I am tolerably serene, very, indeed, when in company of my guardian angel, which I regret ever to quit. A year hence and we shall laugh at all this perhaps, and all that I shall recollect is Mary Anne's marvel of devotion and the sympathy of Bradenham.'

Their Ben was indeed a changed man, as was Mary Anne a changed woman, from a socialite 'rattle' to a dedicated, single-purposed wife. Her husband was going to the top of the tree, or she would know the reason why. She had full confidence in herself. She believed that the second marriage of a widow was seldom a failure, because

she doesn't expect too much and she understands how to give. A young bride unless she was born in the West wants to take everything and give nothing. Every woman in society for years has been taking from Dis. He appreciates better than any man I know the value of a woman who has something to give in return for being given to. Most men have this knowledge but they seldom exercise it because most women don't understand giving —either they don't want to give or they don't know how. Now I want to give and I know how most exactly.

Mary Anne Evans, and Mrs Wyndham Lewis, and 'Rose' of so many men's desires, had been deposed. In a mere two years one of Disraeli's supporters, W. B. Ferrand, would address Mary Anne thus:

My dear Mrs. Dizzy—as this abbreviation has become a household word in England, I am sure you will not think me impertinent for using it.

The next two years saw a steady rise in Disraeli's career. He was not yet forty. After the 'vagabonding' in France, at Caen, he returned to play a waiting game. He refrained from baiting Peel, preferring to support him even on the vexed question of the Corn Laws. He thought that rumours of his attitude to Peel went back to that gentleman by way of his sister. 'I saw Mrs. Dawson; she was most friendly and particularly disagreeable.' Possibly Mrs Dawson resented very slightly her husband's partiality for Mary Anne, and the fact that the *Book of Beauty* for 1841 contained her portrait by Chalon with George's rhapsodic verses attached, calling her 'a very fairy'. In spite of glowing reports of his Parliamentary prowess, Disraeli seems to have made little impression on Peel, who wisely preferred the less flamboyant but utterly dependable young William Ewart Gladstone,[1] on whom he had bestowed the office of Vice-President of the Board of Trade. There was obviously a general feeling that the popular abbreviation of Disraeli's name described him all too well, and it was up to him to live down his reputation for being something of an oddity. Meekly he voted for the Government, even when Peel attempted to conciliate the Free Traders by removing the customs tariff on hundreds of items, and filling its place with the Income Tax. He made speeches of an inoffensive but impressive nature, one of which, on the uninspiring theme of the consular representatives, held the House in thrall for three hours.

It took the cartoonists a long time to notice him. The newly-born *Punch*, whose maiden numbers covered July–December 1841, certainly featured him on its opening pages, as having accused the Whigs of seeking to retain power in opposition to the wishes of the country, and of profaning the name of the Queen at their elections. Later, it perpetrated the occasional feeble joke at the expense of his name: '. . . the discovery of the relationship between Ben D'Israeli and Ben Lomond', was pointed out, and a riddle section enquired whether Ben D'Israeli was a better orator than Ben Nevis; while a humorous List of Wants included: 'Wanted—by Mr. Benjamin D'Israeli, an appointment as ambassador. Distance no object; but a "friendly power" preferred.' It was not very funny, but it was publicity.

Then, slowly, the limelight turned on him. He found his natural level in a small body of youthful Tories, headed by the

---

[1] William Ewart Gladstone (1809–98), son of Sir John Gladstone, 1st baronet. His career is too lengthy to detail, but he is remembered chiefly for his rivalry with Disraeli, his piety, and his powers of oratory.

Byronic George Smythe[1] and the pious Lord John Manners.[2] They were in revolt against the dull materialism of Peel and his followers. Smythe, like Disraeli, wrote novels and verses, and affected a romantic costume and a reputation, rather well deserved, for profligacy. His debts and his women horrified the more respectable members of the party, but Disraeli found him fascinating—the only man who never bored him, as Smythe pathetically reminded him shortly before his young death from tuberculosis and old brandy. He was the last man to fight a duel on English soil, a gesture typical of the splinter-group formed by Smythe and his friends, calling itself 'Young England'.

They were the romantic rebels who inevitably spring up from time to time in a materialistic society. The Oxford movement in religion, the Gothic revival in architecture, the coming pre-Raphaelite group, were all part of the same thing. Medievalism was in fashion among these young men, tinged with a nostalgia for the dying aristocracy and with High Church leanings. Their spirit appealed strongly to Disraeli. When he and Mary Anne were staying in Paris during the winter of 1842, Smythe and his friend Baillie-Cochrane[3] called on them, and found them in a whirl of social gaiety, holding brilliant salons at the Hôtel de l'Europe and being entertained in return by the leading hostesses, who provided such entertainments as orange trees apparently growing out of supper-tables. Disraeli smoked a diamond-studded chibouque with the Turkish Ambassador, and Mary Anne was presented with a dish which her husband had enjoyed in Turkey, specially made for her by the Ambassador's cook. One night they attended a masked ball at the Opera, and Disraeli thought the three or four thousand devils dancing and masquerading 'beyond fancy'. The Young Englanders were full of amused admiration at their friend's splendour. When he could tear himself away from the salons, they conferred with him. Baillie-Cochrane (always known as Kok) was nervous; Disraeli seemed to him too fantastic to be real, and Smythe

---

[1] George Smythe (1818–57), 7th Viscount Strangford and 2nd Baron Penshurst. M.P. for Canterbury 1841; Under-Secretary for Foreign Affairs 1846.

[2] Lord John Manners (1818–1906), 7th Duke of Rutland, politician and poet. He toured the industrial districts of Lancashire with Disraeli and George Smythe in 1844. Various characters in *Coningsby*, *Sybil* and *Endymion* are modelled on him.

[3] Alexander Baillie-Cochrane (1816–90), 1st Baron Lamington. M.P. for Bridport, Lanarkshire, Honiton and Isle of Wight.

wondered whether the view of history they shared was entirely sincere on the latter's part. But his power was irresistible, and by the end of the Parliamentary session of 1843 the Home Secretary was admitting to John Wilson Croker[1] that 'with respect to Young England, the puppets are moved by Disraeli, who is the ablest man among them; I consider him unprincipled and disappointed . . . it would be better for the party if he were driven into the ranks of our open enemies'.

Meanwhile, Disraeli had gone back to authorship and produced his novel *Coningsby*, the first of a trilogy: the chief character was modelled on Smythe. It has been called the first and most brilliant of English political novels. Peel was not amused when he read in it Disraeli's condemnation of his own brand of politics. *Punch*, however, was amused. It published a 'Cartoon for the Merchant Tailors', showing two markedly Hebrew gentlemen dressing up a small Humpty Dumpty-like personage in immaculate evening gear topped by an enormous plumed hat. The accompanying rhyme began:

> The novel of Coningsby clearly discloses
> The pride of the world are the children of Moses . . .

and went on in a similar vein. It was followed on the same page by a skit on a recent Conservative Dinner's toast of 'Our Ancient Institutions', enquiring whether the company present had any idea of what they were toasting. For instance, a few Ancient Institutions were the Feudal System, with the Power of Pit and Gallows, the Application of Dental Surgery, for the increase of the Crown Revenues, to Gentlemen of the Hebrew Persuasion, Hanging, Drawing and Quartering, and so forth. Beside the article stood a dandified figure only just recognizable as Disraeli, blowing a trumpet from which hung a banner labelled *Coningsby*. A later issue showed an equally bad caricature of Disraeli as Young England discovered sitting dolorously before his parlour-fire; 'he grievously waileth as follows:

> I really can't imagine why,
> With my confess'd ability—

---

[1] John Wilson Croker (1780–1857), politician and essayist; introduced the term 'Conservatives' to the Tory party in 1830.

From the ungrateful Tories, I
  Get nothing—but civility . . .
I've flattered Peel; he smiles back thanks
  With Belial's own tranquillity;
But still he keeps me in 'the ranks',
  And pays me—with civility.

He got a full page to himself in the next cartoon, where he appeared as Young Gulliver, making a service bow to the Brobdingnag Minister, Peel; but even the brilliant John Leech had not quite captured his image. Then *Punch* had a go at him with a parody of one of Tom Hood's punning ballads:

Young Ben he was a nice young man,
  An author by his trade;
He fell in love with Polly-Tics
  And was an M.P. made.

He was a Radical one day,
  But met a Tory crew;
His Polly-tics he cast away,
  And then turned Tory too.

Now Ben had tried for many a place
  When Tories e'en were out;
But in two years the turning Whigs
  Were turn'd to the right-about.

But when he called on Robert Peel,
  His talents to employ,
His answer was, 'Young Englander,
  For me you're not the boy.'

Oh, Robert Peel! Oh, Robert Peel!
  How could you serve me so?
I've met with Whig rebuffs before,
  But not a Tory blow.

Then rising up in Parliament,
  He made a fierce to-do,
With Peel, who merely winked his eye;
  Ben winked like winking, too. . . .

A mock commentary on an armoured joust between Peel ('Pawky Bob') and Disraeli ('The Shrewsbury Slasher') reflected an attack on Peel which left the Prime Minister 'stunned and stupefied'. *Punch* further enjoyed itself with a report of a visit

129

made by Indians of the Ioway Tribe[1] to 1 Grosvenor Gate, with jokes about Benjamin's wigwam, the cooling down of the party's excitement by a short reading from *Coningsby*, and a dance of brotherly love in which the Members of Young England joined.

In all this boisterous fun there is no mention of Mary Anne. *Punch*, which had no scruples about racialism and other sensitive topics, forbore to jibe at ladies, apart from ultra-fashionable ones and the Queen, a constant butt. Mary Anne, however, was there, behind the councils of Young England and the publication of her husband's books, her 'literary children'. In a burst of pride, she would tell visitors to inspect 'the room where Dizzy was brought to bed of *Coningsby*'. George Smythe absentmindedly strayed into the bathroom by mistake and plunged headlong into the bath, which was unfortunately full. Returning downstairs in the aspect of a drowned rat, he was met by Mary Anne, who asked him whether he had seen the room where *Coningsby* was born. 'I know nothing of the place of his birth,' replied the dripping Smythe, 'but I *have* been in the room where he was baptized.' Or so ran the story: Mary Anne had a fund of them which she would drop into any awkward silence over dinner. There are glimpses of her in Disraeli's letters to Sa: in May 1843, revisiting Shrewsbury, attending the gay Bachelors' Ball 'the grand lady of the evening . . . in white with a dark wreath of velvet flowers twined with diamonds', and at the Races next day watching Retriever win the Tankerville Cup. Wherever she could go with her husband she went. 'The more we are separated,' he wrote to her, 'the more I cling to you . . . 'tis your approbation and delight for which I am now laboring, and unless I had that stimulus I don't think I could go on.' When they had to be apart, she sent him violets to put on his breakfast-table as mementoes of her, and wrote to him on violet-scented paper. Smythe, writing to Disraeli on Young England matters, begged him to 'lay me at the little feet of Madame'. Disraeli was so proud of the little feet, as perfect as though shoes had never touched them, that he had one sculpted in marble as a drawing-room ornament. It is not, in fact, abnormally small, being about a twentieth-century size 4; but

[1] They were on exhibition at the Egyptian Hall, Piccadilly, and rejoiced in such names as Pigeon-on-the-wing, Roman Nose, and Female-Bear-that walks-on-the-back-of-Another. One of the chiefs, if we are to believe the *Illustrated London News*, was called Neu-mon-ya.

Mary Anne was so often compared to a fairy that she must have bewitched the eye of the beholder into thinking her even tinier than she was; and her wedding-ring would only fit the finger of a child of today.

During these years in which they were, as Disraeli put it, slowly climbing to the top of the greasy pole, they were to be found at most of the grandest Tory country houses, and once at Peel's Drayton Manor. All of these visits were faithfully reported to news-hungry Bradenham. In 1842 there had been a brief quarrel between Disraeli and Sa, who had received no letters for two months, and he told Mary Anne that all correspondence between them had ceased, and it was by no means agreeable to him to resume it. But affection like theirs was not easily extinguished, and soon Sa was able to read the usual starry effusions to her blind father. On their wedding anniversary in 1845 she was writing to her brother and sister-in-law:

My dear Mary Anne and Dis, As I write this date, I am reminded what an important day is this, I breathe a thousand prayers for your felicity. May God bless you both, and give you many many happy returns. We all thank you, dear Mary Anne, for your amusing letter, but especially Papa who desires me to tell you how much he admires your graphic simplicity. He differs from you in one thing, he does not think that Dis could have so completely brought before him the great Rothschild banquet. We fully share in all your fate and all your honours, and quite at our ease with our feet stretched on the fender.

How good you are to think of me—I cannot tell you how *very very* much obliged I am to you, dear Mary Anne. I think it a most extraordinary act of kindness to burthen yourself with such an extra package on my account; I enclose the measure of my head—I am sure the bonnet will be beautiful, but please *not* velvet for that would be quite wasted on me. As you know, I remain in the Grub state all the winter, and never emerge into the light of the world until the Spring.

That Mary Anne's epistolary style kept the Bradenham household in fits of laughter is understandable. While it was left to 'Dis' to give them brilliant descriptions of grand occasions, she added the amusing touches; as when, in 1843, they were staying with Henry Hope at 'beautiful Deepdene'.

One of our greatest amusements were two honey bears, tolerably tame, who I often went to play with; fancy my fright when these horrific-looking pets came howling after me the first time! I went to take a composing draught. Sometimes they are chained, but oftener have their liberty, and use it by frightening the maids and running round the fine galleries—you never heard such a noise. I never kept company with them without witnesses, fearing they might in their fondness hug me to death.

In 1845 they were staying with the Duke of Buckingham[1] at his great house, Stowe, which was being honoured by the presence of the Queen and the Prince Consort. Mary Anne gave Sa an irreverent description of their presentation.

I have left [Disraeli] to try to give you some idea of the splendid spectacle we presented on Friday evening, but you must fancy the greater part of it—we were for the first hour in the vestibule like a flock of sheep, half lit up, and no seats or fire, only a little hot air and a great deal of cold wind; and a marble floor. Fancy dear shivering Dizzy, and cross-looking Mary Anne, in black velvet, hanging sleeves looped up with knots of blue, and diamond buttons. Head-dress, blue velvet bows and diamonds. After a time we passed her Majesty and the Prince, the Duke and Duchess and the rest standing behind, the Duke giving our names exactly the same as an ordinary groom, and we making our curtseys and bows. About eleven, or soon after, her Majesty retired, and then all became joy and triumph to us. First Sir Robert Peel came to us, shaking hands most cordially, and remained talking for some time, then Lord Nugent, introducing his lady, Col. Anson, Sir James Graham, Lord and Lady de Warr, Lord Aberdeen. The Duke almost embraced Dizzy, saying he was one of his oldest friends; and then Sara dear, he offered me his arm, taking me all through the gorgeous splendid scene, through the supper room and back again, 'down the middle and back again'— all making way for us the Queen and your delighted Mary Anne being the only ladies so distinguished. After this I retired to a sofa, with the Duchess, who told me that her Majesty had pointed Dizzy out, saying 'There's Mr. Disraeli.' Do you call all this nothing? The kind Duchess asked me to luncheon the next day and to see the Queen's private apartment.

Mary Anne was suitably impressed with the rooms that lodged Royalty: 'the State bed, the pictures, some of the finest Rembrandts and others in the world . . . china of matchless beauty, tables loaded with works of art from all parts of the

[1] Richard Chandos Grenville (1797–1861), 2nd Duke of Buckingham. M.P. for Buckinghamshire 1818–39. Stowe is now a public school.

world.' She approved less of the more intimate arrangements of Victoria and Albert.

> But how do you think they sleep? *Without pillows or bolster.* Lady Anna assur'd me of this over and over again. . . . The head woman ask'd me if I would like to see the room which had been prepared for Her Majesty. On my asking her what a large red curtain was for, 'Oh,' she said, 'to hang across the staircase when Her Majesty went to the cabinet. On her return the Queen ask'd the woman *where the Prince could go*—but *there was no second convenience!*

(Superior standards of sanitation obviously prevailed at Grosvenor Gate.)

Even on such a grand occasion, Mary Anne was more concerned with the honours paid to her husband than with anything else.

> When Her Majesty pass'd us to go from one room to another, she almost paus'd to look at mine own, who was in his best looks, in shorts [knee-breeches] which nearly all the men were dressed in, black coats, white waistcoats, and so on. . . . My heart, dear Sa, was full of gratified ambition—oh no, of the most devoted love.

At Fryston Hall, in Yorkshire, the home of Richard Monckton Milnes[1] we see Mary Anne through the eyes of another sharply observant lady. Colonel John Spencer-Stanhope's wife, Elizabeth, wrote home to her husband about the members of the house-party.

> . . . last, but not least, D'Israeli and Mrs. D'Izzy. . . . Mrs D'Izzy was in a lace dress, looped up on each side, over pink satin, and a wreath on her head, though I should think near fifty. However, she is very amusing and off-hand, saying everything that comes uppermost and unfeignedly devoted to her D'Izzy. She does not give herself airs, and seems very good-natured. This morning she has been giving us an account of the scenes between Sir Lytton Bulwer and Lady Bulwer, and her own ineffectual attempts to reconcile them. . . .

Milnes, who normally possessed only a woman cook, had specially for the occasion borrowed a chef—'to please D'Izzy',

[1] Richard Monckton Milnes (1809–85), 1st Baron Houghton; statesman and man of letters, friend of Tennyson, Thackeray, editor of Keats's *Life and Letters.*

Lady Elizabeth thought. The visit was more frivolous than usual. One night a guest fell asleep on a sofa, thereby affording the fun-loving Lord Galway the opportunity to black his face while he slept. There were charades and amateur theatricals, in which Milnes played Sairey Gamp.[1] Did either of the Disraelis take part? Lady Elizabeth does not say so, and it is difficult to imagine Disraeli, with his standards of propriety, doing so. Again, Lady Elizabeth dwells on Mary Anne's charm.

> Mrs. D'Izzy I like quite as much as her husband, and think her *equally* clever *in her* way . . . she would love you for your admiration of her D'Izzy, as she calls him, for only my simple and *sincere* tribute this morning brought tears to her eyes. We have spent the whole morning tête-à-tête, and most amusing she has been, but I must keep all the good stories to make myself agreeable to you on my return.

The good stories were many: society delighted in Mary Anne's racy tongue, however much it might pretend to be shocked by some of her remarks. On somebody's commenting at a party on the beauty of a lady's pale complexion, Mary Anne exclaimed, 'Ah, I wish you could only see my Dizzy in his bath! then you would know what a white skin is.' At another country house, at which the Disraelis occupied a bedroom next to Lord Hardinge[2] and his wife, Mary Anne declared to the company at breakfast that she had slept between the greatest soldier and the greatest orator of the day; but Lord Mahon, who was present, felt that Lady Hardinge was not amused. Nor was the unidentified 'wife of the lordly proprietor' of 'one of the most splendid of our Provincial Palaces', according to Sir William Fraser, whose naïve and prim jottings on *Disraeli and his Day*[3] are responsible for so many snippets of otherwise unrecorded information. The lady had, it seems, a deep and sincere sense of correctness, and before the Disraelis arrived had swept from the walls all pictures of a dubious nature; somewhat oddly omitting to remove a conspicuous example of classical nudity in the bedroom allotted to them. At breakfast Mary Anne playfully accused her hostess of having a house full of indecent pictures:

---

[1] Dickens's *Martin Chuzzlewit* had been published in the same year.

[2] Sir Henry Hardinge (1785–1856), 1st Viscount Hardinge, soldier and statesman. He fought with Moore at Corunna, and served under Wellington during the Peninsular War. Later became Governor-General of India.

[3] See Bibliography.

'There is a most horrible picture in our bedroom—Disraeli says it is Venus and Adonis. I have been awake half the night trying to prevent him looking at it!'

The story is apparently true, having been told to Sir William by the son of the house, although it seems unlikely that a lady of rank of that day would carry out a cleaning-up campaign of her walls for the benefit of guests not renowned for their prudery. Mary Anne was the *enfant terrible* of the drawing-room, and got away with it. It is not difficult to imagine the cascades of giggles emerging from that stately bedroom. Nor can one entirely disbelieve the story that Mary Anne confided to Queen Victoria that she always slept with her arms round her husband's neck; it was precisely the kind of marital confidence in which the Queen would have delighted, emphasizing as it did the same kind of married love she enjoyed with Albert, without specific reference to the 'too dreadful animal side of our nature', to which even Mary Anne would hardly have referred in the Royal presence.

One may, however, disregard other stories about the pair; such as the tale that when Mary Anne had become old Disraeli was asked what he could possibly feel for her, and replied 'gratitude'. So many identities have been given to the enquirer that one suspects he did not exist. In any case, it was a question nobody would have dared to put to Disraeli. Likewise, when Mary Anne is reported as having said that he married her for money, but if he were to do it again it would be for love, she was obviously employing her shock tactics; his long letter to her in February 1839 makes it quite clear that he did *not* marry her for money, whatever his early intentions were, and his subsequent letters and verses make it even clearer.

One may discount, too, the implication conveyed by a remark he is supposed to have made, to the effect that Mary Anne didn't know who came first, the Greeks or the Romans. Disraeli's education may have been humble compared with that of the Harrovian Peel and the Etonian Gladstone, but he was a reasonable classical scholar, and Mary Anne worked on his books as editor, critic and proof-reader. She may have teased him with such a statement, but it could never have been meant seriously. When, in 1844, Disraeli wrote to Monckton Milnes about a review Milnes had written of *Coningsby*, he regretted that he had not seen it on the last occasion when Milnes called, for if he had 'we could have discussed together the points of controversy, assisted by Mrs. Disraeli, who has several puissant arguments for you in store, though she, as well as myself, appreciate comments that at the same time indicate the thoughtful mind, the cultivated taste, and the refined pen.' And it was not to a scatter-brained nitwit that he dedicated *Sybil*:

I would inscribe this work to one whose noble spirit and gentle nature ever prompt her to sympathise with the suffering; to one whose sweet voice has often encouraged, and whose taste and judgment have ever guided, its pages; the most severe of critics, but—a perfect Wife!

12

'On thee age creepeth?'

The publication of *Coningsby* and *Sybil* not only established Disraeli's position as a serious novelist but as a serious politician rather than an actor on the wrong stage. In 1845 he delivered a series of slashing attacks on Peel, requesting him to 'dissolve, if you please, the Parliament you have betrayed' and informing the House that 'the right hon. gentleman caught the Whigs bathing, and walked away with their clothes'. Peel lacked the guns to reply to his rival's fire, and old Wellington, who had specialized since Waterloo in making memorable remarks, commented that 'rotten potatoes have done it all; they put Peel in his damned fright'. It was a strenuous summer in Parliament, and caused the Disraelis to feel that another Continental holiday would not be out of place. They travelled, accordingly, to Cassel in French Flanders, took a furnished house for two months, and enjoyed early hours. Mary Anne wrote to Sa that they had walked 300 miles and Disraeli added a postscript that this had particularly agreed with her, 'as she is plump as one of the partridges which we can't purchase here'. It was particularly nice not to have to talk shop. 'We do not know and have not interchanged a word with a single person of even average intelligence on any subject. The names of the Duke of Wn [Wellington] and Sir Robert Peel and all those sort of people are quite unknown here. . . .'

As ever, they revelled in pastoral peace.

As we walk out in the late afternoon, about 5 o'clock . . . we sometimes hear the bells of half a dozen surrounding valleys sounding at the same time. There are oratories and little chapels certainly every half-mile, and a carv'd image or two in almost every field . . . the autumn here of the most mellow nature: continuing fine and mild tho' we live on the top of a mountain. And we never have a fire except in the evenings. We have a pretty little garden wh. grows us mignonette and Alpine straw-berries wh. M.A. picks for me, and often wishes she could do the same for my father. . . . M.A. cannot leave her young pigeons, who live in the house and breakfast with us.

When they were home again, Mary Anne wrote to Sa on 'our dear Dizzy's birthday, bless him', reporting that he was very pleased that Sir Robert Peel had retired to private life.

On 15 May 1846, Disraeli launched a withering three-hour attack on Peel, describing him as 'a burglar of other people's intellect' and 'a committer of political petty larceny'. Neither invective nor satire could prevent Peel and his supporters from repealing the Corn Laws,[1] but Disraeli, with Bentinck[2] beside him, produced a deadly weapon in the shape of the Irish Coercion Bill, and raked up accusations against Peel of having played the turncoat in 1827 over Catholic emancipation. They may or may not have been true accusations—Disraeli later came to the conclusion that they were not—but they split the Tory Party and gained the 'Protectionist' party, as the Tory rebels were now called—led by Lord Stanley[3] with George Bentinck and Disraeli as his lieutenants in the House of Com-mons—enough votes to turn Peel out of office. Lord John Russell formed a Whig government and his position was con-firmed in the 1847 election.

After the summer recess of 1845 *Punch* had depicted the 'Boys of St Stephen's' going home for the holidays in a four-wheeler, with a jubilant Disraeli top-hatted and cricket-batted riding behind, meditating thus: 'Oh! won't I have a jolly game of cricket! fol de rol de rol!' Almost at the same date *Punch* was displaying adjoining views of Queens: Elizabeth, 1580, watching smilingly the baiting of a bear, and Victoria, 1845, adoringly contemplating the mass slaughter of deer by a Tyrolean-hatted Albert ('The Queen was in her easy chair, and looked as sweet as honey, The Prince was shooting at the deer, in weather bright

---

[1] The Corn Laws were passed during 1804–28, imposing restrictions and levies on the import of corn into Britain, by parliaments dominated by land-owners. They caused much distress among the poor, especially during the 'Hungry Forties', and were repealed in 1846 by Sir Robert Peel.

[2] Lord George Bentinck (1802–48), statesman. He had been private secretary to Canning, M.P. for King's Lynn 1826–48, and accepted leadership of the 'Protectionists' in 1846.

[3] Edward Stanley (1799–1869), later 14th Earl of Derby, statesman. His impressive career included two premierships.

A NICE YOUNG MAN FOR A SMALL PARTY.

YOUNG BEN he was a nice young man,
   An author by his trade ;
He fell in love with Polly-Tics,
   And was an M.P. made.

He was a Radical one day,
   But met a Tory crew ;
His Polly-Tics he cast away,
   And then turned Tory too.

Now BEN had tried for many a place
   When Tories e'en were out ;
But in two years the turning Whigs
   Were turn'd to the right-about.

'A nice young man for a small party.' Disraeli disconsolate at the collapse of 'Young England', 1845. *Punch.*

Hughenden Manor before restoration by Lord Henry
Lennox, M.P.

The rear view of Hughenden Manor today, preserved
as it was when the home of Benjamin and Mary Anne
Disraeli.

Rosina Bulwer Lytton,
1852, by A. E. Chalon,
R.A.

The Countess of
Bradford in middle age
by Edward Clifford.

William Ewart
Gladstone in youth.

H.M. Queen Victoria,
after Von Angeli,
presented to Disraeli
by the Queen.

and sunny, The bands were playing polkas, dress'd in green and golden clothes, The Nobles cut the poor deers' throats, and that is all *Punch* knows!') There was no doubt which side Mr Punch was on. The old order was changing, and he had a nose for a winner, person or Party. Early in 1846 he showed Victoria, as lady of the house, dismissing a page-boy-buttoned Peel: 'I'm afraid you're not strong enough for the place, John.'

A little later, Manager Peel was taking his Farewell Benefit on a flower-strewn stage, with Mr Punch waving him off from a box, and a belligerent Disraeli, ringlets flying, shaking a fist from the stalls. By 1847 a cartoon entitled 'The Rising Generation in Parliament' showed Peel, as Headmaster, enquiring of a juvenile Ben, 'Well, my little man, what are you going to do this session, eh?' to which his pupil drawled: 'Why—aw—aw— I've made arrangements—aw—to smash everybody.'

He had, in fact, risen above his previous status as simple M.P. for Shrewsbury. His ambition was to be Knight of the Shire for Buckingham. But this required him to be a County Member who must own land in his own right and Disraeli had none. No. 1 Grosvenor Gate belonged to Mary Anne, and that only for her lifetime. He badly needed a country estate. There was Bradenham, of course, but it was his father's, and Isaac, though blind, was causing his family no particular anxiety in his general health. Ever since the family's removal to that quiet house Disraeli's heart had been in Buckinghamshire and its 'beechen groves'. There he must settle, on his own account, near his beloved family and near enough to London without being on its suburban doorstep. The Red Lion of High Wycombe pointed out the very place to him. Only a mile away from the spot where he had loftily patted its head, in long-ago 1832, stood Hughenden Manor, a pleasant, simple Georgian house high in its own park, with beech groves in plenty, lawns and flowers and grazing land, some 750 acres in all, yielding a comfortable income to its owner. The owner, John Norris, had recently died, and Hughenden Manor was on the market for £34,950.

Disraeli had nothing like that money available. Neither, presumably, had Mary Anne, who had only inherited modest sums from her mother and her uncle Sir James. But, in debt as he was, the prospective landowner was undaunted. He appears to have mesmerized Lord George Bentinck and his brothers,

Lord Titchfield and Lord Henry Bentinck, into lending him £25,000, in a series of protracted negotiations, backed by the generous Isaac. It all took time; Hughenden stood empty. Then death resolved the situation. In April 1847, Maria D'Israeli died. Nine months later, on 19 January 1848, she was followed to the grave by Isaac, aged eighty-one. He left Benjamin one third of his estate of £11,000, the residue being divided between his other children; to Mary Anne went Isaac's precious collection of prints. The home at Bradenham was broken up. Sa retired to Twickenham, to a pleasant Regency house in Ailsa Park Villas (ten years before Charles Dickens had lodged his family next-door for the summer). Ralph departed for London, where he had chambers as a clerk in Chancery, while James kept on the Bradenham Manor Farm. It was ironic that the home at Bradenham should disintegrate just as, on 6 September 1848, a proud Disraeli wrote to Mary Anne: 'It is all done, and you are the Lady of Hughenden.'

He spoke somewhat prematurely, for on 21 September George Bentinck died, and the loan might well have been in serious jeopardy. Bank and solicitors came to the rescue, and with his usual good fortune Disraeli made what proved to be a splendid investment. At the age of forty-three he had lost a mother and, more regretfully, a father, and had gained a magnificent country seat and the prospective leadership of the House of Commons in Bentinck's place.

It was not all honey, however. The clearing up of his father's estate was a considerable task. Isaac had left 25,000 books, most of which his eldest son sold at Sotheby's. It took six weeks to move from Bradenham to Hughenden, and Disraeli wrote wearily to Lady Blessington that recently he seemed to have been living in wagons, like a Tartar chief; which he rather wished he were, as an easier sort of existence. It was, of course, Mary Anne who was doing most of the practical work, taking over the Bradenham furniture and such books as were needed for the new library. To the Bradenham items she added new ones—Aubusson carpets from Maple's, of crimson and yellow, some shields from Mr Lacey of High Wycombe to ornament the hall in proper baronial style, and a marquee for garden parties from Edgington's, the famous tent and flag makers of the Old Kent Road. Ralph and James Disraeli came over and exclaimed with pleasure at their sister-in-law's 'clever arrangements and magic touches'. Hughenden, presumably, had grown shabby with time, and Mary Anne's hearty bourgeois taste was refreshing to the Victorian eye.

There were servants to engage. One Charles Newbury received a character for honesty and sobriety from the Chief Justice's housekeeper; he had been a footman in that establishment. But at Hughenden his life developed complications, and a breathless letter survives, presumably from Charles to the butler, Evans, which sounds as though he had strayed into the paths of intrigue.

> Sir, I am truly sorry of my past crime more partickular of telling you such a falsehood by saying that girl was a fellowservant of mine, as it may be the means of bringing you into trouble about what I know you are quite innocent but I hope their won't be any Blame attached to you and that you will forgive me and except of my umble repentance as I can't find words to express it but it will be a lesson for me for my life and for others I hope I think of coming to see if Mr. Disralia will forgive me tomorrow as I don't know what I shall do if he don't give me a caracter yours respectfully Charles Newberry.

Later Mary Anne acquired a butler called Mr Cheshire, and lost a housekeeper from the Grosvenor Gate establishment. With great hauteur, Mrs Rogers wrote to Mary Anne at Hughenden that she had received Honoured Madam's note and would have answered by return of post

> but waited to be able to name the day that I should leave Grosvenor Gate, which I intend doing this day (Monday). I can assure you Madam On Oath I made use of no abusive language to Susan, I only tould her that she did not give the cats the milk that you allowed them, wich is the truth. She instantly exclaimed 'You are a lying Bald Old Devvel', and threw a glass of beer over me, and also acted as I have before described to you Madam—but I have no doubt it was a premeditated quarrel on her part as she had two persons ready to supply my place one of them your late kitchenmaid, the other a person the name of Ryan, a cook out of place.

A postscript adds that the erring Susan had also called her a 'Toothless Old Beast'. Mr Cheshire immediately took up his dignified pen to inform Mrs Rogers that Mrs Disraeli was very much shocked and surprised at such a scene passing in her 'ouse', and was very sorry that any servant of hers should behave so ill. He continued that Mrs Disraeli did not think that it would improve Mrs Rogers's reputation to bring the case up before a magistrate, and would send a person to supply her place in the morning. Mrs Rogers, meanwhile, was dashing off another condemnation of the incorrigible Susan, whose behaviour-pattern seems to have had a certain sameness. Once again, in the housekeeper's opinion under the influence of liquor, 'she threw a glass of beer over me and then took me by the shoulders and shook me violently, and feeling alarm I scream'd Murder—not satisfied she then threw a cup of tea over me—all this I thank God without [my] raising a hand.'

Disraeli, in London, on the front bench in the House for the first time, with Peel and Bentinck, and in more sober attire than of old, was missing his wife's company. Her lively letters were not so frequent as usual, and he wrote in January 1848:

My dearest Wife, I was very much disappointed by your letter of this morning, as I took it for granted that it wd only be the herald of yr immediate appearance . . . may I soon embrace you.

Another note tells her that she may 'cut down any trees respecting which Vernon [the head gardener] sees his way'. In her opinion, the groves which surrounded the Manor were rather too thick. It was indeed 'bosom'd high in tufted trees', like Milton's visioned towers, and the Beauty who lived there preferred herself and her house to be the cynosure of neighbouring eyes without all that foliage in the way. She had her two devoted gardeners clear paths through the woods, revealing beautiful prospects and allowing visitors to walk through the woodland. Disraeli himself preferred a gentle saunter, and Mary Anne liked to trot in and out of High Wycombe in a pony-cart drawn by the little pony Sir Philip Rose had given her to replace a dead favourite.

Disraeli admired all her innovations to the grounds, proudly displayed to guests 'the Sylvan scene' which was all due to the ingenuity of Mary Anne and especially the walk 'she made with the help of her two old men of the soil'. 'My darling, you have, I am sure, done at Hughenden what no other woman, or man either, could do. You have gained a year in our enjoyment of that place, where I trust every year we shall be happier and happier.'

They were soon entertaining and receiving invitations in return, dazzling the assembled company with the splendour of their costume. However sober he now appeared in the House, Disraeli had no inhibitions about his social wardrobe. In 1844 a Mrs Harriet Stewart made him a waistcoat which she flattered herself 'outdid D'Orsay and out-Heroded Herod, quilted up with suave perfumes . . . and as for the buttons, I don't think they are buttons at all, but Ducks'. Among the items of his wardrobe taken to Hughenden were two white velvet waistcoats and one black, presumably for the display of his array of chains; and Mary Anne kept meticulous notes of her attire at Court functions. One of them was 'a manteau and corsage of rich white satin, lined with azure blue, trimmed with gold lace. Petticoat covered with gold blond lace flounces, and looped up with diamonds, body and sleeves ornamented with gold lace, turquoise and diamonds.' Diamonds, turquoise and white lace also figured largely in a Court costume for 1852. She was sixty years old, and palpably had no intention of admitting the fact by dressing in a way even remotely appropriate to her age, in that era when women of forty retired into caps and shawls. If her eyes were not as bright as they had been, she still felt they could bear the proximity of diamonds, if her skin lacked its one-time clear brilliance, it was still not shamed by white lace, and the hair she twined with 'a wreath of splendid diamonds, green velvet leaves, feathers and lappets' cannot have had much grey in it: perhaps was not allowed to have any. After all, Disraeli dyed his, or rather she dyed it for him. His political opponent Robert Lowe[1] had a facetious comment put into his mouth on the subject of Disraeli's unalterably raven locks by a fellow M.P., according to William Fraser's report:

> BOB to BEN (across the House)
> By all means, if you wish it, we'll take and we'll give:
> To your candid remarks I've a candid reply:
> My hair will be white, so long as I live;
> While yours will be black so long as you dye.

[1] Robert Lowe (1811–92), 1st Viscount Sherbrooke; M.P. for Kidderminster, Vice-President of the Board of Trade and Paymaster-General. He became Chancellor of the Exchequer 1868–73 and Home Secretary 1873–4.

So perhaps Mary Anne applied a little discreet tint to hers. The miniature on which Middleton's posthumous portrait was based shows her face very slightly dimmed from its earlier radiance: like Pater's Mona Lisa, her eyelids are a little weary, and there are heavy shadows beneath the blue eyes, and a hint of thickening below the oval chin. A strange fact which emerged from exploration of the Hughenden Archives is that no photograph of Mary Anne exists in them, or is known to exist anywhere else. There is a famous story of Disraeli about to be photographed; when the photographer approached with the traditional pedestal for him to lean on, Mary Anne ran forward and pushed it away, crying 'Dizzy has never had anyone but me to lean on, and he shan't be shown with a prop now.' The story does not go on to say whether Disraeli was then obliged to sit down or stand up with his arms folded; but certainly Mary Anne did not get herself into the picture as a human prop.

Why did she not choose to stand for the camera and posterity by her husband's side, as she had always done figuratively? The explanation must surely be that she feared the too-candid eye of the instrument, so much less kind to a lady's face than the painter's brush. It was all very well for John Mayall[1] (who also took one of the earliest and most brilliantly revealing photographs of Dickens) to portray Disraeli so superbly, wearing an expression calculated to threaten, command, and generally reduce the Opposition to quivering jellies. But the ladies of the time appear photographically wearing all the charm and vivacity of bag-puddings. The Queen herself, photographed with Albert a few months before his death, when she had no cause for the faintest anxiety about him, wears an expression which might easily be taken for a premonition of early widowhood (possibly, of course, he may have cautioned her against breaking into the jolly, toothy and markedly unregal smile which she occasionally permitted herself). Even in the portrait of herself given by the Queen to Disraeli, which she considered a particularly good likeness and which now hangs in the dining-room at Hughenden, she appears to be extremely cross and to have a bad cold into the bargain.

[1] John Jabez Edwin Mayall (1810–1901), pioneer of the daguerreotype in America. He later came to England and photographed many distinguished people, including the Royal family. He started the vogue for photograph albums by taking 'carte' portraits.

But to the human eye Mary Anne was still lovely, and miraculously young. Someone who very much later saw her presiding at the schoolchildren's summer treat in the gardens of Hughenden remarked that 'as she skipped and ran about with the children, she did not look a day over forty', and was wearing (in her late sixties) 'a crinoline with a petticoat of fine cambric, with innumerable flounces over it, exquisitely goffered. Over it was looped, in a manner calculated to show off her youthful figure, a white dress of French muslin, powdered with purple pansies, her white straw hat trimmed with a band of black velvet, like any young ingenue.'

As for the middle-aged Disraeli, now sporting a tiny Imperial beard, he was following Mary Anne's example of youthfulness; and perhaps smilingly remembered those long-ago verses 'to the Author of *Contarini Fleming*':

> What is this? On *thee* Age creepeth?
> Shall thy glance grow evening-light?
> To a future winter weepeth
> Snow upon thy locks of night
> Shall the morn come when thy fingers
> Cannot brook to beat the lyre?
> When the purple phoenix lingers
> O'er the unillumined pyre?

It was going to be a very long time before the lyre ceased to be beaten; the purple phoenix would find its strength and its temper taxed by a great many years of hovering, and upon the locks of night snow never fell. Mary Anne would see to that.

13

'A spirit I am,
And I don't give a damn'

However soberly Disraeli might behave in Parliament, *Punch* of 1849 enjoyed itself with his origins and appearance in its old irreverent manner, as when, to the tune of 'The Curly-headed Ploughboy', it sang an entirely new Cockney folk-ballad.

A Curly-headed Jew-boy some years ago was I,
And through the streets of London 'Old Clo'' I used to cry,
But now I am a Member, I speechifies and votes,
I've given up all my dealin's in left-off hats and coats;
In a creditable manner I hope I fills my sheat,
Though I vonce vos but a Jew-boy vot whistled through the
    street.

One of the 'Jew-boy's' triumphs had been the political destruction of Sir Robert Peel. But he was essentially too generous a man to crow over a defeated opponent, particularly as they had to share the same bench in the House, with Gladstone, another looming enemy, between them. After an all-night sitting on 28 June 1850, Disraeli went home to Grosvenor Gate, retired to bed and slept until late in the morning. Mary Anne wakened him with the news that it was a beautiful day and a carriage drive would freshen him up after such a night. They went driving in Regent's Park and were surprised to be stopped by two men on horseback. Innocent enough as the strangers appeared, they brought fateful news. Mr Disraeli might be interested to know, they said, that Sir Robert Peel had been thrown from his horse and lay dangerously ill. Then they waited for a triumphant reaction. But Disraeli was shocked. 'Dangerous? I hope not. His loss would be a great misfortune for this country.' The strangers looked surprised—and a little disappointed.
    For four days Peel lay in such agony that his wife was kept

out of his sick-room, in case her uncontrollable grief was too much for his flickering life. On the third of those days, Disraeli attended a morning fête at Rosebank, the riverside cottage of his old friend and flirt Lady Londonderry, where, Marie-Antoinette-like, she served tea from golden utensils in an enormous conservatory. During the festivities Lord Londonderry slipped away, returning later to whisper to Disraeli that Peel's case was hopeless. The next day he was dead.

Now, sentiment apart, was Disraeli's chance to rally the Peelites to his banner, and give the Tory Party a majority in the House. They were not enthusiastic. It fell to Lord Stanley to confer with Disraeli on the possibility of forming a strong Tory party without the help of the too-loyal Peelites.

It was late morning at Grosvenor Gate, Mary Anne busy about her affairs, when a visitor was shown upstairs to the Blue Room. An unusually cheerful Stanley had called to inform Disraeli that they were 'launched': he had promised the Queen he would try to form a Government, with Mr Disraeli as Leader of the House of Commons. Upon which Her Majesty, little knowing how time would change her attitude, interrupted coldly to say that she did not like Mr Disraeli. She had not approved of his behaviour to Peel, and Peel's death had done nothing to alter her views. Stanley was persuasive. 'Mr. Disraeli has to make his position, and men who make their positions will say and do things which are not necessary to those for whom positions are provided.' Reluctantly, the Queen agreed to accept Mr Disraeli's appointment on Stanley's guarantee, with the rider that she hoped he would behave himself, or, in her words, 'be temperate'.

But the party members envisaged by Stanley and Disraeli as being future pillars of the Tories proved disappointing when gathered together. Disraeli thought Henley,[1] his white hope, particularly unpromising, 'sitting', as he said acidly, 'with both his hands on an ashen staff . . . with the countenance of an ill-conditioned Poor Law Guardian censured for some act of harshness.' (Possibly it reminded him of an unfortunate remark made by Sir Robert Inglis in reference to such an act, when a prisoner's wife was not allowed to visit him with free ingress and egress, on which Inglis observed that 'things have come to

[1] Joseph Warner Henley, M.P. for Oxfordshire.

147

a pretty pass in this country when an Englishman may not have his wife backwards and forwards'. The House had collapsed in mirth, and now in Henley Disraeli may have seen another Inglis given to 'cumbersome and weary phraseology'.)

So the Stanley (by now Lord Derby)–Disraeli attempt to form an administration in 1851 failed, and the Whigs continued in office. It was a year of dashed hopes for Disraeli, who was reported as looking 'very much *down*'. His depression was not due merely to political causes. Mary Anne was ill, though well enough to go to the Great Exhibition with Mrs Gollop, friend of one of her Scrope cousins. Disraeli thought the Crystal Palace an 'enchanted pile which the sagacious taste and prescient philanthropy of an accomplished and enlightened Prince have raised for the glory of England, and the delight and instruction of two hemispheres'. Mary Anne was probably more interested in the ideas it gave her for improving Hughenden. Two years later she suffered an illness described as nervous debility, which may have been something like the malaise of 1851. Certainly she was not her usual self, for she had a long and acrimonious quarrel with James Disraeli, from some cause which does not emerge from the correspondence. A previous one had occurred with Sa. Disraeli wrote peevishly to Sa about 'absurd misunderstandings which greatly vex me and prevent me working. . . . I have endless rows on this infernal subject.' James Disraeli was also complaining about his brother for not getting him appointed as a Justice of the Peace; but, as Disraeli pointed out, it was an absolute impossibility, under the current rules, for anyone 'in trade' to hold this office. So long as James was a farmer this applied to him.

James seems to have been one of those people who were fated to irritate Mary Anne from time to time, as both grew older, though the disagreements were usually patched up quickly. In 1853 (in which year she again suffered a serious nervous illness) he wrote placatingly to her:

I am so unhappy that you think I intended to behave rudely to you in London when you called on Sa. The truth is, on the chance of a visit from you I had prepared a grand dinner in the hope that you would do me the honor to partake of it, and really was much disappointed that you did not stay.

I hope in this season of general Love you will forget this

148

unlucky day and accept in charity the affection and contrition of one who is ever yours, &c.

Next year she was the first person to whom he told his most important secret: he hoped soon to be as happy a man as his brother, for he was engaged to a Miss Cave, of Brentry, Gloucestershire, who was generally reckoned 'very clever, agreeable, and accomplished—of course I think that and a great deal more. I hope very sincerely that she will be fortunate enough to gain yr. good opinion.' He added, with consummate tact in view of Disraeli's own marital circumstances, that Mary Anne would think him a far luckier fellow than he deserved, to find a fortune of £7,000 with further expectations. It is sad to have to record that James's happiness was cut short by his wife's death of a miscarriage in 1857, after only eight months of marriage.

James, however, consoled himself fairly soon afterwards with a Mrs Bassett, who is said to have borne him two daughters. His breach with Disraeli became healed (as well it might, for in 1852 he had been granted, at the latter's urgent request, a County Court Treasurership with £900 a year to go with it). There are suggestions of scandals in James's life in the Hughenden Papers, including a letter threatening blackmail—either James, or Disraeli, or somebody would pay up for a lady's dismissal from a post on James's account, or Mary Anne would hear of it. James died in 1868, gravely offending Ralph by leaving him nothing in his will. Ralph and his wife Isabella kept on amiable terms with Hughenden, profiting by such presents from Mary Anne as one of the new light-shades which 'softened the late disagreeable glare of my table', and called her a 'Kind Fairy' for sending it. She, in return, accepted highly personal presents such as bonnets from him, one of which had, in duplicate, 'been smiled on by Majesty', and lace from Swan and Edgar's.

At the end of 1851, Disraeli's fate was swayed by a major decision on the part of Russell who dismissed Palmerston[1] from the Foreign Office for approving without Royal or official consent the *coup d'état* by Prince Louis Napoleon Bonaparte, by which he had made himself dictator of France. The Queen

[1] Henry John Temple Palmerston (1784–1865), 3rd Viscount, statesman. His illustrious career was suitably crowned with burial in Westminster Abbey.

was far from pleased by the sacking. When Parliament reassembled in February Palmerston and his supporters hit back by defeating Russell on an amendment, and Russell promptly resigned. Lord Derby, setting about forming his government, arrived in person at Grosvenor Gate, and, in the famous Blue Room, offered Disraeli the Chancellorship of the Exchequer, which Palmerston had refused. Disraeli was not anxious for it, confessing frankly that he knew nothing about figures, a self-evident fact from his own finances, the successful management of which had been due more to luck than to good judgment. Anyone less typical of an ideal Chancellor of the Exchequer, or of the characteristic Jewish commercial sense, could not have been imagined in a Prime Minister's wildest dreams, and the general opinion was that Derby had gone mad. Obviously the Foreign Office would have been the place for Disraeli, who was so proud of his knowledge of European politics and thought of himself somewhat as a citizen of the world. But the post of Foreign Secretary went to the Earl of Malmesbury. Little wonder that Derby's first Cabinet was to be nicknamed the 'Who? Who?' Ministry, for the old and deaf Wellington could hardly hear a word when the new appointments were read out—and what he could hear he could scarcely believe.

But one person at least was delighted. Mary Anne, at Hughenden at the time of Derby's visit, wrote to 'The Right Honourable the Chancellor of the Exchequer' a loving letter.

> Bless you, my darling, your own devoted wife wishes you joy. I hope you will make as good a Chancellor of the Exchequer as you have been a husband to your affectionate Mary Anne.

She had already given a splendid party for Derby and his ministers, and continued to regard herself as the 'prima donna of Torydom', according to the somewhat catty Lady Charlotte Guest.[1] It was a good thing she had the desire and ability to entertain, for Disraeli was almost too busy to snatch a meal for himself. The Tories, however, were less grateful to Mary Anne than they should have been for the amount of free food and drink they got out of her. There had always been an undercurrent of resentment against the Disraelis amongst certain

[1] She had been the Lady Charlotte Bertie whom Disraeli had once thought of marrying.

factions of his own party, and the Prince Consort had at first thought him 'not a gentleman'. His early flamboyance of dress had been modified and his theatrical manner replaced by a more restrained one and an appearance of semi-somnolence when he was not actually speaking. But he was getting more and more 'Jewish' in appearance, the pallor which Mary Anne had once praised as his greatest beauty becoming sallowness (probably from what he called 'the horrors of a torpid liver'), the prominent nose a cartoonist's gift, the ringlets, rather obviously dyed, as long as ever. He was not, and never would be, completely accepted by the High Tory aristocracy. As for Mary Anne, the eyes of the ladies were as penetrating and unkind to every sign of age in her as the camera she feared, and her high-spirited flow of chatter drew contempt on her. 'It was really shameful,' wrote Lady Charlotte, 'how they turned the poor woman into ridicule in her own house and almost within her own hearing.' They ignored the fact that a certain amount of frivolity from the hostess can cover a multitude of awkward pauses in conversation, and that a lot of Mary Anne's so called gaffes and outrageous statements were deliberate conversational gambits, though others were remarks of a Georgian frankness intended to shock—which they did.

Social gatherings in the 1850s were in no way correspondent to those of today. There were no cocktail parties: no custom of the aperitif which warms up dinners. Wines there were in plenty, served with the food, but ladies were not supposed to partake of more than one genteel glass or so, or to show any signs of exuberance as a result; and when the gentlemen, less inhibited in their drinking, were considered to be on the verge of impropriety, they were deserted in a body by the ladies, to drink tea or coffee in the drawing-room and gossip or yawn until their partners appeared. Mrs Gladstone on one occasion outraged convention by vanishing when the ladies 'rose' and failing to join them in the drawing-room until the gentlemen came upstairs. There was always music for the ladies to entertain each other with, of course, and one wonders whether Mary Anne ever shocked her female guests by rendering some of the ballads of her youth. She was quite capable of it. Among Mary Anne's papers there is a tantalizing scrap of doggerel beginning:

> A spirit I am,
> And I don't give a damn. . . .

The rest she left to our conjecture.

Perhaps she deliberately cultivated her reputation for eccentricity as time went on, on the principle that when one ceases to be beautiful, one might as well be amusing; perhaps she intended, like another famous beauty, to subside into a bath-chair, black lace and epigrams (except that in Mary Anne's case the lace would have been anything rather than black). A highly intelligent woman whose letters until the end of her life continued to be completely balanced and sensible, she had no intention of becoming anything resembling a nonentity; nor did she.

So she laughed when they made fun of her extraordinary remarks, and when Disraeli picked up her hand in company and kissed it, and when she fondled his hair in public. Mrs George Hussey,[1] Churchwarden of the little white Hughenden church which lies a short distance from the Manor, within its grounds, remembered how, when the Disraelis arrived at the chancel door of the church on a Sunday morning, 'it was always an amusement to the Choir when she placed her foot on the step of the door and held it there to be admired by the adoring husband!' Another recollection of Mrs Hussey's was that the Disraelis used to walk in their woods in their old age (no doubt as fondly entwined as always) and that once, when sitting down to rest and admire the sylvan scene, they were warned by a gardener that they were 'settin' on a wiper's nest'. No wonder that in one of her Occasional Books Mary Anne had tenderly bracketed a verse from a poem about loyalty:

> Let no man for more love pretend
> Than he has heart in store;
> True love begun should never end,
> Love one and love no more!

Disraeli had not long been Chancellor when a reminder of an admirer long since lost to sight came to Mary Anne, and probably rather less than to memory ever dear: no protestations to 'Dearest Rose' now, but a pathetic plea for advancement from a disappointed, sixty-three-year-old man.

[1] As told by her descendant, Mrs Ethel Wharton Robinson, of Swanage.

Funtington, near Chichester, March 23rd, 1852.

My dear Lady,

Let me heartily congratulate you on the high position you are destined to attain through the brilliant talents of your husband. When you read what follows you will be inclined to think the above mere words of form, but in that you will wrong me, for I must ever feel the deepest interest in all that concerns you. But to my subject.

If anything should offer to suit a man of moderate fortune, but of moderate intellect, that should be in the gift of D'Israeli, put in a good word for an old friend. I do not mean exactly now, but something might turn up, then please think of
Yours most sincerely,
AUGUSTUS F. BERKELEY.

It was a long time, a whole world away, from the Regent Street Lords accommodation address for clandestine lovers, and the demand for lips, and greater and more tender favours. The sixty-year-old woman must have read it with a smile and a sigh.

In this year of 1852 Mary Anne attended her first Court Drawing-room, wearing the usual riot of blue satin, feathers and diamonds. The diamonds may have been even more profuse than usual in view of a strange friendship which had recently begun between the Disraelis and a very curious lady living in Torquay. She was Mrs Brydges Willyams, a Jewess by birth though a Christian by faith, like Disraeli, for whom she had the sort of passion which would later be accorded to film stars and pop idols. She was eighty, but a prolific correspondent, and the overworked Disraeli for some time ignored the flood of adoring letters which arrived from her. But when at last she wrote on a 'private matter', asking him to be an executor of her will, and what was more, one of her residuary legatees, he not unnaturally began to take an interest. That autumn he visited her, and agreed to what she asked, though advising her to employ her own lawyer. The following autumn Mary Anne (who had been very ill and needed a holiday) went to Torquay with him, and immediately formed a friendship with the old lady, which lasted for the rest of her life. She appreciated Mrs Brydges Willyams's 'constant kind thoughts' of Disraeli. 'I never heard him appreciate so highly as yourself, anyone, man or woman.'

They exchanged letters, endearments, flowers, plants and

presents, and when the old lady died in 1863 Disraeli received over £30,000 in her will. Her last wish was carried out: to be buried at Hughenden. She had wanted to lie in the little church itself, but the vaults had been closed, and the Reverend Mr Clubbe firmly refused to have them reopened. So Disraeli had a special vault built in the churchyard at the east wall of the church, with the intention that both he and Mary Anne would join her there, as they eventually did. When he went out of office, four years before her death, she advised him to take a peerage; a suggestion which Mary Anne was very much against.

> He would not, my dear, go to the Upper House for the world, not for many years. He enjoys his fame too much in the Lower House. He could not take the red ribbon without being knighted, and that would be dreadful—to be called Sir B. Disraeli. The Queen is all kindness to Dis and would give him anything.

His activities in the Lower House might be enjoyable, but they were taxing to his health. Between Westminster and Grosvenor Gate little notes were constantly passing by the hand of a servant—requests from him, comforts from her. 'Will you send me an easy pair of boots, and a great coat? It is very cold,' he requests. Colleagues would scribble messages that he would be home early, or late;[1] but whatever time he arrived she would be waiting for him with a cheerful smile and a good meal or whatever refreshment was appropriate. After a particular triumph over Gladstone in a Reform Bill debate, he was urged to join members of his Party for supper at the Carlton Club, but, Mary Anne told T. E. Kebbel[2] proudly, he had prepared to celebrate his victory with her. 'I had got him a raised pie from Fortnum and Mason's, and a bottle of champagne, and he ate half the pie and drank all the champagne, and then he said, "Well, my dear, you are more like a mistress than a wife." '

To her other ideal-wifely qualities was added that of fortitude: a fortitude which would bear anything for her beloved's peace of mind. One example of this has passed into legend. Mary Anne had driven to the House one day with Disraeli, who was about

[1] A note exists from Lord Henry Lennox saying that 'D. is waiting—has done his work, and will be very glad if you will come down and fetch him home now.'
[2] Author of *Tory and Other Memories*.

to take part in an important debate. A young footman opened the door for him to alight, and slammed it shut on Mary Anne's fingers. She uttered no sound, but smiled her usual smile to Disraeli as he walked towards the House. What was the extent of the damage is to be gauged by an anxious enquiry from the Duchess of Somerset about Mary Anne's *arm*: presumably she had been very badly hurt indeed. And later in 1852 James wrote asking how her fingers were; he had heard of her accident from Sa, and 'it must have been most shocking'. What Disraeli felt, and said, when he came home, is not recorded, but his tribute to her bravery was to detach the carriage door which had done the damage, and preserve it. It hangs now on a wall in the Hall of Hughenden, with its story beside it.

It was such incidents as these which moved Disraeli to write a birthday ode in his wife's honour which from any other husband to any other wife might have seemed extravagant beyond belief; but he meant every word of it, and called it 'A Saint's Day, Nov. 11 1846'—six years before the carriage episode.

> Altho' good Protestants, our jours de fête
> We yet may keep and find full many a saint
> Nicked in our list of love, St. Mary Anne
> Is throned this day, a spirit canonized
> To reign o'er happy marriages; her spell
> A heart devoted, & untiring zeal
> To make our lives as lively as herself,
> Bright with her wit and with her frolick gay—
> A ready Counsellor, her saintship proving,
> By working miracles.
>   An Ave Mary Anne,
> Let all then sing this day, & drop a bead,
> Who finds an altar in a happy home.

One wonders what the departed Mrs Yate, who considered her daughter considerably less pious than she should have been, would have made of this.

In 1856, Mary Anne was at Torquay with Mrs Brydges Willyams, recovering from a bad fall on the way to Hatfield House, where she was to stay with the Salisburys. Disraeli was to follow on. Again he had a 'great speech' on his mind, and Mary Anne, with a pair of blacked eyes and a bruised, scratched face, begged Lady Salisbury to take her straight to her room and say she had a headache, so that he would not see her at close quarters before dinner, and get upset. During dinner itself there was no problem, for 'he has lost his eyeglass, and if you put me a long way from him at dinner he will never see what a condition I'm in'.

Not long afterwards, they went to Paris to escape the English winter and enjoy the Parisian gaieties. Napoleon III ruled there now, he whose huge bulbous nose and tom-cat moustache were as much a boon to the cartoonists as Disraeli's features. (*Punch*, by the way, was suggesting that future Westminsterians would consider the newly finished Big Ben to have been christened after Benjamin Disraeli, Duke of Jerusalem, and, turning its satirical attention to France, was showing Napoleon III as a shopkeeper, begging to announce to his friends and the public that he was back in business.) No one was more welcome to Napoleon than the Disraelis, who had been his friends during his English exile—even when Mary Anne had been Mrs Wyndham Lewis. At a grand dinner at the Tuileries, she was placed next to Napoleon and Disraeli next to his wife, the lovely Empress Eugénie. Typically, Mary Anne could not resist telling Eugénie about the time during their engagement when the Emperor had almost drowned them all in the Thames. They had been invited by Bulwer to a social breakfast at Craven Cottage, his Thameside house, and decided to row there in company with Louis Napoleon and his friend, the Comte de Persigny, having arrived too late to travel with the rest of the company. Louis Napoleon took the oars, with which he was less than skilled, and ran them on to a mudbank in mid-river, where they lodged in constant danger from the swell caused by passing steamboats (not to mention the amusement afforded by their plight to the passengers therein). A very cross Mary Anne had informed the harassed Prince that he was a clumsy creature who should never have tried to row at all; that he was far too adventurous, and should not have undertaken things he could not accomplish. As he was just recovering from the results of two unsuccessful attempts on the throne of Louis Philippe, it was hardly the most tactful observation she could have made, but he took it like a gallant Frenchman, and after all managed not to drown them.

Eugénie's sense of humour was equal to Mary Anne's mischief, and she merely laughed and replied that it was just like him. The rest of the visit was delightful, Mary Anne revelling in parties and routs and opportunities to wear diamonds which almost rivalled the Empress's—and *they*, wrote Disraeli, were like something out of Aladdin's Cave.

Disraeli had been out of parliamentary office since 1852 when his December budget had been defeated, bringing down the Tories. The Whigs had succeeded, under Lord Aberdeen until he resigned in 1855, followed by Palmerston.

In 1857, during the Palmerston administration, Gladstone was urging economy on a nation which had just had its pockets drained by the Crimean War, and Disraeli pleading for the removal of the Income Tax—9d in the pound. *Punch* drew them as acrobats, The Balancing Brothers of Westminster. Disraeli came back as Chancellor of the Exchequer in Derby's second ministry of 1858–9, but it was short-lived and once again he was fretting out of office as Leader of the Opposition (though with the consolation of a government pension of £2,000 a year, which he badly needed). Mary Anne was deeply disappointed. Sa wrote to comfort her:

Remember what great things you have seen, and that we have never known dear Dis experience a disappointment, or more than a disappointment, but that it has proved the very step to greater eminence—nor can we one moment doubt but this will prove so—the pear is not yet ripe.

She was right, of course. She knew her brother better than anyone, except Mary Anne. But she was not long to be his comforter. In September, when Sa was staying at Hughenden, Mary Anne noticed how frail she looked. She had not been really well for years; in 1854 Ralph had reported her as being 'in a terrible state of madness', though just able to recognize him through her delirium. But on 19 December, just before what should have been a merry Christmas at Hughenden, she died. Disraeli had lost 'my first and ever faithful friend', his first playmate in the childhood days of Bedford Row and the grand house in Bloomsbury Square, his adorer in youth, his 'heart's treasure' when she had lost her beloved and he his friend, and he had 'no wife . . . no betrothed'. She had accepted Mary Anne with cheerful friendliness and not an atom of revealed jealousy. Since his marriage she had been his most constant correspondent. He had been able to tell her things he could tell nobody else; things about his worrying debts and about moments when Mary Anne was being temperamental. Her charming, wise, whimsical face beneath its crown of high-piled dark hair still smiles on the family relics at Hughenden, as if she said: 'I was part of this: I was part of him.'

'One of those persons who are the soul of a house and the angelic spirit of a family', Disraeli said of her to Lady Londonderry. When at last he 'reached the top of the greasy pole' and became Prime Minister, Sir Philip Rose said to him: 'If only your sister had been alive to witness your triumph, what happiness it would have given her!' The new Prime Minister replied, 'Ah, poor Sa! poor Sa! we've lost our audience, we've lost our audience.' It was a little unfair to say so, perhaps, as he still had his principal audience in his wife. But by then Mary Anne, too, was declining in health.

Christmas 1859 saw Sa's funeral, and on Boxing Day Ralph and James walked up to the cemetery to see her grave. Perhaps his sister's death hit Disraeli the harder because he could see that Mary Anne would not be with him for ever: was, perhaps, already showing by stranger than usual behaviour that she was moving into the old age she had so firmly resisted.

The Rothschilds, Sir Anthony and Lady de Rothschild (who was Louise to Mary Anne), lived not far from Hughenden at their country house in the village of Aston Clinton. The two ladies often spent evenings together before their husbands came home, Disraeli from the House and Sir Anthony from the Bank. Mary Anne adored Jewish people and considered herself one by marriage—in 1845, when Sir Anthony's nephew Leopold was born, Mary Anne rhapsodized to his mother: 'My dear, that beautiful baby may be the future Messiah whom we are led to expect—who knows? And you will be the most favoured of women.' In fact, Leo became an amiable, horsey squire, who won the Derby and £50,000 with an outsider in 1879; widely known for his philanthropy, a model landlord, he earned from the Rothschilds' biographer, Dr Cecil Roth, a heartfelt tribute in verse.

> Of men like you
> Earth holds but few:
> An angel with
> A revenue.

Mary Anne's prophecy had been broadly on the right lines.

On another occasion in 1845, Leo's mother, Charlotte, the wife of Baron Lionel de Rothschild, had been surprised and alarmed to receive an unexpected visit from an apparently hysterical Mary Anne, who had flung herself into Charlotte's arms, gasping out, all in one sentence:

> I am quite out of breath, my dear, I have been running so fast, we have no horses, no carriage, no servants, we are going abroad, I have been so busy correcting proof-sheets, the publishers are so tiresome, we ought to have been gone a month ago, I should have called upon you long ago ere now, I have been so nervous, so excited, so agitated, poor Dis has been sitting up the whole night writing. . . .

She then asked Charlotte to send the children away (they were no doubt standing in the hall with their mouths open in astonishment) and, swiftly changing to melancholy, announced that this was a farewell visit, as she might never see her friend again.

> Life is so uncertain, poor Mrs. Fitzroy has been so very very ill, Dizzy and I may be blown up on the rail-road or in the steamer, there is not a human body that loves me in this world, and besides my adored husband I care for no one on earth, but I love your glorious race. I am rich, I am prosperous, I think it right to entertain serious thoughts, to look calmly on one's end. . . .

She then produced a document which she said was her will, leaving all she possessed to Charlotte's daughter Evelina, then aged six, in the event of Disraeli's predeceasing her. 'She is my favourite, she must wear the butterfly.'

Mary Anne then left as hastily as she had arrived, and next morning was visited by Charlotte, who returned the will, of which no more was ever heard. This episode happened when Mary Anne was fifty-three, so her alarming behaviour was certainly not a sign of the oncoming of senility; or, presumably, of drink, which never seems to have affected her unduly.

Perhaps the proof-reading of *Sybil* had had an exhausting effect, or perhaps Disraeli's difficult summer in the House had preyed on her mind. It is a far stranger story than any of the so-called shocking anecdotes of her behaviour more commonly known. For one thing, Hughenden is between twenty and thirty miles from Aston Clinton, and imagination boggles at the idea of Mary Anne running from home to the Rothschilds.

No such eccentricity is reported of her, however, at the turn of the 1850s. She was welcomed at many stately homes, including that of Lord Derby, Knowsley. Sir Stafford Northcote,[1] a fellow-guest, wrote to his wife that he found her

> great fun, and we made capital friends in the train, though I could not help occasionally pitying her husband for the startling effect her natural speeches must have upon the ears of his great friends. Still, there is something very warm and good in her manner which makes one forgive a few oddities. She informed me she was born in Brampford Speke, and I told her they must come and see her birthplace some time when they are in Devonshire. What do you say to the idea of asking them to Pynes? It would complete the astonishment of our neighbours.

Lady Northcote agreed, and, whether or not the neighbours were astonished, the Northcotes certainly were when Mary Anne related some of her alleged history to them. Lady Hobhouse, daughter of the family, remembered that as they drove to Brampford Speke, which Mary Anne had expressed a wish to see, she stated that her father was a captain in the merchant service and had made a runaway match with her mother; that she had been married at fifteen, and that she had been a milliner's apprentice.

In January 1861, came a more exciting invitation. It was from the Queen herself, desiring the Leader of the Opposition and his wife to spend two nights at Windsor Castle. Disraeli was highly gratified. 'It is Mrs. Disraeli's first visit to Windsor,' he told Mrs Brydges Willyams, 'and it is considered very marked on the part of Her Majesty to the wife of the Leader of the Opposition when many Cabinet Ministers have been asked

---

[1] Stafford Henry Northcote (1818–87), 1st Earl of Iddesleigh; private secretary to Gladstone, President of the Board of Trade and Secretary for India, Chancellor of the Exchequer and leader of the House in opposition to Gladstone, 1880–5.

there *without* their wives.' After the visit, Disraeli told Derby that both the Queen and Prince Albert had been very gracious and very communicative. The Queen was already falling under the spell of Disraeli's charm and of the flattery he heaped upon her with the lavishness of an Elizabethan courtier. After Albert's death in December 1861, her enthusiasm for him increased.

Two years later an even greater honour was given to Mary Anne. With her husband (still out of office) she was invited to the wedding on 10 March 1863 of Albert Edward, Prince of Wales, and his Danish bride Alexandra, the lovely 'sea-king's daughter from over the sea'. Disraeli was amused and triumphant, and regaled Mrs Willyams with an account of the mortification of the 'great ladies who are *not* asked. The Duchess of Marlboro in despair! The Duchess of Manchester who was Mistress of the Robes!!! Mme de Flahaut only a month ago Ambassadress of France, & a host of others as eminent. None of my late colleagues are invited except Lord Derby & he would go as a matter of course as a Knight of the Garter. *But I am invited!* and what is still more marked Mrs. D too and this by the Queen's particular command.'

The accommodation in the Royal Chapel at Windsor was strictly limited, the occasion one of tremendous importance which caused Tennyson, Poet Laureate since the death of Wordsworth, to burst into poetic eulogy.

> Break, happy land, into earlier flowers!
> Make music, O bird, in the new-budded bowers!
> Blazon your mottoes of blessing and prayer!
> Welcome her, welcome her, all that is ours!
> Warble, O bugle, and trumpet, blare!
> Flags, flutter out upon turrets and towers!
> Flames, on the windy headland flare!
> Utter your jubilee, steeple and spire!
> Clash, ye bells, in the merry March air!
> Flash, ye cities, in rivers of fire!
> Rush to the roof, sudden rocket, and higher,
> Melt into stars for the land's desire!

Whatever the flowers, birds, and March temperatures decided to do about it, the flags, flames, bells and fireworks obliged the Laureate, and the mortification of the slighted ladies was no less on that account. After the inclusion of all the essential guests, only four places remained for the Queen's personal friends, and the Disraelis occupied two of these. The honour may, of course, be partly attributed to Disraeli's behaviour at the death of the Prince Consort. His praises of the dead Albert were excessive: he had described him as 'the only person . . . who realized the Ideal', and prophesied that 'the name of Albert will be accepted as the master-type of a generation of profounder feeling and vaster range than that which he formed and guided with benignant power.' After that, how could the widow leave him out of her son's guest-list?; particularly when he had urged the erection of an Albert Memorial to commemorate the late paragon. During the marriage ceremony Disraeli caught the Queen's eye, and assumed that she was looking to see who was there and triumphing a little in the decided manner in which she had testified her gratitude to the champion of her late husband.

When the wedding was over there was a general stampede for the London train, in the course of which Disraeli gallantly rescued several ladies whose crinolines (enormous at this period) had impeded their progress and separated them from their husbands, and the crush in the railway carriages was such that he had to sit on Mary Anne's knee. They can have cared very little for the proprieties after such a ceremony, of which Mary Anne kept a full description among her papers. The bride had entered to Handel's March from *Joseph* and left the Chapel to the strains of the Hallelujah Chorus.

There is no record of either of the Disraelis having any particular musical tastes on a grand, rather than drawing-room, scale; but in June 1861 they had sat politely through a Royal command performance, at which the Sacred Harmonic Society and Her Majesty's Private Band had given a selection from Mendelssohn's *St Paul* and a Chorus from *Israel in Egypt*.

Royal invitations poured in after the famous wedding; the Prince and Princess of Wales invited them to a morning party at Chiswick, with plovers' eggs on the menu. In fact they lived, as Disraeli said, 'only in a glittering bustle'. From one country house to another they went—Raby Castle, Lowther, Woburn, Ashridge. Mary Anne thoroughly enjoyed it all, but Disraeli's feelings were mixed. He met politicians everywhere, and was able to 'feel the pulse of the ablest on all the questions of the day', but also commented that 'I detest Society really, for I never entered it without my feelings being hurt' and he really disliked the life of the average country-house: eating, drinking, and the slaughter of creatures, which he found disgusting, a reaction most unique in those days. At Crichel, about 1,200 birds were shot, and 'the sky was darkened with their uprushing, and the whir of their wings was like the roar of the sea'. Mary Anne wrote, 'Whenever we go to a country-house the same thing happens: Dizzy is not only bored, and has constant ennui, but he takes to eating as a resource; he eats at breakfast, luncheon and dinner; the result is, by the end of the third day he becomes dreadfully bilious, and we have to come away.' And this was a man who had enjoyed dropping such epigrams as 'that to enjoy a récherché dish, you should have silence, solitude, and a subdued light', and confounding his neighbours at dinner-parties. At one, he was sitting next to a lady of high rank and strong opinions, who was urging him violently that the Government should adopt some firm line of conduct on one of its important issues. Sternly she said to Disraeli: 'I cannot imagine what you are waiting for!' to which he calmly replied, 'At this moment, Madam, for the potatoes.'

Mary Anne never seems to have been jealous of the ladies fortunate enough to sit next to her husband: in fact she looked 'to see if Dizzy is sitting next any pretty women, that he would like to sit next and admire'. It has been said that she entertained a faint jealousy towards the Queen, once that lady's strong feelings for Disraeli became obvious. After all, Victoria was many years younger than Mary Anne, not absolutely ill-looking, and in her young days had caused whispers by her supposed relationship with Lord Melbourne. But no foundation for this can be found. The Queen began the practice of sending flowers to the Disraelis, to one of which offerings Mary Anne sent an appropriately floral letter of thanks: 'Mr. Disraeli is passionately fond of flowers, and their lustre and fragrance were enhanced by the condescending hand which had showered upon him all the treasures of Spring.'

So the house-parties went on, and Disraeli enjoyed them less and less. Unlike nearly all gentlemen of his time, he did not hunt: the Montefiores and Rothschilds rode to hounds, but not

Disraeli, probably on the same principle that kept him away from the autumn shoot. It was not in him to enjoy destroying things, even his political opponents, though he permitted himself the occasional relaxing afternoon of fishing. Another reason, of course, may have been that he was a terrible rider. Only twice is he known to have hunted; during his affair with Henrietta he once told Sa that he had ridden thirty miles across country and stopped at nothing—presumably because he couldn't—wearing a suit of bright green velvet with gold buttons; and Sir William Fraser commented drily that 'Leonora's ride behind her dead lover was a joke to it.'[1] The second occasion when Disraeli rashly attended a 'lawn meet', in Staffordshire, an old friend of Shrewsbury days heard he was nearby and sent to ask him to call, as he himself was too ill to come out. Disraeli refused, and later explained that the reason for his not dismounting was that once out of the saddle he could never have got into it again.

In any case, there were pleasanter country pastimes in his own country home, which by now was transformed almost out of recognition by the efforts of Mary Anne.

[1] *Leonora:* a popular poem by the German Gottfried Bürger, about a faithless lady's nightmare ride to the grave with the ghost of her lover. Maclise illustrated an English translation in 1847.

14

'Lo, brains at last we see,
At the top, where brains should be!'

Simple Georgian manors were all very well, but to the mid-Victorian eye they were far, far too simple. Mary Anne had been giving a lot of thought to the remodelling of Hughenden: a home fit for such a statesman as Disraeli and such a hostess as herself. They called in the architect F. B. Lamb, who specialized in designing buildings in the popular Gothic taste. Largely on the strength of Mrs Brydges Willyams's legacy, Hughenden was transformed into a three-storeyed red-brick building which had no particular architectural distinction either within or without, and certainly no flavour of past times, Gothic or otherwise. The romantic Disraeli thought it restored to what it was before the Civil Wars, 'in which cavaliers might roam and saunter with their ladye-loves'; but the cavaliers would have felt far from easy in this conglomeration of pointed ecclesiastical arches crowned by bishops' heads, Moorish fretwork arches, a 'Tudor'-panelled hall (his Gallery of Friendship, Disraeli called it, and hung it with large and forbidding portraits of the men he had known and admired—Lyndhurst, Smythe, D'Orsay and Bulwer; Byron, whom he had not known, but adored, was also included).

The general décor was riotously cheerful. The furniture blossomed with flowers and beech leaves in tapestry worked by Mary Anne, the carpets were beds of roses, the wallpaper in the green drawing-room was spangled with fleurs-de-lis; there was a great deal of bright blue and gold, and Disraeli's own political pink. Even the ornaments tended to the Sèvres style, bounteously flowered in high relief. In the Library were what remained of Isaac's fine calf-bound books, together with Disraeli's, equally handsome and imposing. 'My collection is limited to Theology, the Classics and History,' he once said;

but the works of Molière were there, and of Swift—the latter disproving somewhat Rosina Bulwer's story that Mary Anne had once asked for Dean Swift's address, so that she could invite him to one of her soirées. Large marble busts of Disraeli in comparative youth, adorned the hall, and family portraits were everywhere: his parents and Sa at various ages, Mary Anne and himself painted by Chalon in the year after their marriage, himself, romantically engaging, by Sir Francis Grant, in 1852, the year he first came to office; the lovely Marguerite Blessington bending swanlike and smiling towards the beholder from her frame. Mary Anne was modestly represented by two miniatures, by Rochard and Ross,[1] as well as by the Chalon; and there is a curious story told by Lord Ronald Gower of an empty frame over the drawing-room mantelpiece. Asking his host the reason for this not very ornamental detail, he was told, 'I had intended her [Mary Anne's] picture to be put there, but she has never sat for her portrait except to Ross for a miniature, but some day I shall have that copied life-size and placed in that frame.' He carried out this intention after her death.

But in 1863 they still had several years left. Now they were happy, strolling in the autumn recess on the broad terrace designed by Mary Anne in the Italian style, and delighting in Mary Anne's German Forest on the hill, and the ornamental trees planted by Disraeli, who hated to see trees cut down and loved to plant them,[2] and the blaze of bright flowers in Italian urns. Small coy marble children adorned the lawns, apt Cupids for a home full of love, and on the lake in the park, where Disraeli had caught a 4½-lb trout and sent it to Mrs Brydges Willyams—who in return sent him some fish from Torquay—swam the swans Hero and Leander, or their offspring. One could not have a terrace without peacocks, according to the master of Hughenden, and peacocks were there, flaunting their blue and gold Disraeli colours, adding their shrieks to the cooing of woodpigeons and the song of thrushes and blackbirds.

Many ladies of her age and station, however enthusiastic they might be as gardeners, would have been content to stand about directing operations. Not so Mary Anne, who put on a

[1] Sir William Charles Ross (1794–1860), miniature-painter patronized by the English and other royal families.
[2] In direct contrast to his great opponent Gladstone, one of whose nicknames was the 'woodchopper of Hawarden'.

short skirt and strong boots and gaiters and went out with the
'old men of the soil', as she had always done. 'I have to go out
planting, too,' she told the future Lord Rosebery.[1] 'I take a
little lunch and some bottles of beer for the workmen and sit
there all day.' Her young friend—he was only eighteen, and she
was then seventy-three—was concerned with the exhaustion
this must cause her. She smiled, and reminded him that mind
ruled matter, and added how 'Dizzy comes back and sees what
I have done when it is all finished and says sometimes "This
is quite delightful, better than anything you have done yet."
And then I feel quite intoxicated for the moment and quite
rewarded.' They would both have liked to live at Hughenden,
always, she said. If necessary they could be happy without
politics.

> But I say, 'No, dear, I will never give you the chance,' for it
> is quite dull in the Country when we are alone together, for
> Dizzy takes his book (he does nothing but read books, old Greek
> and Latin books) and I take my book, but I am so tired with
> planting that I am afraid it often falls out of my hand and I go
> asleep. I never allow Dizzy to come and see me when I am
> planting because he would lose the *coup d'oeil* of seeing it when
> it is finished.

She loved to send presents of the products of Hughenden to
friends. The Scropes in Devon received figs and grapes, and Lady
Northcote at Pynes had hyacinths which had grown 'as if
fairies presided over them', and appeared to her a 'fairy gift'.
People still thought of Mary Anne as fairylike, this little lively
woman with her old-fashioned ringlets and her paint and
powder—for there is no doubt that by now she took full
advantage of the aids to fading beauty which were available.
A mocking contributor to *Punch* in the year when Hughenden
received its face-lift, 1863, complained about these artificialities.

> One shopkeeper sells eyebrows that are warranted to stick,
> while another supplies roses to beautify the cheeks, warranted
> to bear even inspection through a microscope. As for hair dyes,
> they are numberless, and so are curling fluids . . . besides this,

[1] Archibald Philip Primrose Rosebery (1847–1929), 5th Earl of Rosebery.
Politician and sportsman, in 1894 he became Prime Minister and won the Derby
the same year. He was introduced to Hannah de Rothschild in 1868 by Mary
Anne and married her in 1878.

there's the 'pomadore, for beautifying the arms and hands or face, without causing the slightest unnatural appearance', and in addition there's the 'eye fluid', which some genius has invented, and which serves not merely for concealment of crows' feet, but to give great 'boldness, character, and seeming enlargement' to that 'index of character' which we more simply call the eye.

The gentleman also complained of lip-rouge which was off-putting to those wishful to kiss the lips it coloured.

Every lady uncertain of her charms might respectably profit by those much-advertised products made by Mr Rowland: Macassar Oil for the hair, 'imparting a transcendant lustre', Kalydor, giving 'a radiant bloom' to the skin, and Odonto bestowing 'a pearl-like whiteness' on the teeth. As for more homely beauty-aids, Mary Anne would certainly know the skin-elasticizing qualities of ordinary white of egg, which could make one look reasonably radiant and reasonably young under the lights of a ballroom, until the assembly broke up and the effect of the albumen beneath the pearl-powder wore off.

Mary Anne's costume in public, whatever sensible clothes she wore in the garden, was as splendid as ever. A charming little verse from Lady John Manners on 14 February 1868, accompanied an appropriate gift—a hand-made pincushion.

> You are, dear Lady, all confess,
> An adept in the art of dress.
> Your gorgeous draperies fall with grace
> And every pin is in its place.
> But, as we know, you always share
> Your statesman's every toil and care,
> When tired with work, you may let fall
> Your pins; such things occur to all.
> Then from your pocket, Lady, take
> The gift I send for Friendship's sake.
> Then will the happy thought be mine—
> You've used my pins, my Valentine.

Though no evidence remains, one senses strongly from all accounts of these last years of Mary Anne's that she and Dsiraeli were still lovers in every sense. Her first biographer, James Sykes, commented primly on her 'tendency to dwell, whimsically and sometimes indelicately, upon conjugal intimacies', and it was Disraeli himself who repeated with enjoyment her remark to Lady Waldegrave's husband that she had heard him very much praised. 'When and where?' he enquired, and was told, with a giggle, 'In bed'.

In London their life was far from slow. Palmerston's second ministry, which had followed Derby's in 1859, had ended with his death in 1865, when Lord John Russell had succeeded him briefly. In 1866 Derby formed his third ministry with Disraeli once again Chancellor of the Exchequer. The need for parliamentary reform had been recognized for many years and now Disraeli proposed a bill extending the franchise beyond householders.

During the Reform riots of 1866, when the mob beat down the railings of Hyde Park almost opposite 1 Grosvenor Gate, Mary Anne and Disraeli's new private secretary, young Montagu Corry,[1] watched the demonstrations from the drawing-room window, while Disraeli, at the House, was worrying about Mary Anne's safety. He need not have done; Corry sent him a message assuring him that all was well, and 'Mrs. Disraeli wishes me to add that the people in general seem to be thoroughly enjoying themselves, and I really believe she sympathises with them. At any rate, I am glad to say she is not in the least alarmed.' In the following year Disraeli triumphantly pushed through the Second Reform Bill. Concluding his speech to the House, he justified the Bill: 'I do not think myself that the country is in danger; I think England is safe in the race of men who inhabit her—that she is safe in something much more precious than her accumulated capital—her accumulated experience. She is safe in her national character, and her fame, in the traditions of a thousand years, and in that glorious future which I believe awaits her.'

Disraeli and Gladstone had become the most celebrated political opponents since Fox and Pitt; but however they fought publicly, their private relations were cordial, and for Mary Anne, Gladstone had nothing but affection and regard. He often took tea with the Disraelis when he loved to talk of his own happy home life with his beloved Catherine. When Mary Anne was seriously ill (and she was often ill now) Gladstone spoke kindly

[1] Montagu Corry (1838–1903), 1st Baron Rowton, politician and philanthropist. He built Rowton House, Vauxhall, a poor man's hotel, 1892, and other Rowton Houses.

of her in the House. Disraeli was almost too moved to thank him, but wrote afterwards: 'My wife has always had a strong regard for you, and being of a vivid and original character, she can comprehend and value your great gifts and qualities.' There was a quality in all three which drew them together and transcended all pettiness.

That illness had followed a highly successful visit they had made to Scotland, late in 1867, when Edinburgh gave Disraeli a tumultuous welcome and the freedom of the City, and made him an honorary LL.D. of Edinburgh University. 'We were so delighted with our reception, Mrs. Disraeli and I, that after we got home we actually danced a jig (or was it a hornpipe?) in our bedroom.' The recipient of this story, Sir John Skelton, thought Mary Anne like one of the witches in *Macbeth*, and her husband 'the potent wizard himself, with his olive complexion and coal black eyes, and the mighty dome of his forehead (no Christian temple, to be sure), is unlike any living creature one has met. . . . I would as soon have thought of sitting down at table with Hamlet, or Lear, or the Wandering Jew.'

There was, of course, a grand banquet, at which an old friend of theirs, Baillie-Cochrane (once 'Kok', the Young Englander), proposed her health and referred to the help and sympathy she had always given her husband. It was not Mary Anne who replied, but Disraeli. Fixing the coal-black eyes upon her, he told the company: 'I do owe to that Lady all, I think, that I have ever accomplished because she has supported me by her counsel and consoled me by the sweetness of her mind and disposition. You cannot please me more than by paying this compliment to my wife.'

It had been a triumphant visit, but when they got back to London they both fell ill. Disraeli was suffering from gout, and Mary Anne from serious and painful gastric trouble. At Grosvenor Gate, each lay in a different room: they could not even talk to each other, but, because communication was so necessary to them, wrote notes instead. 'Being on my back,' wrote Disraeli, 'pardon the pencil. You have sent me the most amusing and charming letter I ever had. It beats Horace Walpole and Mme de Sévigné.' The letter has, unfortunately, not survived, but she kept all the 'notes from dear Dizzy during our illness when we could not leave our rooms'. How often she

"THE RETURN FROM VICTORY."

(With Mr. Punch's apologies to Mr. Calderon, R.A.)

Disraeli after the Reform Bill's triumphant passage through the Commons, 1867. *Punch.*

PUNCH, OR THE LONDON CHARIVARI.—August 17, 1867.

PUFF AT ST. STEPHEN'S.

Puff. "NOW, PRAY ALL TOGETHER."
All. (*Kneeling.*) "BEHOLD THY VOTARIES SUBMISSIVE BEG,
THAT THOU WILT DEIGN TO GRANT THEM ALL THEY ASK;

ASSIST THEM TO ACCOMPLISH ALL THEIR ENDS,
AND SANCTIFY WHATEVER MEANS THEY USE
TO GAIN THEM!"
Vide "The Critic."

Disraeli as Mr Puff of Sheridan's *The Critic* directing
his parliamentary cast, 1867. *Punch.*

'The new headmaster.' Lord Derby hands over to Disraeli as Prime Minister, 1868. *Punch* cartoon by Tenniel.

Disraeli in middle age.

Mary Anne Disraeli by
G. F. Middleton. A
posthumous portrait
painted in 1873.

must have read and re-read 'Grosvenor Gate has become a hospital but a hospital with you is worth a palace with anybody else'.

Punch reported on 30 November 1867 that 'in the House of Representatives whatever inclination there might have been to attack the Government was dispelled by affliction in the house of Mr. Disraeli'. Gladstone had called a truce for Mary Anne's sake. Everyone knew the illness was serious. What they did not know was that Mary Anne had cancer. Several deaths from it in her family are reported in letters from the Scropes and others. In her case it was cancer of the stomach; agonizing, debilitating, producing more and more frequent haemorrhages, an unmistakable symptom which a watchful, anxious husband recognized.

From Windsor Castle came a note.

My dear Mr. Disraeli,
    I have received the Queen's command to express to you Her Majesty's regret at hearing of Mrs. Disraeli's illness. Her Majesty would be glad to know from the bearer how she is.

It was followed by a telegram making the same enquiry. Her Majesty was reassured. Her Chancellor of the Exchequer presented his humble duty, and thanked her for all her sympathy. 'This morning all seemed dark, and he was told to hope no more; but within three hours of this there was a change, and everything became hopeful: a state of complete composure, but accompanied by increased strength.' Mary Anne did not believe in letting illness get the better of her, and however ill she felt she was determined that Disraeli should not be worried. She had kept the carriage-door accident and the fall at Hatfield secret from him; now the truth was harder to hide.

It was a time when he needed all possible freedom from worry. Derby, too, had gout, and more seriously than Disraeli. In the middle of February, 1868, his doctors warned him that he must retire from office, or become a permanent invalid. Before tendering his resignation (reluctantly enough) he wrote to Disraeli. 'I trust . . . that, if H.M. should send for you, which under the circumstances, I think most probable, you will not shrink from the heavy additional responsibility.' The Queen had already made some tactful enquiries through her secretary about Disraeli's readiness to take up the highest post in the land. In 1868 when he spent two days at Osborne, the Queen was being 'most gracious and agreeable' to him, he wrote to Mary Anne. 'The most successful visit I ever had: all that I could wish and hope.' Events moved fast. Derby dallied somewhat about the actual motions of resigning, and the Queen gently but firmly hurried him up. On 28 February he wrote to Disraeli a kind, congratulatory letter ending:

> Let me beg of you to offer my congratulations to Mrs. Disraeli upon your having attained a post your pre-eminent fitness for which she will not be inclined to dispute.

Nor was she. Her emotion was such that her usual ebullience of expression was reduced to an even more telling simplicity. Her friend Lady de Rothschild was told:

> By the time this reaches you Dizzy will be Prime Minister of England. Lord Stanley is to announce this at the House of Commons today.

Punch, so often sardonic at Disraeli's expense, made itself welcome at Grosvenor Gate by according its own unqualified welcome to the new Prime Minister. In what it modestly described as

> one of the most remarkable cartoons which he has ever presented to a delighted world, he has recorded the event of the day, the rise of an un-aided, untitled, and originally unpopular man to the highest place in the state. The Educator is now formally installed as Head Master, and as at Eton, he receives a Rod . . . which, doubtless, he will be glad to use as little as possible. . . .

Tenniel's[1] cartoon (which is in fact remarkably fine), shows this event taking place: a diminutive Derby hands over the birch-rod of Power to a gowned and capped Disraeli, wearing what somebody aptly called his slaughtering smile. A few pages later he postures before the glass as Hamlet, with a jealous Gladstone lurking in a corner of the green-room; while on the opposite page a poet salutes him as his own hero, Vivian Grey,

[1] Sir John Tenniel (1820–1914), caricaturist and book-illustrator. His illustrations for *Alice in Wonderland* and *Through the Looking-Glass* are his most famous.

and 'My Lord Marquis de Carabas', the gallant nobleman of
Puss in Boots.

> Lo, brains at last we see,
> At the top, where brains should be!
> Ne'er was place won in race
> That so tested pluck and pace . . .
> Is it England's praise or blame
> Such a player wins his game,
> Who can press for success
> Be't by trick, revoke, finesse?
> Is it good or ill,
> This adamantine will,
> With an india-rubber brain,
> And a conscience proof to strain?—
> To VIVIAN GREY *chapeau bas,*
> My LORD MARQUIS DE CARABAS!

On 25 March the Disraelis gave a great celebration party in
Downing Street: not at No. 10 for they had not followed the
usual custom of moving in there; in Mary Anne's state of health
it would have been altogether too much of an upheaval for her,
and in any case No. 10 was, she thought, in a dingy and decaying
state. The party was held in the reception rooms of the Foreign
Office, and so many guests were invited that a printed sheet of
instructions had to be issued, giving 'regulations for Carriages
with Company going to Mrs. Disraeli's Reception'; they were
to set down under the Archway of the New Foreign Office, and
then proceed to Whitehall, to await the direction of the police.

The weather, even in an English March, could not have been
worse. It rained and sleeted and was terribly cold, and even
the most warmly-furred ladies shuddered as they were handed
out of their carriages, for fashion decreed the barest of bare
shoulders, bare arms, and the most diminutive of puff sleeves.
The assembly was as glittering as the ladies' jewels; everybody
of note in London society was present, even the Gladstones.
Bishop Wilberforce, one of the guests, watched 'Dizzy in his
glory leading about the Princess of Wales; the Prince of Wales,
Mrs. Dizzy—she looking very ill and haggard. The impenetrable
man low. All looks to me as if England's "Mene, Mene" were
written on our walls.'

For Mary Anne those fateful words were indeed written on

173

the wall, and her impenetrable man knew it, though neither he nor she can have guessed what a long drawn-out torture was to be hers. She might be with him for only a little longer, now that the coveted heights had been reached, and he was determined to use the rod of power symbolically given to him by Tenniel's pencil.

His influence with the Queen was unparalleled; greater than Leicester's with Elizabeth. And his wife, unlike that nobleman's, shared the Queen's favour. Disraeli, a natural courtier, knew that a Queen was before everything else a woman, and treated her like one. He wrote her wonderful letters, he flattered her in every possible way. If, on her sending him a copy of her literary effort, *Leaves from the Journal of our Life in the Highlands*, he did not really bracket himself with her in the phrase 'We authors, Ma'am . . .', then he said something very like it. She adored him: he was Melbourne, the father-figure of her childhood, all over again; he had gone to Albert's obsequies wearing decent black, whereas tactless Gladstone had worn a most unsuitable *mélange* of colours and materials; he 'spread the butter very thick', and the Queen loved it all—and loved him, in her romantic German fashion. He offered her the Conservative Party as a rock to lean on, and when he kissed the plump, tiny Royal hand on taking office as Prime Minister he murmured, 'In loving loyalty and faith.'

It was a pity that his slightly aery and pantheistic attitude to religion, very far from the earnest preoccupations of his day, separated him from the Queen in the matter of important Church appointments, and that the General Election of that autumn of 1868 was mainly fought on the vexed question of the Irish Church (Ireland, and especially its explosive Fenians, had been one of the sharpest thorns in England's political side for years). From this and other causes, Disraeli foresaw that he would not be Prime Minister for long, and was so sure of it that he resigned after eight months without calling Parliament. But before he did so he performed one of the most chivalrous actions of history. As a medieval knight might have sent to his Sovereign a ring, symbolizing a promised boon, he sent the Queen a long, exquisitely-worded letter. He explained his resignation, mentioned that he was a little tired (he was, after all, sixty-four) and that at his time of life and with the present prospects, 'it is a dreary career again to lead and form an Opposition party'. The normal procedure, at this juncture, as both she and he knew, was that she would award him a peerage and he would thereupon ascend to the Upper House away from the turmoil of the Lower. Instead, he made a startling suggestion:

> . . . next to your Majesty there is one to whom he owes everything, and who has looked forward to this period of their long united lives as one of comparative repose and of recognised honor. Might Mr. Disraeli therefore, after 31 years of Parliamentary toil, and after having served your Majesty on more than one occasion, if not with prolonged success at least with unfaltering devotion, humbly solicit your Majesty to grant those honors to his wife which perhaps under ordinary circumstances your Majesty would have deigned to bestow on him?
>
> It would be an entire reward to him, and would give spirit and cheerfulness to the remainder of his public life, when he should be quite content to be your Majesty's servant if not your Majesty's Minister. . . .
>
> Mr. Disraeli is ashamed to trouble your Majesty on such personal matters, but he has confidence in your Majesty's gracious indulgence and in some condescending sympathy on your Majesty's part with the feelings which prompt this letter.
>
> Mrs. Disraeli has a fortune of her own adequate to any position in which your Majesty might deign to place her. Might her husband then hope that your Majesty would be graciously pleased to create her Viscountess Beaconsfield, a town with which Mr. Disraeli has been long connected and which is the nearest town to his estate in Bucks which is not yet ennobled?

He had put his Queen in a difficult position. There were, as he pointed out to her, historical precedents for such an action. But Mary Anne, though incessantly behind him, had done no political services as such; and her increasing 'oddities' which were whispered about society, and which may have revived some rumours of her early amours and her connections with the Harriette Wilson set, made her not the most desirable of peeresses. She was exactly the kind of person to have started the variously-attributed story about Victoria asking what was the name of the beautiful tune the band was playing, and being told it was 'Come where the Booze is Cheaper'. In fact, as the Queen's secretary pointed out to her, the whole thing was very embarrassing, and might even cause Mary Anne herself some embarrassment as the subject of ridicule. The discussion between Queen and secretary remained strictly private: not for one second was Disraeli allowed to think that his Queen had doubts. She wrote him, by return, a delightful letter saying that she had much pleasure in complying with his request: 'The Queen can truly sympathise with his devotion to Mrs. Disraeli, who in her turn is so deeply attached to him, and she hopes they may yet enjoy many years of happiness together.'

It was a gift not only immensely tender but immensely generous. Disraeli was not so reluctant to return to the Opposition bench as he may have suggested to the Queen; he had years of fighting left in him. But he enjoyed titles and honours, and he could have borne quite happily to have retired to Hughenden and his books and trees and peacocks—and Mary Anne, for as long as she was left to him. With his own hands he gave away his crown to his beloved wife, and she took it in full, glorious understanding of what it meant, that coronet which symbolized self-sacrifice and devotion and true love.

And she enjoyed so much being a peeress. Though his universal nickname had always been an acceptable joke, of late she had become slightly touchy about it, particularly when it applied to her. William Fraser remembered how at a tea-party at Lady Palmerston's, Montagu Corry's father, who was First Lord of the Admiralty, bowed to Mary Anne and said, 'Good evening, Mrs Disraeli.' Unfortunately he had a slight stammer which caused her to mis-hear him. She snapped back, 'I don't mind *your* calling me Mrs Dizzy. I don't allow everyone to do so, I can assure you.' And so it was delightful not to be 'Mrs Dizzy' any more, but a Viscountess to whose husband people would perhaps refer more respectfully in future (though she didn't mind them calling him the 'Jew d'esprit') and to be able to write to him and sign the letter triumphantly 'Your devoted Beaconsfield' on paper adorned with a coronet, and the initial B. In fact, she began embroidering Bs on the furniture, and on book-covers, and everywhere it would go—it even appeared painted on her wardrobe. They both insisted on the new title being pronounced as in 'beacon', not in 'beckon', and Lord Rosebery said that it would have taken more courage than he had to address Mary Anne by any other pronunciation.

The College of Heralds set about designing her a coat of

arms. Her ancestry was handsomely represented by a branch of grape-vine ('a slip of vine argent') for the Viney family, two boars' heads for the Evanses, a fierce eagle and lion as supporters, with castles on escutcheons hanging from their collars. The castles were a compliment to the arms borne by Disraeli's ancestors, the ancient line of Mendizebels. His personal coat of arms bore the same castles, and a bunch of grapes in compliment to his Viscountess.

Congratulations flowed in from friends everywhere, from Derby, from Gladstone, who was genuinely pleased, from the Press. The *Morning Post* eulogized everybody concerned, particularly Disraeli.

> . . . while choosing to remain a Commoner, he accepts the proffered Coronet to place it on the brow of a wife to whose qualities he has borne public testimony, and to whose affectionate aid he has acknowledged himself indebted for much of his success in life . . . none who have hearts to sympathise with the pride a woman can know in her husband's greatness but must feel their pulse beat quicker as they think of the pleasure with which the wife must accept what her hero has so bravely won. . . .

Punch mentioned her for the first time in a congratulatory acrostic.

L ady of Hughenden, Punch, drawing near,
A ffably offers a homage sincere;
D eign to accept it—though playful its tone,
Y *our* heart will tell you it comes from his own.

B attle full oft with your Lord he has done,
E ver in fairness and often in fun,
A dding, as friends and antagonists know,
C heer, when his enemy struck a good blow.
O pportune moment he finds, nothing loth,
N ow, for a tribute more pleasant to both.
S mile on the circlet a husband prepares,
F or his Guide to the triumph she honours and shares!
I n it acknowledged what ne'er can be paid,
E arnest devotion and womanly aid.
L ong may the gems in that coronal flame,
D ecking Her brow who's more proud of his fame.

Seven years after she was dead, and Disraeli had accepted a title for himself, *Punch* glanced back at her unique honour with the suggestion: 'now that the Ladies, thanks to the initiation of Lord Beaconsfield and the Royal condescension to his suggestions, are to be permitted to share the decorations that have hitherto been reserved for their Lords and Masters, we may soon expect an increase in the Orders of Lady Knighthood'. The illustration showed a plume-helmeted, half-armoured damsel of the period being approvingly quizzed by a coroneted Disraeli.

A home-made acrostic came from Lord and Lady Galway.

> B was the bright brain, light of his youth,
> E the eye, eagle-keen, searching for truth,
> A was the augur his fortunes foresaw,
> C the cool helper in weal and in woe.
> O was the circle affection entwined,
> N the new honors and honor assigned,
> S was the subtle in council and fight,
> F the firm faith in the right against might,
> I was the intellect granted by Heaven,
> E the enrichment that later hath given,
> L was the love to the state he has shown,
> D the distinction bestowed on 'his own'.

Even those who might have laughed were impressed; the Queen need not have worried.

15

'Dreams, dreams!'

'The innate and never-ending grief of all those who had adorned Humanity existed in Disraeli. This was written in his face: in his voice: and showed itself through all the brilliant fiction which he produced. What was the heritage of his old age? Was it, as he [Tennyson] asks, Despair?' enquired William Fraser, fascinated by every aspect of his hero.

Partly it was the innate melancholy of the Jew, emerging as youth and strength left him; but in the last four years of Mary Anne's life it was also the knowledge of her suffering and the inevitability of her death. He was saddened, too, by the death of his brother James in December 1868, and when James was laid in the same vault as Mrs Brydges Willyams at Hughenden Disraeli must have known too well whose would be the next coffin to be carried there.

But life must go on as usual; he matched her courage with his. He began to write his first novel since *Tancred* of 1847. It was *Lothair*, a romance based on the conversion to Roman Catholicism of the rich young Marquess of Bute. It proved popular and successful, but its greatest virtue to its author was the interest it afforded to Mary Anne. Here was another of her literary 'children', to hear read aloud at night, to comment and advise on, to proof-read. They spent a great deal of time at Hughenden while he was writing it, and the new Viscountess took a lively interest in parochial matters. In 1869 the little church acquired a new Vicar, the Reverend Henry Blagden, whose wife Isabella arrived pregnant and was actually playing the organ for the service and choir practice when her new daughter decided to enter the world; Mary Anne had only just time to summon the surgeon, Mr Rose, from Wycombe.

May was beautiful at Hughenden that year; 'since this late welcome rain, Hughenden has put on its most lovely spring dress'. In July, when the Disraelis were away, Mrs Blagden wrote regularly to her patroness: there had been a treat for the schoolchildren; 'the woods are quite lovely, and I am told there are numbers of glowworms in the Lady's Walk'. From the country houses they were visiting—Alton Towers, Strathfield-saye, Blenheim—Mary Anne sent the Blagdens pheasant and venison, evergreen for the church decorations at Harvest Festival, and tea, to which, said Mrs Blagden, the Vicar quite looked forward, it was so 'superior'. There was a bazaar at Newport Pagnell, to raise funds for the restoration of the church chancel: Mary Anne was one of its patronesses.

They entertained constantly, in return for the hospitality they were receiving, and engaged a new cook, Mrs Williams. Mary Anne still kept detailed inventories of shopping orders, household contents, lists of plate, down to the smallest sugar-sifter, as she and Mrs Yate had done half a century before. She believed in supervising personally; it was the only way to avoid extravagance when one had two great houses to run. It had won her an unenviable reputation among the tradespeople of Wycombe, who thought her mean. Disraeli had unfortunately taken over Hughenden from a squire of lavish disposition, who was still gratefully remembered as having spent £10,000 a year in the town. Mary Anne had always taken good care that the new squire did nothing of the sort. The villagers told tall stories about her—that she had only ordered six rolls for breakfast when the Prince and Princess of Teck came to stay; how she had ordered a quarter of cheese, and sent it back because Disraeli was recalled to London and wouldn't be eating it—and so forth. But her husband and her servants never went short: on Disraeli's birthday in 1869 he was looking out a bottle of the best Falernian, with which to entertain the new Lord Derby (his father had died shortly before, and Disraeli was cultivating the heir).

In the following May, 1870, at Grosvenor Gate, Mary Anne and Disraeli were rejoicing in Derby's engagement to the charm-ing Mary, Lord Salisbury's stepmother, an old friend of theirs. He sent round a congratulatory note: 'Marriage is the happiest state in the world, when there is, on each side, a complete knowledge of the characters united. . . . Lady Beaconsfield sends you her congratulations thro' her tears—of joy.'

Derby and his bride were guests at Hughenden, and so were numerous other luminaries, including the Prince of Wales, who helped to bag eighty brace of grouse. The dinner menus were comparatively simple—turtle soup (the unfortunate turtles were kept at Hughenden), fillets of salmon, turbot in shrimp sauce, lamb chops, supreme of chicken with asparagus tips, beef à la Provençale—but they were all in fashionable French and on curious little cards showing grotesque scenes of childhood, with extremely ugly infants playing at soldiers and town criers and the like. Disraeli, who was not well himself, must have found so many dinners a little trying, but he enjoyed showing off his estate as much as ever. Constance Rothschild always remembered him so.

> How he loved the place! And how he tried to act up to the character he had imposed upon himself, that of the country gentleman! For dressed in his velveteen coat, his leather leggings, his soft felt hat, and carrying his little hatchet, for relieving the bark of trees from the encroaching ivy, in one of those white hands, which probably hitherto had never held anything heavier than a pen, Mr. Disraeli was *the Squire*. . . .

Women guests smiled a little at Mary Anne's comical get-up (though not when her husband was looking), as they called it. In those days of extreme tight-lacing, bustles and trains, high-piled chignons and 'Dolly Varden' hats, she defied fashion by being seen in what is described as a bright crimson velvet tunic, with Disraeli's miniature pinned above the left breast; and she wore an obvious wig, often awry, as it might well have been if it were the height of some shown in fashion-plates of the period, though the odds are that she stuck to one displaying the bunches of curls she had worn in her youth. It probably did not occur to the smiling ladies that the straight up-and-down tunic may have concealed a figure painfully swollen and impossible to tight-lace. Mary Tudor, three centuries before, and suffering from the same type of cancer as Mary Anne, had pathetically believed herself pregnant. And the 'vain attempts at a somewhat youthful appearance', the paint and pearl-powder and blacked-in eyebrows, disguised a face haggard with starvation, for she could hardly take any food, to Disraeli's distress. 'If she could only eat!' was his constant cry. Yet still she pretended.

Someone who visited Hughenden in her last year remembered her seated in her drawing-room, tiny and shrunken in her brilliant *outré* dress, bedizened with jewels, her face enamelled pink and white: she looked, they thought, like an eastern idol in porcelain.

They were in London for the winter of 1871. Grosvenor Gate was a cold house, but at least in London she could be taken for drives to look at the Christmas shops and shoppers, and have her mind taken a little from her pain. In January of the New Year she went to the pantomime at Drury Lane with Disraeli and the Earl and Countess of Shrewsbury and their children. Disraeli enjoyed the delight of the children, and the pantomime itself: it was *Tom Thumb* featuring the Vokes family, who were brilliant dancers but sang excruciatingly. There was a ballet of charming Watteauesque figures (Watteau frills, flowers and flounces were very much in vogue) and a rather nasty moment when a Giant's head appeared over a wall and snapped up little Tom Thumb, at which the children squealed with alarm; nor were they much reassured when on his reappearance from the Giant's maw he was snatched up by the claws of a huge bird. But then the Clown came on and cheered everyone up, and a delightful evening was had by all.

In February Mary Anne went with her husband to St Paul's, to share in a thanksgiving ceremony for the recovery of the Prince of Wales from typhoid. Unlike his father, who had died ten years before, he made a highly entertaining patient, throwing pillows about, laughing and singing in his delirium. It is a pity that professional etiquette prevented his physician, Sir William Gull, from passing on some of the more startlingly scandalous of his ravings to his other patient, Mary Anne. There were loud cheers as the carriage containing the Queen and the recovered Prince passed through Temple Bar, and the Queen raised her son's hand and kissed it; and almost as loud cheers for the carriage in which sat a pale Disraeli and an improbably pink-cheeked, smiling Viscountess Beaconsfield. The reception given to the Gladstones was distinctly cooler.

In April she insisted on accompanying Disraeli to Manchester for a great Conservative rally at the Free Trade Hall. She sat in the gallery, listening to her husband's brilliant speech and watching him with a look of intense love and sympathy; and from time to time Disraeli looked up to her, for her reassuring approval. After an immensely successful meeting she drove back to the home of Romaine Callender, leader of the Manchester Conservative Party, in one of the stately new houses in Victoria Park. Disraeli, who had been delayed by admirers, came in later. When she heard his carriage-wheels on the drive, the seventy-year-old Mary Anne rushed out of the drawing-room to meet him in the hall, threw herself into his arms like a bride, and cried 'Oh! Dizzy, Dizzy, it is the greatest night of all. This pays for all!'

She herself paid for the fatigue and excitement of that visit. When they got back to London she collapsed, and the seriousness of her condition could no longer be hidden, at least from those near to her. But she struggled up again, and on 7 May was attending a party at Lady Waldegrave's.[1] She could not get through the evening, but left priding herself on not having given away her illness; and the next day attended a Court at Buckingham Palace. Sir William Gull had said she could go, much to Disraeli's distress, for only he knew how weak she was; and he was right, for at the Palace she was taken ill again, and he, with the aid of some court-ladies, had to smuggle her out.

Disraeli wrote to Corry, who was managing affairs at Hughenden, that 'to see her every day weaker and weaker is heartrending; to witness the gradual death of one who has shared so long and so completely my life entirely unmans me.' Yet politically he was in fine form, following up his speech in Manchester with an even more brilliant one at the Crystal Palace in June. One of his main themes was an improvement in the condition of the people, a preoccupation of his since the beginning of his political life and voiced in *Sybil*. It was not a popular theme. The crowded state of England's cities had caused appalling slum conditions, in London more than elsewhere. Untreated sewage had until recently run into the Thames, making the taking of tea on the terrace of the Houses of Parliament a pleasure no longer possible—the least of its evil results. The Prince of Wales's recent illness had probably been caused by infected water. Rats the size of kittens still played in the sewers of Paddington; and the new Drainage Age had only

[1] Frances, Countess Waldegrave (1821–79), daughter of the singer John Braham; she married four times and was a leader of London society.

just begun to take effect. 'Air, light and water' were what the people needed, said Disraeli, and made his famous classical quip 'Sanitas sanitatum, omnia sanitas', provoking a Liberal comment that he and his party were pursuing a 'policy of sewage'.

He took Mary Anne to Hughenden for Whitsuntide, hoping the air and scenery might help her. But by now she could scarcely stand the journey. Every little roughness in the road jolted her and brought on her pain, so that long drives in the country were impossible. Antonelli, one of the servants, pushed her about the grounds in a bath-chair, which amused her a little, as did Antonelli's imperfect English: he informed her that he heard a nightingale whistling in the garden, and she told Disraeli that she thought 'whistling' a capital word for bird noises.

She insisted on going back to town with Disraeli after the recess, and actually continued dining out. At the Foreign Office, where they had held the great party for Disraeli's Premiership, he was seen helping her step by step down the long staircase, tenderly supporting her, almost carrying her. Her last dinner-party was on 17 July, at Lady Loudoun's house, to meet the Duchess of Cambridge. It was obvious that she was in acute pain, and the guests were amazed by her heroism. She bore it, literally, with a smile, more concerned with the inconvenience she might be causing Lady Loudoun. Disraeli took her home, and she never went out in London society again.

In July he was writing to her from the House, as she lay ill at Grosvenor Gate:

I have nothing to tell you, except that I love you, which I fear, you will think rather dull. . . . Natty [Nathan Rothschild] was very affectionate about you, and wanted me to come home and dine with him; quite alone; but I told him you were the only person now, whom I could dine with; and only relinquished you tonight for my country. My country, I fear, will be very late; but I hope to find you in a sweet sleep.

Her last note to him (or the last known) was written on 26 July.

My own Dearest—I miss you sadly. I feel so grateful for your constant tender love and kindness. I certainly feel better this evening.
Your own devoted Beaconsfield.

During the shooting season Lord Cairns[1] sent them some pheasant, and Disraeli was delighted that she actually ate some. Otherwise, he thought she was too ill even to move to Hughenden. She was haemorrhaging badly again, and he feared whether even her buoyant, gallant spirit could survive so much. 'We have not been separated for three and thirty years', he told Cairns, 'and, during all that time, in her society I never have had a moment of dullness. It tears the heart to see such a spirit suffer, and suffer so much!'

Such a spirit, indeed; for she made him resume their drives, to beautiful retreats previously unvisited by them in Middlesex and Surrey, marvelling at how London was growing, from the small place it had been in their youth, and at the suburban outcrop of villas stretching their antennae in every direction.

What miles of villas! and of all sorts of architecture! What beautiful churches! What gorgeous palaces of Geneva![2] One day we came upon a real feudal castle, with a donjon keep high in the air. It turned out to be the new City prison in Camden Road [Holloway] but it deserves a visit—I mean externally. Of all the kingdoms ruled over by our gracious mistress, the most remarkable is her *royaume de Cockaigne*, and perhaps the one the Queen has least visited. Her faithful servants in question, preparing their expeditions with a map, investigated all parts of it from Essex to Surrey, and Lady Beaconsfield calculated that from the 1st of August to the end of September she travelled 220 miles.

This note, with its third-person references and its gentle hint that the Queen was not getting about enough among her humbler subjects, was probably intended for Victoria herself, but because of some distraction remained unsent. Disraeli thought that these urban and rural rides had made a distinct difference in Mary Anne's health, and that they might risk going to Hughenden. 'There is a streak of dawn. . . .' Even now, he could hope; she meant him to hope. 'If she could only regain—not appetite—but even a desire for sustenance, I should be confident of the future.'

In August Mrs Blagden wrote to report that the Manor

[1] Hugh McAlmont (1819–85), 1st Earl Cairns, leader of Conservative opposition in the Lords after Lord Derby's death in 1869.
[2] His flowery description of the new, gaudy, plate-glassed gin-palaces, paradises of the poor.

garden was in full beauty—she had never seen the geraniums so brilliant—and Disraeli was sorry that they would 'go home in the fall of the leaf'. It was October before they reached Hughenden.

Mary Anne was still unable to eat, but Disraeli continued to believe that if he could make her touch the delicacies Corry had sent down for her, all would be well. There was some improvement in Mary Anne—not in the appetite, but in continued absence of pain, and consequent enjoyment of life. Their evenings were as quiet and pleasant as usual. He read to her, and sometimes she dozed; and at others, surely, amused herself by going through those great bundles of correspondence she had kept since her very first letter to 'Dear Mama': 'Our school is broke up and I am very comfortable. . . .' And there were all those tributes from admirers—and some comic efforts of hers, from Clifton days.

> Oh! Byng! thy vows have no more truth
> Than hers who did of late, forsooth,
> Beguile thee of thy gay gold ring . . .
> Then Byng, Oh, Byng! conceal my name,
> Love and live happy if you can,
> Away from me—your M . . . A. . . .

Byng (unfortunately unidentifiable) replied in kind and with commendable resignation.

> To be remembered when we part
>   Is all that I will ask of thee,
> To bear an interest in your heart
>   Is all save hope that's dear to me.
>
> I wish in token to recall
>   A word, a smile, a look of thine,
> Too dearly do I prize them all
>   For time to bid their powers decline.
>
> Then keep the ring, and keep the charm,
>   For those whose hearts less truly beat,
> And only what thou art remain,
>   'Tis all I ask till next we meet.

Was it Byng or someone else who had poetically deplored her lack of wealth?

I would a lovelier lot were thine; for then my heart's emotion
Co'd pour unnam'd at Riches' shrine the soul of love's devotion.
Yet what hath wealth to do with love, whose type the *Rose*
    doth blossom,
As sweetly near the humble cot, as in an Eden's bosom?

There were more poems from her Clifton days—sheaves of
them—poor Wyndham's, of course: too many to read with
tired eyes. And here was George Dawson, rhyming her at
Pantgwynlais, 'with a flower and a rhyme for each word'.
The flowers were withered, but the words were left.

> Accept this bouquet of picked flowers,
>   Not made, I own, by fingers fairy,
> I cull from Covent Garden's bowers
>   The *rose*, companion old of Mary.
>
> With it the wind's own flower you see,
>   'Tis not the worst among the many.
> I'm right, you surely will agree,
>   To send *ane*-mone to Annie.
>
> Clematis delicate and white,
>   Among the rest its leaves I find 'em,
> In doing so I know I'm right,
>   The *winding* plants are apt for Wyndham.
>
> The lily of immortal fame,
>   Over thy heart its hostile hue is,
> What better present could I name
>   Than orange *luce* for Tony Lewis.

It must have seemed to her a hundred years since anyone
had referred to Wyndham as Tony. And here were much later
things—a bundle of letters from the charming rattle, Arethusa
Milner-Gibson, whose husband had been a Privy Counsellor
and President of the Board of Trade. Arethusa had written so
many amusing letters, on romantic notepaper decorated with
painted and gilded scenes of angels and cupids and German
schlösscher. Here was a New Year Card with 'M. A. Disraeli'
painted by Arethusa's Alice, 'with more patience than taste',
and here the information that Arethusa had been confined of
such a nice, fat, dear little girl; and an invitation to an evening
party on All Fools' Day, 1850—only, if Mr Disraeli were coming

Arethusa wouldn't send cards to the Charles Dickenses and John Forster, whom she fancied he would not like to meet. How Arethusa (who was now dead) had admired Disraeli! 'I must write to congratulate you upon Mr. Disraeli's splendid speech [on Protection, February 1846]. I hear of nothing else —not only London but all the country rings with it. . . . How happy you must be.'

And of course there were invitations from Royalty and menus from Royal banquets; very resistible now. Then great piles of Disraeli family correspondence, and funny verses and riddles Mary Anne had found to amuse Isaac, who had so loved a parlour entertainment. Could she still do any of Mr Richard Miller's Conjuring Tricks, which could be performed by either Lady or Gentleman: such as the Magic Scrap-Book, which was empty one minute and full of flowers the next, and then of soldiers? or the Welsh Rabbit trick—'live rabbit produced from a saucepan toasted over flames'? Yes, she had probably kept her sleight of hand, if only she could find the energy. 'Thy hand, fair Lewis, by the Graces taught. . . .'

And here were tiny envelopes of hair, with her own scrawled writing, 'Dear Dis's hair', but at so many different ages, so shining black at first and later so much duller, when the black came out of a bottle, and the very first one, 'Dear Dizzy's hair given to me by his mother, August 27th 1839.' Into another tiny envelope she placed a plain gold ring, too small to go on the smallest finger of a woman of the twentieth century: 'Dizzy's wedding-ring, taken off today because my hand and finger is swolen. July 6th 1872.'

Her fingers were still swollen, and she did not like to look at them very much; but she still had the portraits, and her beloved's lovely verses, like the one he wrote when they were engaged.

> Thick tresses, Nature's auburn boon,
>   That scorn to wildly flow,
> White shoulders, rounder than the moon,
>   In all her harvest glow.
>
> A face as fair as summer skies,
>   When western winds rejoice,
> Heaven's ether tints her light blue eyes,
>   Birds warble in her voice.

Even now, her husband looked at her from the other side of the fireplace as he had looked then. Beauclerk and Berkeley and all the others, they meant nothing now. She hesitated over that long peevish letter from George, then, unable to resist the implied tribute, wrote on it: 'Mr. Beauclerk. To be kept.' He had been dead a year.

And there was so much to be thankful for, so much that other wives had never known. Their husbands tired of them, were unfaithful or short-tempered. Lady Charlotte Bertie, for instance, who had married Wyndham's colleague at Dowlais, in such an atmosphere of fervour that she had to chide him for kissing her in the middle of Piccadilly, could look back and say:

> I remember this day fourteen years, and how wildly I was loved then, and how everything I then did was not only appreciated but overrated. And now am I not even misunderstood? Why should it be? My heart is unchanged, and though my energies are diminished that could hardly be otherwise by the course of years and the wear and tear of spirits. Perhaps I have laid my heart and soul too open, and have been too devoted. Had I been more reserved, may be the airy nothings of every move-ment of daily life would not have been thus subject of cavil. But I can do no more. . . .

This was the common experience of wives when the flame cooled; but it had not been Mary Anne's, even when her looks were gone. Perhaps Disraeli *had* had the perfect wife; but she had had the perfect husband. Poor Lady Charlotte had made the wrong choice. And then there was Rosina, long since bitterly estranged from Bulwer, vindictive, almost mad, heaping public and private abuse upon the man she had once adored, and upon everybody else except her beloved dogs, like Fairy, who had caused such acrimony and had been supposed to call Mary Anne 'Auntie'. Rosina was alive still, no longer beautiful, an em-bittered alcoholic. Mary Anne had been very, very lucky.

However, it would never do to look as though she were living in the past. It would depress Disraeli too much. They must invite and receive, and they did. They had arranged to call on Philip Rose and his wife on 13 November, but the snow came and frightened Disraeli off the journey, 'tho' my wife was inclined to face it', he apologized. Mary Anne was determined that people should come to her, even if Disraeli would not take her to them. From 21 November to 25 November she entertained a house-party: the John Mannerses, Lord Rosebery, Sir William Harcourt[1] and Lord Ronald Gower. Harcourt and she had always flirted; once, at Grosvenor Gate, she had seen him gazing appreciatively at a near-nude painting, and had observed, 'Yes, it oughtn't to be allowed in here—but it's nothing to the Venus that Dizzy has up in his bedroom.' '*That* I can well believe,' responded Sir William. On the second night of his stay she gave him a French novel to take up to bed with him, and he absent-mindedly packed it and felt like a felon when he unpacked his bag at Trinity College. He wrote her a charming letter advising her that he was sending her a consignment of Trinity audit ale,[2] which she enjoyed so much. She had always had a robust Georgian taste for beer, and had once entertained Wellington on it to show him what a good and pleasant drink it was.

In his charming bedroom on the top floor of the Manor, with its light rooms and beautifully moulded ceilings (now the delightful flat of Hughenden's custodian), Sir William Harcourt perhaps thought less of his French novel than of his hostess: 'sadly altered in looks since London—death written in her face —but, as usual, gorgeously dressed,' as Lord Ronald Gower reported. All through dinner Disraeli's whole attention was concentrated on her: 'Mary Anne was constantly appealed to.' She did not appear at breakfast or attend service at the church with the guests, but joined them for lunch, and afterwards the whole party went for a walk through her miniature German Forest, she leading the way in her little pony-chaise. That evening, at dinner, she chattered away about her pets, her horses, her peacocks. Anybody would have thought that her husband, not she, was the invalid, from his groans and his face of suffering and woe after she had gone to bed. She was late down next morning, after a bad night, but was wonderfully brisk and lively, and had her late breakfast with her guests in the library. She was smiling cheerfully as she and Disraeli waved them goodbye from the arched portico at noon, but

[1] Sir William Harcourt (1827–1904), scholar and statesman, Liberal M.P. or Oxford 1868. He served on Royal Commissions on naturalization laws, was a champion of religious equality, and an authority on international law.
[2] A famous drink, highly popular with scholars, from Cambridge, which was then a seat of brewing as well as of learning.

Lord Ronald went off filled with gloom because he knew that he 'would never again see poor old Lady Beaconsfield'.

It was her last social appearance. A chill struck her, followed by congestion of the lungs and pneumonia, and she collapsed in the first week of December. Disraeli wrote to Philip Rose, 'I am totally unable to meet the catastrophe.' He moved into her bedroom, and hardly left it until the end.

A telegram came from the Queen: 'I see by the papers that Lady Beaconsfield is very ill am most anxious to know how she is today, pray answer by telegraph.' Mary Anne was up and sitting by the fire when it was delivered. 'What is it? What is it?' she testily asked. 'A message from Her Majesty to know how you are,' replied the servant. 'Bah!' said her Ladyship, picking up a spoon from the table by her side and throwing it at the innocent telegraph form.

There were two more telegrams from the Queen. 'I am truly grieved at this report.' 'Have received your sad letter and feel deeply for you how is she this morning.'

She surrendered to death at last, on Sunday, 15 December, with her husband by her side, as he had been for three and thirty years. Her death certificate gave her age as seventy-six —four years short of the truth, confirming that she had never told Disraeli her real age.

For the last few days she had been delirious, imagining scenes and people from the past; but in one lucid interval she asked for young Montagu Corry to come to her, and the distracted Disraeli sent for him. 'She will not let me go out to fetch you. Come. D.'

Once, when Corry visited her bedside, she told him that they had persuaded her to send for a clergyman (presumably Mr Blagden from the estate church). 'He told me to turn my thoughts to Jesus Christ,' she said, 'but I couldn't. You know *Dizzy* is my J.C.'[1]

As the dying so often do in delirium, in the last week of her life, when the disease reached her brain, she turned against the one so dear to her, and raved against him to Corry, who listened, helpless, knowing that Disraeli was listening too, outside the door, in tears.

On 16 December a letter with the Royal crest arrived at a darkened, mourning Hughenden.

[1] From the diary of Lord Rosebery for 14 May 1899.

My dear Mr. Corry,
   The Queen is so anxious to hear some account of the last hours
of Lady Beaconsfield. Could you write me such a letter I could
show Her Majesty. . . . Poor Mr. Disraeli, I feel for him so much.

Jane, Marchioness of Ely, was writing the letter the Queen
could not bring herself to write personally, so deep was her
grief for her beloved statesman. When Corry replied, he must
have given the Queen the substance of what was told to Henry
Lucy, who attended the funeral. Mary Anne had said that
people need not die unless they gave way to death, and for her
part she never would. She refused to go to bed when her last
illness came on, and died in her chair. Her last drink was a
draught of Cambridge audit ale, Harcourt's gift.

The condolences which poured in must have alternately
consoled and harrowed the widower. From the Queen came an
expression of heartfelt sympathy in his first hour of desolation
and overwhelming grief. She, who had also lost the dear partner
of her life, knew what he had lost and what he must suffer;
and the day of Mary Anne's death was the anniversary of the
Prince Consort's.

Royalty, colleagues, opponents, friends were united in their
sympathy. Telegrams came from the Prince and Princess of
Wales, and Disraeli wrote back to tell the Prince how much
Mary Anne had been gratified by an invitation to Sandringham.
She had said, 'It would have been a happy incident in a happy
life, now about to close. I liked his society; I delighted in the
merriment of his kind heart.'

Gladstone stretched out a hand, metaphorically, across the
floor of the House.

You and I were, I believe, married in the same year. It has been
permitted to both of us to enjoy a priceless boon through a
third of a century. Spared myself the blow which has fallen on
you, I can form some conception of what it must have been and
be.

Rosebery wrote of the 'sad and pleasant memory' of his last
sight of Mary Anne. Even the public joined in Disraeli's sorrow;
one letter was a touching condolence from an anonymous
woman, that 'you may, in your hour of sadness, like to know
that you are thought of and felt for in homes where your step

192

is strange'. The Press and amateur poets poured out effusions varying from the sentimentally romantic to the grisly (death-knells, charnel-houses and pearly gates) and the unconsciously funny, which Mary Anne would have been the first to appreciate:

> She has left this wide world—one of troubles and cares—
> To partake of a crown which by birthright was hers.
> To put on sweet robes of a pure spotless white,
> And to live in a land that hath never known night.

It was not quite her conception of a party, with no diamonds and blond lace. Nor would she have seen herself 'attuning her harp to loftiest songs of praise'; she had never cared much for hymns. The most extraordinary effort at consolation began:

> Let trodden serpents writhe and hiss,
> Or coil themselves in wrath despairing;
> The hand that smites us we should kiss,
> For God, who grieves, our grief is sharing.

Another poet began:

> There's mourning in the Manor Hall,
> There's a pall o'er the family crest. . . .

It went on to make up in music-hall rumbustiousness what it lacked in scansion, and would have pleased its subject by referring to her as a 'Graceful Belle'. Disraeli's favourite was probably the simple 'In Memoriam. Mary Anne Disraeli':

> The light that helped to give him brilliance, gone,
> The joy that made his well-earned fame so fair,
> From his proud worship and affection, borne
> To some diviner life and loftier care.
>
> Her sweetness gave him strength, her fondness zeal,
> To scale and storm ambition's stony height,
> And reach by ceaseless effort that ideal
> Which dreamy youth had mirrored in his sight . . .
>
> And when he reaped the glory of success,
> The tribute that was his, he nobly set
> On her, whose perfect faith and tenderness
> To him was brighter than a coronet.

The Press gave her every tribute that even her husband could have wished. She was recognized, as no politician's wife had been before, as the power behind his own power. *The Times*, 16 December 1872, wrote:

> Who would have supposed, 35 years ago, that the coming history of English political life would take a direction from the unselfish affection of a woman, and a woman not marked by any unusual capacities? Society would have been as little likely to single out the widow of Mr. Wyndham Lewis as destined to play an important part in life as the politicians of the day would have been inclined to see in Mr. Disraeli the future leader of the Tory party. Yet the marriage which sprang from that affection was an historical event.

On the day of the funeral, 20 December all the leading London newspapers were represented at Hughenden. It was a pity she could not have had a fine day for this, her last occasion. The roads, paths and fields were saturated with rain, the leaden sky wept incessantly. It was like a humble village funeral rather than that of a great lady. Tenants from the estate carried her small coffin, draped in a pall of black velvet, the few hundred yards down the Manor drive and the path that led to the little church in the park. Behind them walked the widower, the chief mourner, with Philip Rose and Montagu Corry behind him. Then came Alfred Leggatt, who had attended Mary Anne in her last illness. The black-clad, wet procession seemed in strange and sad incongruity with the Christmas decorations in the tenants' cottages, the garlanded windows, the doors hung with holly wreaths.

As the coffin was borne into the church, Isabella Blagden, at the organ, played Mozart's *Agnus Dei*. Disraeli was ushered into a pew opposite the pulpit, where, bending low with his face to the wall, he passed a few moments in the indulgence of a grief which was shared by not a few of the congregation. 'The heavy gloom of a dull leaden sky hung over the church and the mourners, when something like a ray of light appeared to have settled on the coffin. Friendly and loving hands had during the brief interval placed upon it a cross, several wreaths, and bouquets composed of white camelias, azaleas, and other exotics.' Among them was a simple wreath of white flowers from Mrs Blagden.

The service over, the flower-covered coffin was carried outside. Many years before, in 1856, Mary Anne had written but not delivered a note to Disraeli:

> My own dear Husband,
>   If I should depart this life before you, leave orders that we may be buried in the same grave at whatever distance you may die from England. And now, God bless you, my kindest dearest. You have been a perfect husband to me. Be put by my side in the same grave.

He would be, when the time came. Now, they opened the vault at the east wall of the church. There were the coffins of Mrs Brydges Willyams and of James Disraeli, so recently put there. When Mary Anne's was laid in place, there was room for but one more. Disraeli stood for ten minutes looking down at the coffin, then he went home, if home it could be called any more, walking slowly, unconscious of the damp and the kind murmurings of his friends. Now he was alone indeed, and would be alone for the rest of his days. When he went through her papers, she died again, a hundred times, for him. If he bothered to read the letters from her old lovers, they can have provoked no anger in him, for they still exist. 'Fickle Rose' she may have been to them, but to him only 'my kind and faithful Mary Anne'.

With her death he had lost the Grosvenor Gate house and £5,000 a year. Montagu Corry, who looked after him like a son, found him rooms at Edwards' Hotel in George Street, Hanover Square, near the church where he had been married. He tried to find consolation in living in a house which, in his youth, had been Lady Palmerston's; at least, he thought, he would labour in rooms where a great statesman had been inspired.

His Party feared that the death of his wife might end his career in politics; but it was his career that saved him from utter melancholy. He constantly wrote to people of his heaviness and misery, and told Malmesbury, with tears standing in his eyes, that he hoped some of his friends would take notice of him now in his great misfortune, 'for I have no home, and when I tell my coachman to drive home I feel it is a mockery'. His friends, and they were many, rallied round, giving quiet dinner-parties for him. He had Mary Anne's miniature copied by G. F. Middleton, as a half-length portrait, and it went into the empty frame over the mantelpiece at Hughenden which had intrigued visitors, and looked down, as it looks down now, with that typical expression of sweet gravity which masked the laughter behind her deep eyes. One delicate hand holds a Paisley shawl of soft pink against her bosom, contrasting with the 'white shoulders, rounder than the moon', and long pearl earrings set off the column of her lovely neck. Many years after her death, the pink shawl was found at Hughenden, put away in a drawer and forgotten, spoiled by moths and mildew.

And so Disraeli began to rebuild his life. In the same note in which she had asked him to be buried with her, she had entreated him, with her own loving generosity, 'Do not live alone, dearest. Some one I earnestly hope you may find as attached to you as your own devoted Mary Anne.'

She knew he was the kind of man who cannot live his life fully without a woman's fond companionship. 'My nature demands that my life should be perpetual love,' he had said in his fiery youth. Mary Anne was right. With no disloyalty to her, for he knew that she would have approved, he began, unconsciously, perhaps, at first, to look for her successor.

There were two sisters among his acquaintance who became close to him during the early years of his bereavement. Lady Chesterfield and Lady Bradford had both been noted beauties in their day, and he had known them longer than he had known Mary Anne. Lady Chesterfield, a widow, was seventy, two years older than Disraeli. Selina, Countess of Bradford, was fifty-three, and still beautiful, though a grandmother. It was to her that Disraeli was attracted, but her husband, a sporting peer, was still very much alive. Disraeli, rather tactlessly, began to woo her through her available sister; like the man in the poem, 'while he sang Euphelia's praise, He fixed his soul on Chloe's eyes'. Euphelia (in this case Anne) was not flattered, for it was perfectly clear to her that when he proposed marriage to her it was only to be nearer to her sister; and Lady Bradford, who was happily married and no doubt wanted to preserve a reputation for respectability, was embarrassed rather than pleased to receive ardent, passionate letters from him, sometimes two or three a day by messenger—letters such as he had written to Henrietta so many years ago, a reckless young man head-over-ears in love. He told her she had a sweet simplicity, blended with high breeding; an intellect not over-drilled, but lively, acute and picturesque; a seraphic temper, and a disposition infinitely sympathetic. It was not unlike an idealized portrait of Mary Anne. He added, poor man, 'I am certain there is no greater misfortune than to have a heart that will not grow old.'

He wrote love-letters to Selina up to the time of his death, but she never gave him any real encouragement. Not so the dowager Lady Cardigan, who had once been the dashing, disreputable, blazingly lovely Miss Adeline Horsey de Horsey. In 1873 she began to write him an increasingly glowing series of letters which ultimately amounted to a proposal of marriage. Presumably her beauty had declined, and her eccentricities were noted—the Queen strongly disapproved of her—for Disraeli allowed the correspondence to lapse, and must have been relieved to hear that she was going to marry the Comte de Lancastre.

Of all the ladies he gathered round him—even going so far as to form an Order of the Bee (for Beaconsfield), in which each honoured lady received a bee-shaped brooch—only one truly reciprocated his devotion: his Queen herself, the Faery Queene, as she loved to hear him call her (though she was by now over 40 inches round the waist). She received him at Osborne in 1874 with such warmth that, he said, 'I thought she was going to embrace me. She was wreathed with smiles, and, as she talked, glided about the room like a bird.' He had gout at the time, as he often had by now, and she, who had kept the dying Charles Dickens on his feet for an hour, actually asked Disraeli to sit down. Soon he was sitting in her presence whenever they talked alone. While he was at Balmoral, and too ill to get up, the Queen came and visited him in his bedroom. 'What do you think of receiving your Sovereign in slippers and a dressing-gown?' he asked Lady Chesterfield. In reversal of the usual order of things, she sent him flowers; primroses, which he wore on his breast at a banquet glittering with stars and ribbons, rivalling all other decorations because it came from his gracious Sovereign. He believed that 'everyone likes flattery: and when you come to Royalty, you should lay it on with a trowel'. Yet his flattery of the Queen was not insincere. He liked and respected her, enjoyed amusing her with his wit and managing her with his exquisite tact. Well might he congratulate himself, as he did, in having a female Sovereign. 'I owe everything to woman; and if in the sunset of life I have still a young heart, it is due to that influence.'

One of the surprising facets of Victoria's character was a sympathy for the sufferings of animals. (This might not be easily guessed from Landseer's groups of herself and her family surrounded by slaughtered game bleeding all over the Balmoral upholstery.) When she discovered some of the awful truths about vivisection, she wrote to Disraeli asking him to stop it, and he, so much in sympathy with her, immediately set about bringing in a Bill which would at least help to control what he described as 'this horrible practice'.[1] She also heard with disgust of the barbarities of seal-slaughter, and Disraeli, by way of the Board of Trade, obliged her by establishing a close-season for the seal fishery. He was Prime Minister again —had been since 1874, old and ill, but full of power and cunning as ever.

He was now mainly concerned with colonial expansion and 'Imperial consolidation'. In 1875, the reins still firmly in his hand, he seized the chance to buy a large block of shares in the Suez Canal. The Canal was the new route to India, and important to Britain. Disraeli dealt successfully with the Khedive of Egypt and with the French government, but there was the little matter of four million pounds to be found if the shares were to be bought. To Disraeli it was a trifle; no more trouble than the purchase of Hughenden. He sent Corry round to the Roths-childs, who at once, on the security of the British Government, supplied the money; 'and the entire interest of the Khedive is now yours, Madam,' Disraeli wrote to the Queen. She was enchanted, 'all smiles', and she entertained him to dinner.

In 1876, when he was seriously ill (he observed facetiously in the House that from his colleagues' demeanour they thought the Burial Bill, which was under discussion, a rather fitting subject for him), she insisted that he should move to the Upper House, where he would be under less strain, and she created him Earl of Beaconsfield, the title he had not accepted earlier for Mary Anne's sake. As though in return, he brought in a

[1] The Cruelty to Animals Act, 1876.

Royal Titles Bill and made her Empress of India. Just as Mary Anne had done, she wrote him a little letter of thanks with her new title proudly inscribed as the signature: 'Victoria, Regina et Imperatrix'. At the ceremonial dinner, the usually black-clad Widow of Windsor appeared smothered in gems from India. Tenniel in *Punch* drew him as a wily, persuasive old Eastern trader offering the housewife Victoria New Crowns for Old.[1]

He had five more years to serve, and they were not easy years for a man of over seventy, suffering from gout, asthma and Bright's Disease. Russia attacked Turkey, Gladstone pursued an anti-Turkish policy which Disraeli thought might easily involve Europe in total war. In 1878 the Powers of Russia, Turkey, Germany, Austria-Hungary and Britain met together at the Congress of Berlin. Disraeli managed his country's affairs brilliantly, and handled the notoriously difficult Chancellor Bismarck with superb tact. Agreement was reached over the vexed question of the ownership of Cyprus.[2] Disraeli and Lord Salisbury, who had been his companion throughout the Congress, returned home like conquering heroes. Downing Street was draped with scarlet, and a great bunch of flowers from the Palace awaited Disraeli. To the cheering crowds he said, 'We have brought you back, I think, Peace with Honour.'

It was flattering, but exhausting to be so popular. Applauded and mobbed everywhere he went, he was still regarded by the public as the dazzling, epigrammatic lady-killing dandy he had not been for years.

> A Premier who saunters and gossips and glitters,
>   Has an epigram ready for any girl-rose,
> Marks the sunset that blushes, the red-breast that twitters,
>   Deserves, *Punch* declares, his autumnal repose.
>
> For him, while from county to county he's vagrant,
>   Wherever caprice may incline him to go,
> May the claret be sound and the pineapples fragrant,
>   And the pretty girls Tories from Chignon to toe!

In 1880 the Conservative government fell over the problems of the depressed state of agriculture. And the triumphant

---

[1] The cartoon can be seen in the study at Hughenden.

[2] Strangely enough, Disraeli had foretold this thirty years before, in his novel *Tancred*, and now his vision of Venus's Isle becoming part of the English Mediterranean kingdom had come true.

Gladstone wrote, 'The downfall of Beaconsfieldism is like the vanishing of some vast magnificent castle in an Italian romance.' His occupation was gone, and on the whole he was not sorry. He sat, in his red dressing-gown and red fez, in the red and gold drawing-room of his Curzon Street house, near the home he had shared with Mary Anne; and gazed into the fire, and dreamed. 'Dreams, dreams!' they heard him murmur. He travelled painfully to Hughenden, spoke to no one but his servants and his peacocks, who pleased him best when they basked on the lawns in the sun, mercifully silent, for 'in the morning they strut about, and scream, and make love or war'. He began a new novel, called *Endymion*, possibly as a compliment to Lady Bradford, who was named for Selina, the Moon Goddess. He wandered among the rooms where chairs embroidered by Mary Anne still stood, bright as ever, and where her bridal face gazed pensively out at him; while on another wall a young Selina nursed a miniature spaniel, her long ringlets touching her white bosom. The Queen surveyed him, plain, pudgy and cross-looking. He had written not long before to Jane Ely, 'I love the Queen—perhaps the only person in this world left to me that I do love.'

On 10 March 1881 he gave his first and last dinner party at 19 Curzon Street. Many old friends were there, but not Selina, who was out of town. Drugs given him to ease his pain kept him conscious and even cheerful and he had a surreptitious cigarette. The doctors had strictly forbidden smoking; the March weather was terrible. A week or so later, on his way back to Curzon Street from the House, he was caught in an icy blast of wind, too fierce for his old frame. He caught a chill and developed bronchitis. His valet Baum, and Baum's wife, who had been his nurse, gave way to a trained nurse and a regiment of medical men.

England began to worry. 'May the Almighty be near his pillow!' wrote Gladstone, in his diary, ever chivalrous in his rival's tribulations. Disraeli was very near the end, and knew it, but he joked to the last. They suggested to him that the Queen might like to visit him. 'No, it's better not,' he said. 'She'd only ask me to take a message to Albert.' But spring flowers from her filled his sick-room.

He fought death to the end: and the last coherent words

anyone heard him say were, 'I had rather live but I am not afraid to die.' About midnight on 18 April he woke from a calm sleep and raised himself, looking for a moment as he had looked so often in the House, when he rose to reply during a debate. Then he lay back, and died.

When Corry and Philip Rose read his will, they found a clause which cancelled Gladstone's decision for the Westminster Abbey funeral of his dead rival.

I desire and direct that I may be buried in the same Vault in the Churchyard of Hughenden in which the remains of my late dear Wife Mary Anne Disraeli created in her own right Viscountess Beaconsfield were placed and that my Funeral may be conducted with the same simplicity as hers was.

They obeyed him, of course. Mary Anne had been buried at Christmas, Disraeli was to be buried soon after Easter, eight years later. The funeral may have been intended to be private, but both the church and the grounds were packed. Among the distinguished mourners were the Prince of Wales, the Duke of Connaught and Prince Leopold, representing the Queen, whose presence at the funeral of a subject was prevented by Royal etiquette. It was a pity, because she longed to look once more at the face she loved, nobly aquiline in death. Instead, she sent two wreaths of fresh primroses: 'His favourite flowers from Osborne, a tribute of affection from Queen Victoria.'

Victoria's servant takes his rest,
Well-earned, and on his faithful breast
Victoria's primrose wreath.

said one of the many elegiac poems.

They opened the vault and laid his coffin beside Mary Anne's, with his brother James and Mrs Brydges Willyams nearby. Ralph Disraeli and his fourteen-year-old son Coningsby were the only family mourners.

When the funeral was over the Queen lost no time in going to Hughenden from Windsor. For her they reopened the vault, and she laid a wreath of delicate porcelain flowers on the coffin, above his heart, where he had once worn her living primroses like a proud Order. Then she took tea in the library, where she had many times taken it with him; and went up to the small homely study which he called his workshop, and sat there for an hour, sometimes silent, sometimes weeping. In the same room today, a glass shade covers a cluster of brown withered primroses from one of her wreaths.

The Queen drove sadly back to Windsor, past the tiny church, and the graves so strangely situated outside the eastern wall; and perhaps she envied Mary Anne, who was no doubt reunited with her 'Dearest Dis' in spirit as she herself would one day be with her own 'Dearest Albert'. 'Marriage is the greatest earthly happiness, when founded on complete sympathy,' Disraeli had said. He, of all men, had had reason to know.

APPENDIX

Mary Anne's adopted daughter

James Sykes, in his book *Mary Anne Disraeli*, states that 'Mrs Lewis had no children of her own, but adopted a little girl, who lived with her until her marriage with Disraeli, and became subsequently Mrs Riches, of Cardiff . . . she was only three years old when adopted by Mrs Lewis.'

No reference to this adoption has come to light in the Hughenden Papers—curiously, in view of Mary Anne's habit of keeping every scrap of correspondence relating to her life. But in a letter inviting Mary Anne and her mother to Bradenham for Christmas, 1838, Disraeli adds an invitation to 'Eliza', and allots her a bedroom. Nine years later, on 30 July 1847, a letter to Mary Anne appears with the heading 'Belle Vue, Penarth.'

My dear Madam,

I cannot help congratulating you upon your [illegible] since I find that your health is excellent as ever. I do so because last week I was shocked by a report of your death, which called Mrs Lewis and Miss Williams up to town. It seem'd too true, and you can have little idea of the extraordinary sensation it created among all classes—I had not given the world credit for such genuine attachments—but every voice was raised in praise of the many good deeds you had done here—everything seem'd to be remembered affectionately and perfectly by all—and when I look [illegible] upon my dear husband and on our dear children, and felt more than I can speak—but it was, in that thinking I owed *them*, even under Providence, to you.

I wrote to Mrs Price, and had the gratifying news that you were quite well—thank God for it.

We are staying here for change of air, with our little family, and have enjoyed our holidays very much, and all have benefited very much from them, but I shall be glad to return to our dear little home next week—we have the prospect of more ample means ere long. . . . I hope you have received the calendar

from Virginia . . . my little Norah is a perfect lady at the table.
. . . I am very happy in them and in Mr Riches. I most sincerely
wish you may enjoy a long life of health and happiness. Believe
me, Madam, your grateful obedient servant

Eliza Riches.

This letter suggests that the writer is a person who has been
a servant, or at most a particularly favoured ward, rather than
an adopted daughter.

Sykes also states that 'Mr Lewis had a natural daughter,
married and living in Ireland at the time of his death.' No
further clues to either of these girls have yet been discovered.

SELECTED BIBLIOGRAPHY

Baily, F. E., *Lady Beaconsfield and her Times*. Hutchinson, 1935

Bermont, Chaim, *The Cousinhood: the Anglo-Jewish Gentry*. Eyre & Spottiswoode, 1971

Bessborough, Earl of (ed.), *Lady Charlotte Guest: Extracts from her Journal 1833–52*. John Murray, 1950

Blake, Robert, *Disraeli*. Eyre & Spottiswoode, 1966

Cecil, Algernon, *Queen Victoria and her Prime Ministers*. Eyre & Spottiswoode, 1952

Disraeli, Benjamin, Earl of Beaconsfield, *Novels*. Longmans Green, 1919

Elletson, D. H., *Maryannery: Mrs Lincoln and Mrs Disraeli*. John Murray, 1959

Ellis, S. M. (ed.), *Unpublished Letters of Lady Bulwer Lytton to A. E. Chalon, R.A.* Eveleigh Nash, 1914

Falk, Bernard, *The Berkeleys of Berkeley Square*. Hutchinson, 1944

Fraser, Sir William, *Disraeli and his Day*. Kegan Paul, 1891

Iremonger, Lucille, *And his Charming Lady*. Secker & Warburg, 1961

Jerman, B. R., *The Young Disraeli*. Princeton University Press and Oxford University Press, 1960

Lee, Elizabeth, *Wives of the Prime Ministers*. Nisbet & Co., 1918

Leslie, Doris, *The Perfect Wife*. Hodder & Stoughton, 1960

Maurois, André, *Disraeli: a Picture of the Victorian Age*. John Lane, 1927

Monypenny, W. F., and Buckle, G. E., *The Life of Benjamin Disraeli, Earl of Beaconsfield* (6 volumes). John Murray, 1910–20

Pearson, Hesketh, *Dizzy*. Methuen, 1951
Sadleir, Michael, *Blessington d'Orsay: a Masquerade*. Constable, 1933
Sykes, James, *Mary Anne Disraeli*. Benn, 1928
Wilson, Harriet, *Memoirs*. Peter Davies, 1929

OTHER PUBLICATIONS
Punch
The Illustrated London News
The Times
Heath's *Books of Beauty*

MANUSCRIPT SOURCES
The Hughenden Papers, by permission of the National Trust

INDEX

In this index BD = Benjamin Disraeli, HM = Hughenden Manor, MA – Mary Anne Disraeli, WL = Wyndham Lewis

Disraeli, Benjamin—*cont.*
59, 73, 110, 111, 124, 140; and Berkeley, 72; and Chequers Court, 73; and gold chains, 84; and his mother, 91; and Rosina Bulwer, 96; engaged to MA, 98, 99, 105; and broils between MA, her mother and her brother, 98–9; borrows money from MA, 99; and John Viney Evans, 104, 105; his marriage, 105, 107; and honeymoon, 107–10, 122; only marital quarrels financial, 111; and his father's blindness, 111; and the poor, 112; and Chartism, 112; his 'two nations', 112 (*see also* Sybil); his epigrams, 113; and social reform (1840), 113; his character assessed by MA, 114–15; and Charles Dickens, 116–17; and 'progress', 117; and the Sugdens, 117 & *n*; and his mother-in-law's finances, 118; and Peel, 123–6, 128, 131, 137–9, 146; has no flair for finance, 124, 150; 'vagabonding' in France, 125; and George Smythe, 127; and 'Young England' splinter-group, 127, 128; in Paris, 110, 127, 156–7; caricatured in *Punch*, *q.v.*, 128–30, 139; a classical scholar, 135; and Milnes's review of *Coningsby*, *q.v.*, 135–6; at Cassel, 137; his local aspirations, 139–40; and Buckinghamshire, 139; buys, and moves into HM, 140; and its surroundings, 142–3; his losses and gains, 140; entertains friends, 143, 173, 200; his 'social wardrobe', 143; his hair dyed by MA, 143–4; and Peelites, 147; and Stanley (*later* Lord Derby, *q.v.*), 147–8; and his brother, James, 148, 179; Chancellor of the Ex-

chequer, 150, 157, 169; his sartorial flamboyance and theatrical manner modified, 151; and Mrs Brydges Willyams, *q.v.*, 153, 154; and Income Tax, 157; at Windsor Castle, 160–1; and Prince of Wales's wedding, 161, 162; and Prince Consort's death, 162; not musical, 162; detests society and country-house parties, 163; did not hunt, 163–4; but fished, 164, 166; and HM remodelled, 165; and planting and felling trees, 166 & *n*; loved HM, 167, 181; and Reform (1867), 169; and Gladstone, 169–70, 173, 192, 200, 201; visits Scotland and is honoured, 170; and MA, both ill, 170–1; and Lord Derby, *q.v.*, 172; Prime Minister, 172, 198; and religion, 174; resigns premiership, 174; persuades the Queen to create MA Viscountess Beaconsfield, 175–6; his coat of arms (later), 177; and MA's cancer, 179, 183; and his brother James's death, 179; and the new Lord Derby, 180; the 'Squire', 181; and a pantomime, 182; to St Paul's for a thanksgiving, 182; speaks on the condition of the poor and on public hygiene, 183–4; on drives near London, 185; speaks on Protection, 188; and MA's last days, death and funeral, 191–5; his grief and loss, 195–6; his new London home, 195; saved by his career, 195; consolation, 195–6; looks for MA's successor, 196–7; on flattery and women, 197–8; and animals' sufferings, 198; and colonial expansion and the Empire, 198; and Suez Canal

Disraeli, Benjamin—*cont.*
shares, 198; and Burial Bill,
198; created Earl of Beaconsfield, 198; makes Queen Victoria Empress of India, 199;
and foreign affairs, 199; and
Congress of Berlin (1878), 199;
and Bismarck, 199; 'Peace
with Honour', 199; in retire-
ment, 200; his death and will,
201; directs that he be buried
with MA, 201; his funeral, 201
  Health, 56 *n*, 96, 105, 113,
  148, 170, 197, 198, 199, 200
  Literary works mentioned:
  Coningsby 119 *n*, 128, 130, 135,
  137; *Contarini Fleming*, 46,
  145; *Count Alarcos*, 95; *Endymion*, 117, 200; *Henrietta Temple*, 50–1, 56–7; *Lothair*, 179;
  Revolutionary Epick, The, 53
  n, 54, 55; *Sybil, or The Two
  Nations*, 59, 112, 113, 136, 137,
  183; *Tancred*, 179, 199 *n*;
  Venetia, 59; *Vivian Grey*, 38,
  43; *Young Duke, The*, 38, 44
  Political career, 43–6, 59–61,
  73, 89, 111, 117, 120, 122, 125,
  126, 131, 137, 139, 142, 150,
  154, 157, 169, 182, 183–4,
  188, 199; Chancellor of the
  Exchequer, 150, 157, 169;
  Prime Minister, 172, 198
Disraeli, Major Coningsby (BD's
nephew), xii, 201
D'Israeli, Isaac (BD's father),
40 *n*, 41–2, 43, 61, 88, 90–1,
102–3, 107–9, 111, 139, 140
Disraeli, Isabella (wife of Ralph
Disraeli), 149
Disraeli, James (BD's brother),
40 *n*, 42, 43, 88, 91, 140, 148–
9, 155, 158, 179, 195, 201
D'Israeli, Maria (*née* Basevi,
BD's mother), 42, 43, 91, 140
Disraeli, Mary Anne (*née* Evans,
1792–1872, 'Mrs Dizzy', *latterly*
Viscountess   Beaconsfield):

personal details, xi, 4, 6, 10,
11, 13, 14, 29, 37, 85, 91, 97,
118, 130–1, 167; the men in
her life, xi (*see also* Admirers
and lovers *below*); birth, 1, 4,
5; christening, 1; parentage,
1–2; and BD, xi, 11, 37, 38,
39, 44, 60–1, 61–2, 70, 72, 74,
81, 84, 88, 89–101, 105, 113–
14, 120–1, 123–4, 135–6, 142–
3, 150, 154, 168, 170–1, 172,
179, 184–6, 189, 191, 195, 202;
her papers, 2, 63, 186–7; her
sense of fun, 4, 10; and her
mother, 5–6, 62, 98–9, 105,
118–19 (*see also* Evans, Elean-
or); childhood, 6–7; at Brampford Speke, *q.v.*, 5–6, 7; her
Devon 'burr', 6; and Queen
Victoria, 6, 132, 135, 160–1,
163, 175–6, 191; her handwriting, 6–7; visits to Exeter,
7; and death of grandparents,
8; moves to Gloucester, 8; and
her brother John, 9, 24–6, 29,
33, 45, 62, 98–9, 104; at
Bristol, 9, 10; rumours of her
early life, 10; 'money-wise'
and a good housekeeper, 10,
14, 33; her Occasional Book,
10–11, 14, 34, 75–6, 90, 92,
152; first meeting with BD,
11, 37 (*see also* BD *above*);
'a flirt and a rattle' (BD), 11,
37; her medical maxim, 11;
verses from rejected suitors,
11–12; at Clifton, *q.v.*, 12;
her conquest, 12; and Wyndham Lewis, 12–69, 74–6, 81,
83; her first marriage and
honeymoon, 18; at Green-
meadow, *q.v.*, 19–21, 31, 33,
35; and the Williams sisters,
19, 20, 21, 24, 34; and Scropes,
20, 99; studies French and
Italian, 20; hunting, 21; and
a greyhound, 21; her hospitality, 21, 27; and Sir Charles

Disraeli, Mary Anne—*cont.*
Morgan, 21–2, 22–3; was she
unfaithful to WL?, 22, 23, 26;
plays the guitar, 23, 24; her
fine voice, 23; proud of her
femininity, 23; and schizophrenia, 23–4; could not
produce a child, but loved
children—and dogs, 24; her
'adopted' daughter, 24, 203–4;
her daily routine, 24; her views
of the Irish, 25; her ball at
'Pantgwynlais Castle', 27;
electioneering for WL, 28, 31;
in London for half of each
year, 28, 29; at Riding School,
29; and WL and brother
John's debts, 29, 33; growing fat, 29; and a house in
town, 31; and WL's with-
drawal from second Cardiff
election, 31; and her home in
Mayfair, 32–3; her Grand Ball
(1827), 34; starts a school in
Greenmeadow for local children, 35; and useful and lively
charities, 35; indefatigable,
35; touring on the Continent
(1830–1), 35; at Bulwer-Lytton
soirée, 37; first meeting with
BD, 11, 37; at a Rothschild
soirée, 39; first note from BD
(1832), 39; her love for her
brother, 45; has influenza
(April 1833), 47; but gives a
déjeuner in May, 47; and Lady
Charlotte Bertie, 47; and
Maidstone election, 60–1; at
Bradenham, 61, 88, 89–94,
98; and Isaac D'Israeli, 61,
88, 90–1, 103, 108–9, 140; and
'Sa', 61, 88, 90, 148, 157, 158;
and Wyndham in his fifties,
62; at Brighton, 62, 117;
her jewellery given by WL,
62, 110; her accommodation
addresses and secret meetings,
64; keeping doubtful company,
65; newly-widowed, 69; hates
married men, 71, 81; and WL's
death (1838), 74–6; falsifies
her age, 75 *n*, 85, 191; and
Rosina and Edward Bulwer,
37, 76–8, 79–80; in Wales,
settling WL's affairs, 81, 83;
turns to BD for comfort, 81;
her reputation in danger, 83;
gives BD a set of gold chains,
84; her wealth, 85; her age and
appearance on second mar-
riage, 85–7; her portrait as
Mrs Disraeli, 85; eulogies, 86;
makes most of mourning fashion, 87; gets an analysis of
her character from a pro-
fessional, 87–8; her twin characters of self and BD, 87–8,
114–15; and D'Israeli family,
88; sings ballads and lyrics,
90; her story of the Cheltenham dog, 92; engaged to BD,
but postpones decision on date
for wedding, 98; broils
between herself, mother and
brother, 98–9; lent money to
BD, 99; BD's long remon-
strance and her reaction, 100–
1; 'names the day', 101; Lady
Battersea on their engagement, 103; and brother John's
illness and death, 104; on
Time: past, present and
future, 105; refuses to postpone marriage, 105; comforts
her mother, and prepares for
wedding, 105; her second marriage, 105, 107; and honeymoon, 107–10, 122; dislikes
extravagance and borrowing
money, 110–11; her only marital quarrels financial, 111;
prepares BD for his election
campaign, 113; as hostess and
companion at parties, 113–14;
talks politics with BD and
criticizes his writings, 114;

Disraeli, Mary Anne—*cont.*
a perfect wife, 114, 136; and
the Sugdens, 117 & *n*; at
Deepdene, 119, 131–2; canvassing for BD at Shrewsbury,
120–1, 130; no more unfaithfulness, but only flirtations,
121; her temptations, 121–2;
writes to Sir Robert Peel on
behalf of BD, 123–4; and BD's
debts, 124; 'vagabonding' in
France, 125; 'a changed
woman', 125; on second
marriage of a widow, 125; in
Paris, 110, 127, 156–7; not in
Punch, 130; and 'Young
England', *q.v.*, 130; her fund
of stories, 130, 134; amuses
Bradenham with her letters,
131; at Stowe, *q.v.*, 132;
presented to Queen Victoria
and Prince Consort, 132;
criticizes royal domestic
arrangements, 133; at Fryston
Hall, 133–4; Mrs Spencer-
Stanhope on, 133–4; the *'enfant terrible'* of drawing-rooms,
135; apocryphal stories about,
135; edits, criticizes and proof-
reads for BD, 135–6; travels to
Cassel, 137; her inheritances
modest, 139; inherits Isaac's
prints, 140; 'Lady of Hughenden', 140; and her servants,
141–2; loses Grosvenor Gate
house-keeper, 141; improves
HM surroundings, 142; and
BD's appreciation, 142–3; her
pony and pony-cart, 142; her
attire at Court functions, 143;
her hair-colour at sixty, 143,
144; still young, 145; at a
summer garden treat, 145;
ill in 1851 and 1853, 148, 153;
visits Great Exhibition (1851),
148; her nervous debility, 148;
quarrels with James Disraeli
and with 'Sa', 148; and Ralph

and Isabella Disraeli, 149;
delighted at BD's appointment as Chancellor of the
Exchequer, 150; entertains
Lord Derby and his ministers,
150; her conduct at her
parties, 151; and eccentricities,
152, 159–60; and an old admirer, 152–3; her first Court
Drawing-room, 153; and Mrs
Brydges Willyams, *q.v.*, 153–4,
155; 'more like a mistress than
a wife' (BD), 154; her fortitude, 154–5, 155–6, 171, 184,
185, 192; at Hatfield House,
155–6; and Napoleon III,
156; disappointed, and comforted by 'Sa', 157; declining
in health, 158; and Louise de
Rothschild, 158; adored Jewish people, 158; and Charlotte
de Rothschild, 159; welcomed
at many stately homes, 160;
Sir Stafford Northcote on,
160; and her alleged history,
160; guest at Windsor Castle,
160–1; invited to Prince of
Wales's wedding, 161, 162;
and music, 162 (*see also* 23,
24 & 90); royal and aristocratic invitations, 162–3; jealous of the Queen, 163; remodelling HM, 165; and Dean
Swift, 166; an active gardener,
166–7; and the future Lord
Rosebery, 167 & *n*; loved HM,
167; and cosmetics, 167–8; her
costumes in public, 168; and
BD—still lovers to the end,
168, 189; her conjugal intimacies, 168–9; and Reform
riots (1866), 169; and Gladstone, 169–70, 171, 173, 177;
now often ill, 170; visits
Scotland with BD, 170; and
BD both ill, 170–1; has cancer,
171; her joy at BD becoming
Prime Minister, 172; celebra-

Evans, John Viney ('James', MA's brother), 4, 6, 8–9, 17–18, 24–30, 76, 98–9, 104
Evans, Mary Anne, *see* Disraeli, Mary Anne
Evans, Mr (MA's grandfather), 5, 7, 8
Exeter (Devon), 1, 4, 5, 7, 10

'Fairy' (Rosina Bulwer's dog), 77–80, 189
Falcieri, Battista ('Tita', BD's manservant), 61
Forester, Lord, 120 & *n*
Fraser, Sir William, 84 & *n*, 134, 135, 143, 164, 176, 179
Frederick William, King (of Prussia), 110
Fryston Hall (Yorkshire), 133–5

Galway: Lady, 178; Lord, 134, 178
George IV (*formerly* Prince Regent), 27, 32, 35, 69
Gladstone, Catherine (wife of W.E.G.), 151, 169, 173, 182
Gladstone, William Ewart, 126 & *n*, 135, 146, 154, 157, 166 *n*, 174, 182, 200; and BD, 169, 173, 192, 200, 201; and MA, 169–70, 171, 173, 177
Gloucester, 2, 8, 9, 83, 119
Gore House set (*see also* Blessington, Lady), 36, 71 *n*, 85 *n*, 116
'Governor, The', *see* Lewis, Rev. William Price
Gower, Lord Ronald, 166, 190, 191
Grant, Sir Francis, P.R.A., (portrait painter), 166
Great Exhibition (1851), 148
Greenmeadow (near Cardiff, renamed Pantgwynlais, *q.v.*), 12, 14, 18, 19, 20, 27, 28, 31, 33, 35
Guest, Lady Charlotte (*formerly* Lady Charlotte Bertie, *q.v.*), 150, 151
Guest, Josiah John, 47, 189
Gull, Sir William (royal physician and MA's doctor), 182, 183

Harcourt, Sir William, 190 & *n*, 192
Hardinge, Lord and Lady, 134 & *n*
Hardwicke, Lord and Lady, 84 & *n*
Hatfield House, 155–6, 171
Henley, Joseph Warner, 147 & *n*, 148
High Wycombe (Buckinghamshire), 45, 46, 61, 142
Hope, Henry, 119 & *n*
Hotham, Lady, 65, 66
Hughenden Church, 152, 154, 179, 194–5, 201
Hughenden Manor (Buckinghamshire), xi-xii, 24, 41, 97 & *n*, 139, 140–3, 148, 155, 158, 160, 164, 165–7, 167, 179, 181, 182, 190, 199 *n*, 200; remodelled by MA and BD, 165–7; the library, 165–6; the pictures, 166, 196, 200; the gardens and park, 166; dinner menus at, 181; Hughenden Papers (archives), xi, 39, 57, 63, 116, 144, 149

Inglis, Sir Robert, 147–8
Irish: Catholic Association, 31; Church, 174; Coercion Bill, 138

Jewish aristocratic families, 113–14
Jews excluded from Parliament until 1858, 43

Kebbel, T. E., 154 & *n*

Lamb, F. B. (architect), 165